Acclaim for
~*Homo deva*~

"*Homo deva* is more than another excellent book on human development and evolution. Mary has put her attention to the precise breakthrough that most of us do not yet notice. That is: We are becoming a new species! This has been my understanding but never before have I read a book outline the stages of our new species-hood that is arising everywhere, but is very rarely realized. I believe it will be seen in retrospect as a step as great as from Homo Neanderthal to Homo sapiens sapiens 50,000 years ago. Bravo, Mary! Essential reading for all evolutionaries and everyone interested in the future of humanity."

— Barbara Marx Hubbard, President,
Foundation for Conscious Evolution

~

"*Homo deva* is at once rich and profound in its exploration of new ways of being. In a time that suggests that we have no alternative but to grow or die, Mary Belknap offers a pathway into our future selves that is both practical and achievable. To dialogue with the ideas in this book is to discover the evolving self that is latent in every one of us."

—Jean Houston, Ph.D., author,
Jump Time and *The Possible Human*

~

"This breathtaking vision of the evolutionary step now facing humanity provides hope and courage as we meet our current struggles. Dr. Belknap also gives practical guidance: From her personal sharing, to experiential exercises, action-oriented suggestions, and a comprehensive resource list, she invites us not only to understand the challenges in this evolutionary shift, but offers us ways to engage it. I read *Homo deva* as a hopeful song from our collective future."

— John Firman, psychotherapist and co-author,
The Primal Wound and *Psychosynthesis: A Psychology of the Spirit*

Homo deva

Evolution's Next Step

Mary M. Belknap, Ph.D.

Lifethread Institute
Vashon, Washington

Revised Edition

Homo deva: Evolution's Next Step
Copyright © 2004 and 2015 by Mary Belknap

Lifethread Institute
PO Box 2285
Vashon, WA 98070

206-304-2250
Lifethreadinstitute@gmail.com

Cover and book design by Cypress House
Developmental editing by Patricia Heinicke, Jr.
Copyediting by Mary Gail
Proofreading by Nancy Morgan

Publisher's Cataloging-in-Publication

Belknap, Mary.
Homo deva : evolution's next step / Mary M. Belknap. -- Revised edition. -- Vashon, Washington ; Berkeley, California : Lifethread Institute, [2015]
pages ; cm.

ISBN: 978-0-9962505-0-4

First published in 2004.
Includes bibliographical references and index.

Summary: The author suggests that members of Homo sapiens are developing into a new creative species called Homo deva. The era of Homo deva will take us across a major evolutionary threshold, as people learn to express a full integration of intellect and higher intuition. The author describes three phases through which we will journey during our species transition, a biopsychospiritual shift upward in identity.--Publisher.

1. Transpersonal psychology. 2. Developmental psychology. 3. Spirituality. 4. Mind and body. 5. Consciousness. 6. New thought. I. Title.

BF204.7 .B45 2015   2015937271
150.19/87--dc23   1505

PRINTED IN THE USA
2   4   6   8   9   7   5   3   1

The mission of Lifethread Institute:
Breath for the 21st Century

To
my mother
Martha Jackson Morgan, M. A.
with love on her 80th birthday

You were my first human friend,
steadfast homebase,
and the first subscriber
to H.D. Newsletter in 1988.

Thank you for your
faith in the future.

The following few pages
present a preview of this book.

Health Advisory

Viewing these pages
has been known
to lift one's spirits.

Proceed at your own pace.

We have all the time we need,
And there is not a moment to spare.

Reasonable People

Reasonable people are asleep at 5:00 A.M.
On Saturday yet here I sit at the window writing
Sonnets to my planet, while a voice within hums
Softly, wondering if I've finally lost it—
Perhaps so, but consider this—if you chose your bliss
To follow, wouldn't it also sing of passion in the
Wee hours to a Great Attractor breathing with you
In the soft curving beauty of timespace?

FIGURE 1.
OUR FAMILY: HOMINIDS —
PAST, PRESENT, AND FUTURE

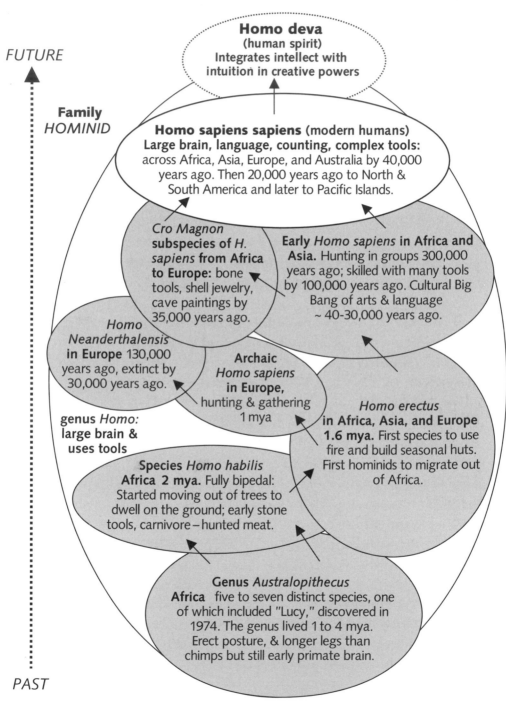

mya = million years ago

Our Planet, Our Self

Earth is in the final process of transformation, by which it will vitalize its fifth great energy center. The four earlier centers are commonly known as minerals, plants, animals, and humans. All of Earth's energy centers are highly interdependent ecosystems. Each great center or kingdom has its own rhythm, yet they all interact and interpenetrate deeply. They share a unified breath of the planetary life.

We of the *Homo sapiens* kingdom are constituted of the first four energy centers of Earth: mineral, plant, animal, human. Our bodies remember the tidal rhythms of the seas, and the seasons of the grasses. As humans, we have had almost a million years of growing and learning. Now we face the ecological climax of our species. The choice is to open our minds and hearts to the next stage of Earth life, or become unviable.

The fifth physical kingdom is emerging, and will correspond to the *throat center* of the planet. We who are alive today are crossover specimens, living at the threshold between the planetary heart (*Homo sapiens*) and the planetary throat. The core quality of the fifth kingdom will be **creativity**, including creative expression of solar energy.

Each energy center's vibration oscillates in response to those of the others. Those oscillations that become visible to the human eye are called *incarnated* or *objective reality*. There is much beyond that optical range. The fifth kingdom, *Homo deva*, will link Earth's heart to Earth's throat.

FIGURE 2.   OUR PLANET, OUR SELF

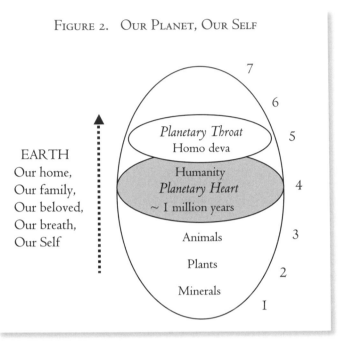

Already in Existence:	*Planetary Centers*	*Approximate Age*
1 Mineral kingdom	Earth's base-of-spine	4 billion years
2 Plant kingdom	Earth's sacral center	2.5 billion years
3 Animal kingdom	Earth's solar plexus	600 million years
4 Human kingdom	Earth's heart center	1 million years
modern humans	heart-of-Heart	40,000 years
our civilizations	crown-of-Heart	6 to 10,000 years
Now Emerging:		
5 *Homo deva*	**Earth's throat center**	next 2,000 years
The full fifth kingdom		next 40,000 years
6 and 7		
To be continued	Earth's ajna center	To be continued

Preface 2015

We have traveled twelve years along the evolutionary spiral since this book was first written. I am pleased to see that the basic ideas of *Homo deva* have become more recognizable and relevant during the period 2003 to 2015. Many new practices are appearing to help us embody the three natural phases of transition to a new humanity — *intuition, innovation,* and *Identity.* The specific practices of this transformative process are being developed by millions of persons — through alternative health practitioners, teachers seeking to help each student become their authentic Self, community self-help groups, new social media, scientific evidence of multi-dimensionality, online webinars connecting spiritual pilgrims, more published reports of near-death experiences (NDE's), ecumenical dialogue and retreat centers, businesses whose mission includes "triple-bottom-line" for sustainability, and personal relationships where persons have conscious intention to respect the Soul of each "other." In this second decade of the 21st century, we have begun to realize that humans can even "teach" our DNA to activate what is best for our individual and collective well-being. All these movements are contributing to a marvelous co-creative time to be alive on Earth!

Here are a few recent resources that I have appreciated and learned from. I am pleased to pass them on to you:

- The Shift Network (theshiftnetwork.com) offers webinars, books, author introductions, and other resources from diverse traditions
- *The Intuitive Way* by Penney Peirce
- *The Bond* by Lynne McTaggart
- *Emergence: The Shift from Ego to Essence,* by Barbara Marx Hubbard

At the same time, the challenges that this book described a decade ago have become more severe, more visceral, and more personal. The challenges in health, relationships, community, economy, politics, international arena, and climate change aren't staying abstract on the page! They are unfolding in your lived experience or in the life of someone you/we love. For many people, the *dissonance* between our *Homo sapiens* local self and our Divine Self (or Inner Self, Essential Self) is twirling outward. That dissonance will continue as long as humanity has not yet reached "ignition" for a critical mass of the new species to incarnate. When left unchecked, the dissonance becomes *fission* — with experiences of ripping apart at both individual personality and cultural levels. Our species' cultural climax is inevitably producing two major vectors during these early decades of the 21st century: *fusion* toward an integral **unity of Spirit**, and *fission* into separate fragmentary lives (mental, emotional, and physical).

Those persons who learn to infuse and experience daily life from their best Self, moment by moment, are noticing a greater fusion in the shift upward in their lives — toward a more integrated sense of meaning and purpose. You may recognize yourself as one of the new wave who collaborate and help to co-create trust and respect. The cultural-psychic shift of December 2012, which was described in the mainstream media, also helped anchor this major seed of Hope and Love through the dimensions of Earth life. The organic germinating of that seed has already produced new international programs in conscious evolution, sustainable community, integral hearts, cultural transformation, conscious living and dying, inter-ethnic peacemaking, and emergence of the divine feminine. Our growing ability to be more *Real* with each other — through both the love and the fears — helps us build deeper resilience, resonance, and compassion. These deep waves are inevitably spreading through humanity. As the waves become more tangible (more "objective"), we manifest our divine nature, and thus the divinization process of incarnating *Homo deva* (or as other authors describe it, *Homo universalis, Homo noeticus, Homo spiritus*) continues. As more and more people recognize themselves as part of the new species, that Self-recognition naturally counter-balances the tendency toward fission and entropy.

The years 2004- 2014 were our **Decade of Decision**: A significant portion (fractal) of humanity in many nations chose Love, Wisdom, and Co-Creation over fears, acquisitions, and dominance. We have successfully shifted the first wave (Intuition) toward the tipping-point. A Soul-identified fractal of our species is even now welcoming the incarnation of *Homo deva* on all levels (regardless of what words they use), and thus chooses divinization each day. The mental-emotional-physical embodiment of *Homo deva* will, I believe, precipitate much deeper in this next decade, the time of the second wave (Innovation). The years 2015- 2025 are our **Decade of Destiny,** when thousands of evolutionary pioneers begin to emerge visibly through their work on local community and regional levels. Their deep compassion, coherence, and integrity will become a steady beacon of radiance from the one Soul of humanity, bringing the song of the one Heart into dimensions of daily life.

The free-will choices that millions of persons make today...and everyday in the next few years...will make a big difference in how many *Homo sapiens* remain in the "vale of fears." You and I and most of our friends are learning to share our hope and love, and thereby transform our lives. The unified-field of well-being and abundance — of love and joy — is available for all. This next decade is truly a time to reach out to your friends and relatives, and share what you are seeing. The path of Love~Compassion~Joy is open to everyone who chooses to let go, and surrender to the grace of Life Itself.

Hugs to you all. ~ *Mary Belknap, Vashon Island WA, 2015*

Think of this book as a friend's journal about the future, complete with field notes and drawings to help the imagination. The story is about you and me, our culture, and where we are going in the next two decades.

It is a true story, not a novel in the sense of a developed fictional plot and narrative line. Hints of the story's climax have begun to appear in articles, professional journals, and the back pages of daily newspapers. This is not a footnoted treatise on a subject that is amenable to hard proof. Calling down the future is more an art than a science, though it partakes of both. The hard data will come in the next few years, but before the data, we need the story. Our story concerns *who we are as humans*, and the steps we are taking beyond *Homo sapiens*, to *Homo deva*. To tell this story fully, we all qualify as experts. You do not have to be a specialist in evolutionary or biological science, or in meditation or theology, in order to take the next steps for humankind. You do need to look deeply and consistently at who you are in the world, and what the future of the world means to you.

A friend remarked that the story of *Homo deva* is like the folktale of the young child who watches a royal procession walk by and then blurts out, "But Momma, the emperor has no clothes!" Our story is a modern parable in the same genre. There is something that we, as a culture and as a species, have been spending a great deal of energy to *avoid* looking at. We have reached the time for looking because there is now a way out of our impasse. You, dear reader, will be one of those who help finish the tale.

~

Remember when you were a teenager in junior high school and you started hearing stories about what high school was like? Some of the stories were exciting, and others were downright scary. It sounded like an immensely bigger place, a larger pond in which you needed to find your way and make new friends. You weren't sure if you were going to like it, and yet you could hardly wait. You were clearly outgrowing your current pond.

Each of us has gone through that kind of transition—moving into unknown challenges and stresses, new ways of relating to people, new concepts to digest and assimilate, and new opportunities to express ourselves. With each of these steps, we deepen our awareness of who we are as a person. Our identity expands like a tree, with branches stretching, adding height and width, blossoming outward. We make choices, and each choice energizes deeper threads of our identity.

Now is one of those times for growing and blossoming, for making choices, and expanding the identity. However, much more than one individual person is facing the transition of identity. The being that is preparing to enter the next level of learning is our own species, humanity. We humans are about to leave the familiar level where we have been growing during the past few millennia, in order to enter a larger pond, the *next level* of Earth's evolution.

The transition is not going to be easy. It qualifies by every definition you can find as a "growth crisis": a biological climax, an ecological impasse, and the start of an evolutionary epoch. What separates us in the gray dawn of the 21st century from the new epoch and its abundance of positive energy is a very thin, yet very dark, membrane. The membrane consists of humanity's deepest and most concentrated fears. Our goal in this decade is to move through that membrane with as many human beings intact as possible.

At the same time, today is just the first day of high school for earthlings. We don't need to know everything right away. We just need to know where our first class is, where the restroom is, and how to open our lockers. The rest will follow. There are teachers to help us. There are friends to walk with. Some of our peers have been here longer and can give us tips about how to proceed. Does this sound OK? Let's take the first step, which is a look at the horizon.

The journey ahead concerns our whole human family. In looking at Figure 1, "Our Family: Hominids — Past, Present, and Future," you will realize that we are talking about some long time horizons. For now, we will be focusing quite specifically on the years 2005 to 2015 — the next decade. The major premise of this book is simple but not yet widely accepted: Between now and 2020 is a major homestretch for our species, not just culturally but in terms of evolutionary survival. You have probably read many similar pronouncements from an environmental, psychological, political, or spiritual perspective in the past few years.

However, this time the message comes all the way down to the physical life that we live every day, the biological reality of who we are. The next step involves our emergence as a physical / mental / spiritual new species. The species is called *Homo deva*. *Deva* comes from the Sanskrit language and means "divine or good spirit." The incarnation of *Homo deva*s will embody a unity between hominids and nature, both the physical world and the spirit world.

Given this book's premise, you are probably wondering what its attitude is. Is this book going to join the doomsayers and sound a woeful alarm, will it confidently predict a mystical triumph, or will it join the fundamentalists' scenarios of an end-time catastrophe?

Actually, the answer is none of the above. The message here is one of practical concerns, deep love for human beings, and specific suggestions for steps to take. We *Homo sapiens* traditionally rise together and help each other when we face an immediate crisis or a specific targeted challenge. Two examples that come to mind from my own half-century of life experience are (1) the coordinated airlift response in the 1960s and 1970s to help European peoples receive food and supplies when various totalitarian regimes blocked road access, and (2) the international space flight projects in the late 1960s to develop the scientific and social infrastructure to put humans on the moon and later into space stations. Both those projects were triumphs for the spirit of *Homo sapiens*.

Eventually, our progress on the way to *Homo deva* may require that we adopt similar projects during the current decade. Yet, the first step toward that kind of undertaking is for us to get acquainted with the idea of the transition itself. The number one priority of this initial book about *Homo deva* is to share the basic idea, the seed thought, as widely as possible. Meeting that objective will allow many people to play with the idea, interact with it, fertilize it with their own experience, and thus help the concept germinate.

There are suggestions in this book to encourage each of you, from whatever background or age, to dive in and explore these fundamental ideas. The world needs you. You can help develop some of the implications of *Homo deva* in your own daily observation, your reflections and discussions, occupational activities, interactions with family and friends, and meditations and prayers. We need cross-fertilization of many kinds of ideas and practices in order to release a new level of problem solving and creativity. Through our collective efforts in the next ten years can come a wonderful co-creating of the future for all our children.

As a teacher and psychologist, my training leads me to look at how to share knowledge and elicit learning in diverse ways. My intention in this book is to present several angles of information to help you see the concepts implicit in the premise of a new species, and in particular some of the implications for children who are suffering with chronic illness. I am sharing with you what I see and believe about our future. The first central concept is that with the emergence of *Homo deva*, thinking and feeling will encompass a longer timeframe than humans are accustomed to. Indeed, that kind of expansion is what each kingdom brings to the evolution of Earth. You, a verbal and literate *Homo sapiens*, can think, plan, and create in much longer timeframes than a deer, cat, or even a chimp can. Likewise, the emerging species will be able to think, plan, and create through much greater timeframes than *Homo sapiens* now can. Each kingdom is a major quantum step upward in neural organization. This is the nature of our growth and development as part of life on Earth.

The ideas in the following pages are designed to welcome you to this new world of longer timeframes and to suggest ways that we might create our future on Earth within that greater context. Such a context implies the fulfillment of two potent aspirations that most humans share: to bring *lasting peace* to our planet, and to nurture the deepest *beauty, love, health, and creativity* within each individual.

The next steps are up to all of us as a family.

Berkeley, 2003

CONTENTS

LIST OF FIGURES

Here is a brief introduction to my own journey
and how this book germinated for 20 years.

WINTER SOLSTICE, 1981

Map in the Snow

I happened upon the antechamber of humanity's next step in a rather sudden manner on the evening of December 21, 1981.

Although I had been in rigorous study and disciplined contemplation for more than six months, the core mental expansion occurred during a two-hour period on the evening of the winter solstice, 1981. What was quite new on that evening was that my mind opened without strenuous effort into dimensions that I had no words for. The extensive inflow was literally beyond language, into energy patterns and vortices that had clear meaning but unfamiliar dimensions. The multiple dimensions appeared "friendly" and totally accessible to my own pace of exploration.

The experience was not mystical in the normal sense because I was not seeing visions perceptually or having emotional uplift. The expansion did not stimulate my emotions directly, although there were secondary impacts days later. It was as if someone opened a sidedoor into the Nonverbal Library of the Future and gave me a free pass for two hours. What bibliophile could resist that?!

For the record, it is pertinent to note that there was no fatigue factor, no pharmaceutical intervention, and no strange diet. I was a healthy 35-year-old, non-smoker, non-caffeine drinker. (I did, then as now, occasionally overindulge on peanut butter, but my family does not subscribe to any theory about its spiritual properties.)

At 10:00 PM on December 21, 1981, I was still familiar to myself, a health educator who wanted more than anything to help reduce the violence in the world. I sat by the window of my home in Silver Spring, Maryland, watching snowflakes fall quietly onto the white landscape of the backyard. By the light from the back porch, I saw a squirrel appear on a tree trunk and then move cautiously toward the ground. He was probably searching for the acorns that I had seen him bury weeks earlier. For some minutes, I watched the squirrel. As he moved back and forth on the tree trunk and made several fruitless forays out onto the snow, I felt a great wave of compassion for him—searching for a meager meal amidst the cold winter habitat.

Over the next hour, the squirrel continued to search and dig in the snow, and my mind continued to open. A great many humans were spending their lives like that squirrel, scurrying within a small space, looking for the next meal, often fighting each other for subsistence, territory, or national or corporate pride. What did they need in order to create peace, to enrich their lives, to gain hope?

By midnight of that evening, I was another person. Or rather, my brain awareness had made a quantum *click* into identity (something, somewhere, sometime) that I had never glimpsed, or experienced, or read about before. It was as if I were watching the squirrel through infinite gentleness and patience from a *million years away*, seeing all the myriad patterns that connected his life to all other lives on the planet, both from the past and the future. The gentleness and the patience were core qualities that flowed from the very nature of the identity. Multiple dimensions were simultaneously hitting my human mind like large snowflakes against the windshield of a fast-moving car. The impact was harmless, yet awesome in terms of our relative velocities and the exquisite artistry of the individuated structures. I was totally entranced by the goodness, truth, and beauty of life on Earth.

Through those higher snowflakes, a *knowing* about the future of humanity stretched out in front of me as clearly as a map engraved on the snowy landscape, like Indra's net flung across the stars. The map was sparkling with many facets, full of promise for a beautiful future of life on Earth. Yes, the future included struggles and pain, yet there was also much joy and celebration. And the joy was as serious as the pain.

Grounding the Map

That initial insight (inner seeing) into humanity's future has never faded over the subsequent decades. From 1982 to 2002, I worked in the professional world—serving as operations director for several nonprofits and as an administrative assistant, becoming an attorney, and working as a state training specialist in juvenile justice.

While all the external professionalism was going on, in a way I had a second job of investigating the *knowing* that had been handed to me. My analytical mind was fully engaged in learning more, from books, other people, and my external business transactions, about this next step for humanity. Through steady, daily, trial-and-error steps, my mental growth and development continued; in a way, it felt as if I was re-learning to be human, starting as a baby and bringing my brain-heart-mind "online" with this greater identity that was breathing "me." I slowly learned to make new and consistent *thread connections* between my brain and the higher mind, spiritual will, and identity that is our birthright—between the human and beyond-human aspects of ourself.

From my training in educational psychology, I realized even that first evening in 1981 that this experience was quite different from sudden "aha!" insights or bursts of creativity. During 10 years of graduate school and then work as a consultant, I had experienced my share of those. On that 1981 solstice night in Silver Spring, I had taken a quantum jump of unexpected mental magnitude, a step of willing surrender to a more inclusive identity—all the way through aspects of personality—and had tapped into an inner (higher) *be-ness* that was totally full of infinity and totally empty, into a knowing that was calm and limitless and, at the same time, deeply practical, generous, and experienced in problem solving.

The difficult part came later, in subsequent weeks, months, and years, when I needed to explain who I was to other persons and to express myself again as an individual human making choices (and mistakes) in daily life. Verbal language was insufficient, and I didn't know how to ask for help. Both the professional and personal sides of this challenge have been daunting, and they continue to this day.

On that solstice night in 1981, in the heartbeat of two hours, I realized in great detail that we are becoming another species. We are crossing a major threshold, beyond changes in consciousness — a threshold as big as the one 40,000 years ago — to welcome a new biological branch of the family tree. And in fact, I realized, an initial cohort of the new species was here already, but many of these children were struggling with illnesses caused by the "gap" between now and the future. They were demonstrating much greater sensitivities, on all levels, and as a result were often getting terribly squeezed, sometimes unto death. The words to describe these new cousins-from-the-future hadn't been created yet. My job was to help create the words. To put it mildly, the prospect of this task blew my mind. My analytical mind was confused and bewildered, but willing to try.

During the first hour, I recognized that I had entered Phase 1 of a three-phase process for the emergence of the post-*Homo sapiens* species. The evolutionary change had entered an acute episode, where thousands of persons were entering Phase 1 in the 1970s and 1980s. Phase 1 involves awake-brain awareness of being a part among many planetary nodes, of being inextricably linked with all of humanity — our species in all its past growth, present challenges, and future glories. In the same hour, I intuitively knew that Humanity as a whole will enter all three phases by about year 2025, and that the United States will have a central part in evoking the transformation, although the threshold is happening in all nations. The evocation of this species-wide step would help fulfill a deep part of our nation's spiritual purpose. And this evocation would challenge us in deep and painful ways to face our national limitations and points of resistance.

One intriguing element about that night in 1981 was the tone of my reaction. I felt neither elation nor excitement. Those came much later. No, the initial response was hesitation, a marked reluctance about being handed such a strange seed. I didn't know what to do with it. Was it my responsibility to stay in that house in Silver Spring and meditate for the next decade about this species change? What was the *highest and best use* of this information, the most effective way to help protect and nurture the children ... including my own child?

It took me a full year before I had glimmers about what to do next. It was another three years before I was able to allude even indirectly to that solstice experience in a conversation with a friend.

During the subsequent years, I steadily worked to ground the seed idea, to find ways of making it as real as possible — by serving diverse populations in need: in hospitals, juvenile justice centers and group homes, affordable housing programs, in superior court as a law clerk, and as an administrator for programs with homeless shelters for families, child-care centers, and language programs for immigrants. In all these contexts, I attempted to bring the identity of *Homo deva* — with its gentleness and patience — to the work of healing Earth's children.

By now, after several decades of working objectively in the world, the birth of hope implicit in that winter solstice experience has permeated my bones. I know beyond a shadow of doubt that we are living in a very special moment in the history of life on Earth. We as *Homo sapiens* at the dawn of the 21st century are participants in an immense transitional threshold that will open into unknown and wondrous steps beyond. Yes, there are many problems to solve. Yes, there is widespread resistance. But, as you will read in this book, there are many resources and companions on the trail to help us face the task together. And we have all the resources that we need to do the job now. As a team for Earth's future, we are truly greater than the resistance.

Although the species transition seemed more puzzling than exciting to me on that night in 1981, it certainly does look exciting now! It has been a long journey from that winter evening of watching a squirrel in the snow to sitting at a computer in the early 21st century, drafting a book. My main experience right now is relief. The expanded view that has been pulsing inside me like a drum for years is finally ready to be shared more widely, to interact with others' views, to blend with and benefit from others' wisdom and gifts, to share in others' joy and courage, to become more coherent with the light of day — and to serve our beloved species and planet.

Homo deva

Introduction

Through much of the nineteenth and twentieth centuries, there was often an implicit, and sometimes explicit, assumption that *Homo sapiens* is the capstone of evolution. Many writers trumpeted that the continuance of life on Earth depends on the fate of the two-legged primates with verbal and written language, the "knowing" (*sapient*) ones.

Earth is deeper and wiser than *Homo sapiens* has yet dreamt of. The evolutionary and cultural changes during the past 1 to 2 million years have brought us from our hunter-gatherer Stone Age societies into complex, multinational, highly technological cultures. How are we doing now, as *sapient ones*? How would you rate our overall performance as wise beings? And where do we go from here?

Look again at Figure 2 (page xii), "Our Planet, Our Self." This illustrates the progression of the kingdoms and energy centers, which is a natural, biological process. It is also a divine process, because universal (or at least, planetary) energies are involved. As the planet develops, the growing edge moves upward from one great energy center to the next. The primary period of anatomical growth for *Homo sapiens* climaxed about 200,000 years ago with the biological climax that brought our bipedal stance. The primary period of cultural growth for the species was about 40,000 years ago, concomitant with spoken language. Cultural change has run its course. We now must reorient spiritually/physically in order for the species to survive.

In this reorientation, your memories, my memories, and our species' memories are steadily becoming at-one, or synchronized. The term *at-one* is not used here only in its mystical sense of atonement. I am also referring to a scientific resonance of wavelength and quantum energy, frequency, and bandwidth, in which our brains are learning to significantly reduce inter-entity resistance or "noise." In a mathematical sense, this means achieving maximal degrees of freedom; and in physics terms, this means bringing friction to a point approaching zero. Humans are thus becoming able to tune consciously to the overtones, harmonics, and *chord progressions of thought* generated at the species and planet level. The ultimate result is a new branch of the family tree, whose full members I am calling *lifeseeds:* persons with tremendous energy to assist in the healing of our planet and all its life-forms. Lifeseeds will be people at the third phase of the emergence of *Homo deva.*

To bring this capacity within reach of a critical mass of humanity, we need to traverse the developmental boundary from *Homo sapiens* to *Homo deva.* This is easy to say, but quite a challenge to do. Yet this transition is critical—no, it is absolutely essential—if we are to create a viable future for our children and grandchildren. In order to describe the transition most cogently, I have chosen to use the model of the energy chakras. Two alternative models, which also appealed to me, were the primary physical forces (gravity, electricity, magnetism, nuclear, and particle physics), and the biological phases of cell mitosis, where chromatin in the nucleus separates into segments or chromosomes. A central tenet of my work and my life experience is that all three of these models are describing the same reality; and all three are intimately involved in the threshold we are currently traversing. We, as members of an emerging species, are entering a new planetary chakra, we are learning to express through and with new levels of physics, and we are beginning to govern the genetic code of cells. The healing of Earth's children will integrally involve all three of these realms.

The model of the energy chakras, which I have chosen as a way of describing the 21st-century threshold, has been around for thousands of years. One excellent book that I refer you to in this regard is Wauters (1999); there are many more at your local bookstore or online. As you may know, of the seven major energy centers within a living being, the *heart* is the fourth center, the pivot. The *throat* is the fifth center, mediating between heart and head. Within this model, we are evolving upward from the heart of Earth, into the throat of Earth. The new branch of the family tree will include very creative hominids who will express directly and potently the *throat energy* of our beautiful planet. Earth's heart energy, expressed most fully by *Homo sapiens*, is now ready to move upward, to energize and vivify Earth's throat energy, expressed by *Homo deva*. Our species will need to partner with *Homo deva* as the next higher species. And through this partnership of friends, the greater wholeness that we all sense inside will be released to blossom through Earth's peoples. That is the core of this book's message.

The time has arrived for the next great shift for humanity, beyond our cultural big bang to the *creative big bang*. Many implications of this step have been discussed and debated during the past forty years. Those implications will be further researched and investigated, reflected on, meditated about, and prayed on during the next two decades. If our species is to survive the transition in a healthy state we will need all of those responses, because we are in for a very bumpy ride during the next decade. What appears as a natural process when seen as a planetary growth spurt can bring major trauma for some of the species, nations, and families involved. In this book, we will look at some of the biological, physical, cultural, and spiritual changes that are approaching in the transition period.

During the past half-century, we entered Phase 1 of a three-phase process. The transition we have entered involves a species *shift in identification*. During Phase 1, many people became aware that they are a living part of the planet, and in fact that all living beings on the planet together form a single entity, a species-and-Earth energy system. Thousands of people have had this experience during the past several decades through study, travel to other countries, learning other languages, student exchanges, meditation and other spiritual practices, near-death experiences, international employment and education, and guided imagery for pain management and other conditions. Many of these people have become active in social justice, environmental, transnational exchange, and green economy organizations.

During the past two decades, we have moved as a species into Phase 2 of the process. In this phase, thousands and gradually millions of people integrated a consciousness of planetary caring and dedication into their personal lives. They regularly commit time, money, and personal energy to bettering conditions in their community and the larger world. Their emotional identification has expanded to embrace all of humanity and our planet-home. And that identification is expressed tangibly through *daily intention and innovations*. The individual's emotions and personal will are aligned in efforts to better life for all peoples.

There is a third phase, a phase of biological links between individuals and the planet. It is a phase of beyond-human identity precipitating directly to physical / spiritual form. Individual humans are evolving beyond the limitations of both consciousness and will. The third phase grounds the planet's evolutionary shift through the greater energy of a new biological species. Some spiritual traditions call this "opening the direct path." Without this third phase, the consciousness and "human potential" movements of the 1970s and 1980s would continue to float two feet off the ground and would lack the traction required to bring tangible, worldwide changes. We might say that the third phase involves a species-wide step of enlightenment, but it is not the kind of enlightenment that seeks to leave the world. Phase 3, which humanity is now entering, will produce a *steady-state enlightenment* on an ecological level because it is vitalized by the planet's own lifethread. Through the process of solving humanity's ecological / spiritual crisis, we participate in incarnating the lifethread of Earth. *Homo devas* are the messenger and the message of that lifethread, the carrier-waves for peace on Earth. The family of humanity is rapidly approaching an actual birth in which *Homo sapiens* will be the midwife for the new sibling called *Homo deva*.

The transition that we are looking at has been described in many ways during the past fifty years. You have probably read books and attended programs that anticipated the transformation. The books listed in the Resources section at the end of this volume are a small sampling of the many wise elders who have led us to this step. We are now entering the homestretch. Unanticipated events can, and often do, happen in the homestretch. The homestretch is a time of acceleration, a time for precise focus of one's energy, and a good time to breathe steadily and link together with friends.

The nature of our goal has altered significantly since we turned the corner into the new century. It is no longer a question of "if" the change will come, and no longer a question of "when." The issue has come down to *how* it will happen. How are we going to make the transition to the next era? Will we reach the major thresholds of the years 2020 and 2025 with about 6.3 billion people still on Earth, or only 4 billion, or even fewer? The stakes are high. Given the current major strains on Earth's ecosystems, the lack of coherent collaboration between nation-states, and the general absence of corporate commitment to planetary and human stewardship, we are looking at a potential for serious die-off and violent disruptions in our species. We need to link closely together and look at ways to prevent that from happening.

The key is this: Our coordinated actions now are critical to the future for all children of Earth. Humanity as a whole will fully enter Phase 3 of this evolutionary transition sometime between 2020 and 2025. The United States will have a central part in making the transformation happen. The relationship between the United States and the United Nations will be critical during this period. Phase 3 also requires us to face directly our own national resistance to this evolutionary step. That resistance includes what we want to see and what we don't choose to watch in the mass media, how we participate in co-creating the "objective events" on the 6:00 news.

The transition will be much more than a shift in consciousness, although that is an important element. We might even say that such a shift in consciousness is necessary for species transition, but it is not sufficient. It is only the initial step. The quantum step (or "jump time," in Jean Houston's term) is a fully objective shift in the evolutionary process:

- It is a *biological step* to the next significant level of planetary functioning, beyond minerals, flora, fauna, and hominids.
- It is a *spiritual step* to the next significant level of planetary manifestation.

Both those statements are true and will be physically demonstrated. In the next few years, empirical studies about the cognitive, affective, and physiological functioning of *Homo devas* will appear among a wide variety of disciplines, such as biology, gerontology, genetics, immunology, learning theory, developmental psychology, pediatrics, physics, and astrophysics.

Nature is picking us up (by the scruff of our neck in some cases) and carrying us to the next quantum step in Earth's evolution. But each of us still has a choice. We can move upward of our own free will and take volitional steps into the new era. Or we can be carried, yelling and resisting, as part of the remnant of *Homo sapiens* who choose to stay in the separatist mode (or "dominator culture," in Eisler's description). The choice is ours. We are at a fork in the evolutionary road. We need to choose—together *and* individually.

People with whom I have discussed the idea of *Homo deva* over the past twenty years generally think that it has explanatory power. They say that the concept's implications for both health and ecological issues help re-frame many of the trends that have puzzled them in the past few years. As several 20th-century scientists have remarked, humanity cannot solve all of the problems that we have created at the same mental level where we created the problems. We need to *grow to the next level*, in order to look outward and see possible solutions. Problems produced by rationality demand suprarational solutions. Moving into identification with *Homo deva* provides a leverage point from which we can gain new insights about the problems and challenges facing our families, friends, clients, communities, nations, and our species. *Homo deva* can become a beloved friend and mentor to *Homo sapiens*, and someone we can trust implicitly to have our best interests at heart.

In the process of gaining that greater perspective, we will also develop strategic plans that fit our many unique communities. Such plans will incorporate the best available wisdom from interdisciplinary teams. These plans need careful discussion and review by the wise teachers of our species from many cultures and nations.

The mental development of *Homo deva* will be a central component of the creativity of Earth. Because individual *Homo devas* will express and embody the *throat of the planet*, their innovations and high-voltage energy will help us solve many of the problems now plaguing humanity. The impetus for these innovations will emerge through many people in over two hundred countries on all six continents. These individuals will serve as visible core threads of species unity by the year 2020 and, in a very real way, are already serving in this capacity. The term *core thread* implies a dynamic, living energy field between the part (a person) and the greater whole (humanity and planet). My best estimate at this time is that ten thousand people will have traversed all three phases of the step to *Homo deva*, to become lifeseeds, by the year 2020. You will probably know some of them, or even be one of them. Perhaps your children or grandchildren will be among them. And the rest of us will benefit by the positive acceleration in our own steps that this energy field of innovation will stimulate. The rest of humanity will be enabled and empowered to take whatever steps are next for each individual.

In fact, you and I and our friends are helping right now to bring this incredible change into our world. You are an integral part of a very deep evolutionary shift. From another angle, you are bearing witness to a very deep period of spiritual revelation. That is the beauty of the epoch of our new species: The truth of science and the wisdom of spiritual (and indigenous) traditions across all cultures will be shown to be integral parts of the great transition from *Homo sapiens* to the kingdom beyond.

The description of this shift may also suggest to you why there is very concentrated and dark resistance at this time. We have all seen in the past few years a virulent and violent resistance at both international and community levels. All of humanity's subconscious fears about taking this next evolutionary step—the fear of running out of energy, the fear of being left behind, rage and envy about disparities in energy / wealth, and fears about the great unknown that we must eventually face—all are rising to the surface concurrently. The archetypal fears of *Homo sapiens*, collectively, will be on full visceral view during this decade.

I have a strong hunch that you have already chosen to step into Phase 1 of the species transition. You and your network of family, friends, and like-minded colleagues are working to make the world a better place, not just a place to plunder and gather the "most toys." You contribute time, money, and passion to worthy causes that you believe in, some of them nonprofits and / or environmental organizations (see Appendix 6 for some representative groups). Indeed, many of you are dedicating yourselves to bettering the world in daily life through vocational and avocational choices that reflect deep caring for our species as a whole.

How do we help more people click into Phase 1, and then move toward Phase 2? A critical mass of humanity needs to make this shift to Phase 2 together, and we need to do so within ten years. This introductory book is intended to suggest some of the issues and implications of the transition to *Homo deva*. Many other researchers and educators are presenting related work on the great turning or the world change; some of them are referenced in the following chapters. From among all of us, we will find the wisdom and focused intention that we need.

∾

A suggestion: Some readers may find it helpful to read this book twice—once for a transfusion of energy, and a second time for the more practical and strategic implications. The optimism in these pages is real, inclusive, and grounded. It is meant to be digested at whatever pace and rhythm works for you. And it is here to stay.

Part One of this book, "Cultural Climax of the Human Family," presents an overview and a closer look at the nature of an evolutionary climax. First we will examine some specifics of our species' *cultural big bang* of 40,000 years ago, and then the agricultural revolution of 10,000 years ago. How have these events prepared us for this next great biological and spiritual emergence? What can we anticipate about the *creative big bang?*

Part Two, "Our *Homo sapiens* Children," presents a specific description of twelve persons who are suffering from the multiple stresses of species transition. When I met them or heard of their situations, these young people (ages eight to thirty) were struggling—either with chronic illness, emotional dysfunction, behavioral acting out, chronic poverty, or other problems. I describe some soft indicators that suggest many of our *Homo sapiens* children are physically embodying the tremendous stresses of our species' transition. Their individual suffering is a highly amplified microcosm of the species macrocosm.

Part Three, "The Biophysics of Our Imminent Divinity," brings together some theoretical material on the implications of *Homo deva* for our view of divinity. The basic question it addresses is: How do we prepare, physically, mentally, morally, and spiritually, for *Homo devas*, divine humans, living among us? Will we be able to welcome these innocent messengers and joyfully accept their powers of creation? If a critical mass of *Homo sapiens* does not welcome the newcomers among us, the *Homo devas* will not survive.

The chapters in Part Three explore this question through concepts such as mind-body integration and spirit-matter synthesis as examples of complex lasers. During the coming decade, these fields of nature's energy are moving into significantly greater coherence between frequency (wisdom), wavelength (caring), and quanta of voltage (unified will). As our species' capacity to govern light and love becomes fully coherent among millions of persons internationally, the *unified field of will* can emerge safely for the first time, thus welcoming the next kingdom. The issue of unified will is a pivotal aspect of *Homo deva's* viability in our world. This step is both very abstract and very personal: How do we, as a species, as communities, and as individuals, prepare for the appearance of *Homo deva*? Listen to how you answer this question for yourself, and you will learn much about the future. It is time to recognize our own inner allies and adversaries.

Part Four, "Our *Homo deva* Children," returns to a discussion of our young people, this time from the perspective of the emerging species. I examine some of their specific characteristics; one chapter, for example, presents a rough estimate of demographic distribution at the year 2000 among the *early-Homo deva*, *mid-Homo deva*, and *high-Homo deva* stages of development. This part of the story is meant to stimulate discussion, debate, and further dialogue.

Finally, Part Five, "Your Next Steps," includes a number of suggested topics and exercises to help you move forward with your next steps. Whether you are approaching the idea of *Homo deva* from the viewpoint of a teacher, parent, counselor, businessperson, or for your own quality-of-life issues, the exercises are planned to be thought provoking and fun at the same time. Hopefully, they will *stretch the boundaries* of who you see yourself to be.

Each section includes several schematic figures that are intended to help you get acquainted with the concept of a new species. Seven appendices provide additional background, directions for research, and more in-depth treatment of some of the ideas. You will find a resources list that presents a diverse sample of wise elders from several disciplines and fields of study. They and many other colleagues are helping guide us on our collective journey during this critical time. Many of these authors and explorers have excellent bibliographies and Internet links to provide further direction. You will likely have names to add to the list, of other people whom you think will be, or that you wish might be, involved in this effort. Whichever resources give uplift to your heart are the ones that will also help the world.

There are a couple of researchers and writers whose work shares a close kinship with mine, while the external areas of our professional focus are different. I would like to mention, in this regard, the work of Jean Houston, Thomas Berry, Barbara Marx Hubbard, and Angeles Arrien. Although I had not met any of these four individuals when this book was first published (2004), I felt as if we had been acquainted for a long time. It is also curious, in terms of the unfolding of consciousness, that I had not read any of the books by these four authors until quite recently (in 2001). The themes we are all exploring are so clearly parts of the one work.

Because my professional focus during the past two decades has been on serving children and youth in hospitals, or those incarcerated, or those receiving emergency social services, I did not keep current with developments in these other areas. Yet it is true for this sample of four pioneers, as well as for the others listed in the Resources section, that the work each of us is doing has intimate cross-fertilization effects; we have all been nourishing each other for years on the level of greater mind, and for that I am grateful.

You may already be familiar with the work of these particular pioneers. But in case you are not, here is a capsule introduction: Jean Houston's areas of focus include extensive cross-cultural research on aspects of the cultural transformation; expanding our view of the arts and communication media as a central part of the transformation; and the growing impact of the Internet as an expression of our species' collective mind. Thomas Berry's areas of focus are the ecological crisis, our function in the history of the universe, and our species' opportunity to become an ethical and healing presence on Earth; he also provides crucial insights into the role of educational institutions during the planetary passage. We all become ethical ecologists in Berry's hands.

Barbara Marx Hubbard's areas of focus are in community building, in the many facets of our national political transformation, and in developing training tools for adults to link to what she terms the "universal human." Her theorizing is quite long-term, in considering future evolution of humans beyond the solar system. She has recently begun a community-based endeavor in "conscious evolution" in Santa Barbara, California. Finally, Angeles Arrien's area of focus is on the multiple aspects of the path we are on, as persons, tribes, and larger groups; she describes in exquisite and colorful detail the roles of teacher, healer, visionary, and spiritual warrior, and their mutual contributions to the whole. Her cross-cultural view, including the wisdom and compassion of native peoples, is crucial to our mission.

I recommend to you the work of these four and their associates and, beyond them, the work of all those listed in the Resources. Their books and Web sites provide leads to other aspects of their work. We will need a diverse, collaborative, and networked approach for the effort required in this decade of decision. It is a time to celebrate our many talents and dedicated commitment to help heal all of Earth's children.

PART ONE

CULTURAL CLIMAX
OF THE HUMAN FAMILY

Chapter 1

EVOLUTION IS KNOCKING AT OUR DOOR

The rumor that human evolution is finished is wildly exaggerated. We need to step back and examine our family tree from the planetary perspective. Two million years ago, we were on our own as a distinct species—no longer a tree-dwelling primate like our cousins the chimps. The pre-humans and pre chimps had parted ways from a common ancestor sometime in the mists between four and seven million years ago (mya). Even today, the gorillas, chimps, bonobo chimps, and humans all share in common 98 percent of their DNA heritage. That fact implies quite directly that there was a common ancestor species for all primates, almost certainly less than ten mya. At a relatively recent fork in the trail, about 2 mya, our branch of the family tree gave us the crucial 2 percent genetic difference from all of our hominid cousins. Much more recently, by 200,000 years ago, we were definitely a separate species, described as anatomically modern humans.

That crucial difference of 2 percent nudged us on, as we moved out of the forest and onto the savanna, and later the prairies. We learned to walk upright, migrate long distances, vocalize language, adapt to diverse and severe climates, and live as tribal bands on several continents. During the succeeding thousands of years, we adapted tools for survival, for communication, for commerce, and for creativity.

Our tools were diverse and powerful, including bone clubs, baskets for carrying food, fire, medicinal herbs, folktales and oral legends, cave paintings, domestication of animals, agriculture, wagon wheels, logboats, alphabets, musical instruments, quillpens, currency, clocks, steam engines, trains, electrical generators, cars, transistors, airplanes, atomic fuel cells, silicon wafers, satellites, solar panels, modems, GPS and cell phones. The 2 percent difference has led us to blossom in great and marvelous external adaptation, particularly during the past 30,000 years since our *cultural big bang.*

We have learned to be more than animal in social ways as well as technological—to train teachers for our young ones, to gather in councils and courts to deal with our conflicts, to seek comfort from healers and in hospitals for our times of illness, and to turn to rituals and places of worship for our times of loneliness, when we face separation and death, when we ask "why?" We have learned to wage prolonged and systematic war as no animal could, and to negotiate peace with all the considerable ardor that a human can muster.

We have gone beyond our animal-self in several other important respects—learning to enjoy face-to-face sex, to develop hundreds of kinds of currency as abstract media of exchange for goods and services, to project our dreams and fears through books and movies where we can "lose ourselves" in tales of other times and places. We have developed cosmologies describing the birth of the Universe, and we have sent technologic probes with messages of greeting beyond our solar system. The past two hundred millennia have been good to us as a species.

The most recent 30 to 40 millennia have been a steady acceleration of *Homo sapiens'* impact on Earth, truly the ascent of humanity. We are now the dominant life form on the planet, at 6.3 billion and growing. That dominance is both a trademark of our success and a source of our possible extinction in the drama of survival.

Here we are, 6.3 billion strong in the first decade of the 21st century. We survived Y2K (remember?), and then chaos broke out. Financial markets teeter... Urban homicides... New York and Washington terrorism... Anthrax poisonings... Crisis of authority between USA and U.N. What is happening? We are experiencing—in our bodies, our families, our tribes, and our cultural events—a mega-species shock, a shock that will only subside as we face the bigness of our future and recognize the real challenges and the grace that lie ahead. As we learn to look with deep eyes or "sacred eyes," in Keck's (1992) term, we see that a deep shift is happening. With this larger shift, our tremendous energy as a species will be liberated—energy for healing, innovation, community building, and celebration of life.

We have always been a hardy species. Over the past 40,000 years, we have developed multiple ways of expressing caring, innovation, and creativity. Yet, those qualities have often been submerged beneath the brutality of warfare, of neglect, of competition for resources.

Name your poison: fear, jealousy, greed, arrogance, loneliness, distrust, hatred, envy, rage, revenge, doubt, cynicism, and contempt. All those are wounds of the human heart. It is a central tenet of our story that those poisons are ready to be collectively lifted. The human heart seeks to lift the toxic load, and liberate the goodness and truth and beauty held inside all of us. We have the intelligence, the caring and compassion, and the courage to do it. We know about critical mass, and the hundredth monkey. We understand the holographic effect of healing microcosms, and energizing primary nodes in a network. Whether we as individuals feel ready or not, the next step is pulsing inside us, steady as a divine heartbeat. The shared wisdom of our friends, neighbors, and future selves can guide our daily choices across this new and unfamiliar landscape.

What are we lacking? The unified will to do the lifting of those poisons out of our systemic life. You remember, from biology or developmental psychology, that when any level reaches its deepest crisis, the solution can be found on the next higher level.

Query: Where can humanity's heart gain leverage to lift those poisons out and fully dilute them? Those poisons are threatening to swamp our species and drag us down into the entropy of self-destruction. Answer: The leverage comes from the next higher developmental level, from humanity's throat; and in a deeper sense, from the throat center of the planet. The practical solutions to our energy crisis, the wise guidance from young bodhisattvas in many cultures, and the unified field of physics made accessible and economical all come from the same source: The next evolutionary level. At each stage of evolution, we look upward and reach for greater wholeness. The next level reaches down and magnetically attracts our ascent. The upward movement of growth and the reaching downward movement function as partners. This step is no exception.

How shall we describe the next level? For now, let us call it the fifth planetary energy center, Earth's fifth major chakra, the fifth physical kingdom of our world, which is ready to emerge. You are part of the solution, dear reader. Through thee is born a living thread of the planetary synthesis of heart-to-head. Through thee arises a breath of the divine fusion of Earth's throat that we are calling human-deva, *Homo deva*. The dual name utilizes the familiar format of genus and species. To benefit from Eldredge's (1998) reminder, "Think of genus as 'general' and species as 'specific.'" *Homo deva* is the direct incarnation of Earth's throat.

We are entering a biopsychospiritual transition within the genus Homo, which will produce the new species *Homo deva*. It is time to open your deep eyes, and breathe the air of Earth made whole and holy. Today is the time to open your own throat and sing the song of peace and justice that you seek in the world. Through the passion, wisdom, and harmonizing of your voice with others, the voice of Earth is rising—we become the change that needs to happen.

Evolution is once again knocking at our door. For several centuries it has been a quiet, persistent knock that has sounded through our species' beautiful wisdom traditions and, more recently, through our scientific search for truth. With compassion to yourselves, hear this message: Both paths were necessary. The past couple of centuries were not a digression or mistaken path. The pulse of evolution truly needed us to grow up in heart and mind both, in knowledge and experience, before we would be ready to co-create the next step of Earth's growth. The sound that you hear is a knock at the door of our collective heart-and-mind, and it has been patient for a long time. But we would now ignore it at our peril.

As many researchers and authors have described in various ways, the fork in the road has arrived. We each get to choose which evolutionary branch we journey up during the next ten to twenty critical years. If we choose the path of unified Earth family, we will help bring forth the coherent vision, the wisdom, compassion, creativity, strength, courage, faith, perseverance, and aligned action to become a thoroughly divine species. We have choices ahead.

The many problems facing humanity have been extensively researched and documented (and the Resources section gives many excellent books and calls to action of the past decade or two). The crises don't need repeating here. What is clear is that it is now time for us to move on. Another major fork in the road has arrived. The ascent of mankind has reached the critical threshold, ready for another evolutionary punctuation mark. We cannot solve the problems created by *H. sapiens* at the level of *H. sapiens*. It is biologically impossible.

Again, as happened 40 millennia ago, part of our nature is stretching upward. This time, it is more than 2 percent of our makeup, more than a tiny fraction of the current species who will make the transition to the next life form. Many writers have described the great step that is approaching; this time it is pulsing within the brains and hearts of millions of humans. The evolutionary whisper tells us that human ways alone cannot bring viable peace between our tribes, between our children. *Homo sapiens* technology alone cannot express the wisdom and generosity needed for humanity and the planet to co-exist as an integrated and viable ecosystem.

But somewhere inside, you already knew that.

Natural selection is a powerful teacher and mentor, the very best that has ever existed. Evolution is calling to us once again, saying to the pioneers among us, "It is time for the next species…" Sadly, many people are too numb or too frightened to recognize that message. They will cling to familiar ways—just as our chimp cousins did long ago, just as our nearer European cousins, the Neanderthals, did more recently. The numb ones in our 21st-century culture will scramble desperately to survive, will scramble to propose extremely shortsighted things like drilling for oil in Alaska's wilderness in order to sustain fossil-fuel addictions for six additional months. The numb and fearful ones will continue to support early–*Homo sapiens* habits like restricting women's access to literacy (when a mother's literacy in any culture is a top indicator for her children's health). They will seek a thousand other short-term solutions in their desperate attempt to keep the acquisitive *Homo sapiens* identity intact and defended. Whatever their gender or nationality, their religion or political stripe, the future for these persons is shrinking daily. Pursuing these outmoded solutions, habits, and morés will lead nowhere fast; and unless they change objectively in the next very few years, their viability as a sub-species will fade away.

The fork in the road beckons. The message drums in our brains and hearts—we must move on.

∿

The next step, beyond *Homo sapiens*, will do more than bring better tools to improve our infrastructure for the 21st century. The next step will produce more than effective national or state planning, more than integrated educational goals, more than enlightened consciousness, more than fighting terrorism "over there," paying off the federal debt, developing exotic antibiotics, genetic engineering, nano-robotics, or multinational e-commerce. Most certainly, the next step will be beyond the cosmetics of "kinder, gentler politics."

Heaven knows, the human family can benefit greatly from each of these endeavors. However, what is now emerging is deeper. To offer a simile: Humanity's next step is to current human politics as thunder above Half Dome is to clapping your hands loudly. We can make a great deal of cultural noise down here by ourselves—but we are now approaching the human / planet interface where our creative and healing powers will increase by an unprecedented quantum step.

Evolution's next step involves a mental, emotional, behavioral, biological, planetary, and soul transition initiated by and expressed through a subset of individual humans. The people of this subset are serving as trailblazers and wilderness guides for the rest of our kin. Some of you, your generation and your children's generation, will provide sufficient momentum in over two hundred nations to lead our species across the threshold by the year

2020, and into the next chapter by 2025. If you haven't already done so, you are hereby invited to join as part of that critical mass.

This book suggests that we of the 21st century are the crossover specimens, the first fruit of the transition to the next 10,000 years. And, for purposes of digesting such a quantum leap and developing strategic plans for the more immediate horizon, you are welcome to think of the evolutionary transition as being only 1,000 years, or 100 years, or a mere 10 years. Whichever horizon evokes the inner doorway for you — that is what this book is talking about!

We as a global family are reaching toward a place much more grounded than a "new age" of consciousness. We are rationally and deliberately going to cross the event horizon into the next evolutionary epoch. This is a very literal event horizon in the physics sense of the term. We are crossing from a realm of blackhole entropy, where things wear out and energy dissipates, into a realm of syntropy where life generates and nurtures more life. And it is also an event horizon in the full biological sense, a quantum step in mental and physiological functioning that will bring a natural integration of *H. sapiens* and the next higher level of Earth life. Through that synthesis, the next species is now being born, on all continents of the planet.

This book does not ignore the very real problems we are facing. The resistant part of us (individually, in groups, in tribes, and collectively as a species) is very acquisitive, aggressive, and articulate; and it is threatening to get out of control. In order to open a new pathway beyond that resistance, we need help. Where can we find such help? Perhaps from the future.

We need to ask for help from our future-self. Or, if you prefer the mystical view, we need to ask for help from above. As a critical mass of humanity begins to realize this simple and profound truth, the path will open wider. We need to open our eyes to our "cousins of tomorrow," and thereby strengthen the link between intelligent creative powers. That link is nurtured through intuitive / analytic innovations. By such innovations, the wisdom of year 2025, or year 2100, can be accessed, organized, disseminated, taught, and shared.

If that idea sounds too good to be true, then you're in luck. The book you are holding was written with you in mind.

Here is the premise: As a global family, we are beginning to glimpse the species-and-kingdom beyond humans—much as humans stepped beyond the animal kingdom. And much as modern humans, such as Cro-Magnons, stepped beyond the Neanderthals in the Near East and Europe. Both steps took biological maturation, emotional stabilizing, and neurological stretching in terms of greater brain organization. Those steps took courage and steadfast will, a day at a time. We have now reached the cultural climax of the human family, where the limitations of culture itself are the boundary. It is a more accelerated version of the kind of step we took about 30,000–40,000 years ago, when we expanded our capacities to include spoken language, visual arts, and complex tools. We will describe this process in more detail in later chapters.

From what I see thus far, the tightest part of the cultural climax will last another ten years. The duration and depth of the climax will depend on how thoroughly we move forward. It also depends, to a great degree, on how many of the "we" actually do move forward. And lastly, the climax depends on how we see the act of creation ahead of us. We are, after all, re-creating ourselves.

One reason that you and your friends and neighbors are all moving at high speed in your daily lives, and yet don't have a clear sense of where we are going, is that we are prime pioneers. What hasn't been described before is that we are moving across a threshold that is much higher and deeper than humans normally think of themselves. We are moving into extraordinary new territory. Until now, we haven't seen how truly BIG the territory is.

The people who are recognizing the quiet message to move on, those who actively seek a hopeful new beginning, are explorers. By reading this book (and any of the books in the Resources section), you are joining that cadre of beyond-human explorers. You are explorers not just of a new century or millennium dawning, but also of ten millennia into the future. We are living in an historic time that will soon provide hard evidence for the hypothesis of "punctuated evolution" (proposed by the late Stephen Gould and others). This step goes far beyond discussions of who is liberal/conservative, high-tech or agrarian, and who are proponents of sustainable communities or operational resilience for companies on Wall Street.

Take a long, slow breath here. We are talking about the planet's natural growth and development, an epochal shift. If this concept makes sense to you, then perhaps you are ready to become an early guide of the next epoch. The guides are people who can help their neighbors and others in their local community to take their own steps forward, one day at a time. We will all need partners and guides during this critical decade, to teach each other how to traverse the new territory of Earth's next quantum step. It may be reassuring, at times, to recall that evolution moves one day at a time — consistently and faithfully — one day at a time.

Does this idea of a new species sound too outrageous to contemplate? If so, that is OK. The idea does take some getting used to! And the concept won't fit for everyone. Some people are having a good life and are not seeking any bigger view. Maybe he is practicing divine detachment, with enlightenment that needs to float two feet off the ground for a while longer. Or she has lived in a gated community for the past two years, and hasn't been near a newsstand lately. The idea of a new species is literally out-of-tune for them. The idea would introduce unwelcome dissonance to those people, and that is not my intent. It is important to clearly state here that I trust the timing of individuals and their sense of whether the seed idea is ripe for them.

My intention with this book is to touch people who are ready for a bigger view, those who have been shaking their heads a lot during the past three years, wondering what happened to the optimism that glimmered for a while after the Berlin Wall came down, the Cold War ended, and we started a new century. I seek to connect with those who want above all to trust human beings. And yet, they realize that in practical situations such a stance can be inefficient and frustrating, if not outright dangerous.

Perhaps you, too, realize that what passes as consensual reality is getting increasingly outrageous, and the trend is accelerating. After working with suffering people for thirty years as an educational psychologist and juvenile justice professional, and studying many disciplines of science and wisdom traditions, I have found that the idea of a new species lifting us to Earth's throat center makes eminent sense. Indeed, it makes more sense than many resolutions passed by our Congress in recent sessions, or the trends and ads presented in the mass media. Given that, I send you sincere best wishes for whatever road you choose. I hope that the following pages provide food for thought as you proceed in this decade of decision.

You are invited to remember: Mary believes that it is time for you to claim your birthright as an evolutionary pioneer.

~

Chapter 2

THE RECENT 10,000-YEAR JOURNEY

About 30,000 – 40,000 years ago, our ancestors brought forth upon several continents a new way of being. This epochal shift has been called our cultural big bang. It is the period when Stone Age humans suddenly began to create and express themselves much more elaborately (see Klein; Arsuaga; Leslie; Tattersall for related archaeological and paleoanthropological research). DNA evidence reported in the summer of 2002 supports Richard Klein's hypothesis that genetic mutations about 50,000 years ago may have provided the basis for our capacity for language. And about 10,000 years later, only an eyeblink in planetary time, the cultural big bang occurred. It appears that vocal language probably laid the foundation for our tremendous expansion in artistic, tool-making, and regional self-expression capacities.

If we can say that human "culture" began 40,000 years ago, then early "civilization" began only 10,000 years ago. Humans successfully began the cultivation of agriculture and domestication of animals about 10 millennia ago or 8,000 BCE (Before Christian Era). This was in the dawn of recorded history. This chapter in our collective story is an important time-marker. The hominids of ten millennia ago were clearly relatives of ours. They were early humans. They walked and ran in a smooth bipedal manner. They talked in several languages. They lived, birthed children, raised crops, and died in communities. We have discovered evidence of the permanent shelters they built, some of which had elaborate heating systems.

Think for a moment about those early humans of 10 millennia ago. Living in settlements, no longer nomadic followers of the animal herds, they raised their children, consulted their elders, celebrated good harvests, had rituals of burial for their dead, waged war on their neighbors, and looked to the sky and to nature for inspiration for their paintings, carvings, jewelry, and tokens of trade. They were, in every anatomical measure, the same species as we are. These were our kin, the early *Homo sapiens*.

Naturally, the humans of 10,000 years ago were using modes of transportation, methods of construction, education and healing practices, and many other sociocultural tools that were more rudimentary than those we are accustomed to. Yet, our kin at the dawn of civilization had dreams of finding more than survival. They searched and found ways to cultivate crops and healing herbs, to develop wagon wheels, to make technological innovations and spiritual connections that allowed them to build incredible ritual sites such as Stonehenge about 5,000 years ago (3,000 BCE), and to develop new areas of commerce and trade to improve their daily lives. Between these ancestors and our century, there is continuity but also a great step forward. It is crucial to keep in mind both the continuity and the quantum step.

Modern civilizations are considered to have begun about 6,000 years ago, with humanity producing large urban centers and hundreds of languages. Similarly, we can describe contemporary civilizations as emerging more recently—about 3,000 years ago in Asian and African tribes, and 600 years ago among European tribes. What we have named the Renaissance is an example, among several, of the acceleration of human cultural development. Within the span of a century or two, roughly 1400 to 1600, there was a great creative flowering in the West. The innovations in the arts and sciences of that era significantly increased our self-expression, stimulated the human exploration of much of the physical world, and enhanced our ability to regulate or manipulate our habitat in ways that were inconceivable to earlier generations. Within the past 500 years, we as a species began to blossom as masters of the world; that is, *Homo sapiens* became governors of all spaces on Earth.

Today we are approaching a comparable step of expansion, but in a different dimension—the dimension called Time. While the past 10,000 years of civilization enabled us to explore and gain mastery of space on Earth, the new epoch will enable us to explore and gain mastery of time. We have made tremendous strides in the past 10 millennia. Can you imagine a comparable degree of change lying ahead of us, just around the corner? Imagine for a moment some of the kinds of innovations that will be possible for creative people who can think centuries ahead, as we think of 5-year school curriculum plans or 5-year corporate strategic plans. From this perspective of greater time vision, the challenge is to look so deep that the very future can reveal to us some solutions for today's critical problems.

The Current Challenge

The unique challenge of the early 21st century is to solve a sufficient number of humanity's problems that we will be able to keep our species viable. The problems we currently face were largely created with our intellect and our emotional passions—especially our territoriality, possessiveness, and material acquisitiveness (which are, to a large degree, secondary effects of our fear of death). These tendencies have produced great inequities of wealth and resources, as well as the unprecedented growth in human population.

In our present situation, moving across a knife-edge path at the climax of human culture, our species is encountering severe turbulence. *Homo sapiens* are having trouble finding a stable direction, finding ways to relieve stress, ways to solve local, national, and international ecological, health, and social problems. Notice again in Figure 1 how many of the species preceding ours are now extinct. Current estimates are that 37,000 species per year are going extinct from a worldwide pool of about 10 million species. Yet, several scientists have posed the obvious question, "Why should we care?" In reply, Niles Eldredge (1998), Thomas Berry (1999), and others remind us from a biological perspective that we literally have been living outside of Nature since the invention of agriculture 10,000 years ago. It is not so much that we don't "care," but that we don't "see." With the limits inherent in *Homo sapiens* vision, our passion for the future is limited to our immediate self, offspring, and community. The urban and suburban population centers shield us from the critical role of long-term functioning ecosystems in keeping human beings alive and healthy.

How many species can the world afford to lose before the biomass system begins to implode? Estimates vary, and the parameters are too technical for our discussion here. The bottom line is that humanity and its ecosystem / culture are having serious trouble. But we are having trouble not because we aren't smart or courageous or dedicated. We are having trouble because we haven't been looking big enough: High enough. Wide enough. Deep enough in the daily lives of our children.

We clearly have a lot of work to do. This initial book about *Homo deva* is focused toward all the dedicated change agents at the local level who are shoveling out the barn on a daily basis: the teachers, court service workers, social workers, nurses, staffers at local nonprofits and NGOs, city and county employees who maintain a beam of compassion and dedication in public service in the midst of dark conditions, and all those still holding the torch of idealism for community building. These people are extremely dedicated, yet most of them don't see clearly why the path has recently become so difficult ... and so dangerous.

One way to explain the suddenly steeper slope of our path (e.g., rates of violence, severe county and state budget crises, accelerating rates of chronic illness among adolescents and young adults) is that we have reached the transition phase in birthing the new species. Anyone who has been a participant or family member at a birthing knows that the transition is a crucial and often frightening time. The transition is an acute and sacred place of passing between nonlife to life, from potential to actual energy. That phrase also accurately describes the current decade for humanity. We are literally entering a new stage of physical life and death on Earth.

The changes will necessarily encompass more than a new global culture, a new political order, new educational systems, new economic models, new technological infrastructures, new religious mythos, new medical paradigms, and a unified field from theoretical physics, made manifest. All those and their practical applications are certainly needed, and many good people are working in each of those areas, bless them.

And yet, all those areas of innovation and focus derive from our identity as a species. Self-identity is a key component now, as it was at the beginning of our 10,000-year journey in civilization. When we stopped roaming as hunter-gatherer tribes and settled into villages and began agriculture, we numbered 5 million. Those 5 million people created civilizations 10 millennia ago. And in the process of beginning urban civilizations, they stepped forward as an "I", they forged an identity. Those early *Homo sapiens*, on six continents by then, were evolving the basics of a fully developed species personality. They were creating the ego of humanity, the integral self-organizing principle that has brought us such tremendous progress in exploring and regulating the world. We conquered most infectious diseases and the barrier of distances with that strength of species-ego.

Now, that same ego has become our nemesis. Our rampant exploration and resource depletion have made domination the rule of our culture. Me and mine, and us vs. them have become the hallmarks of our predicament. As Eisler (2000), Kozol (2000), and LaDuke (1999) have eloquently described, the tide needs to turn in order for our children to walk into a viable future. Rather than domination, we need partnership models, integral dialogue-building, and respect for indigenous voices in order to reach toward those who are wedded to domination and also toward those who are ready for a major change.

We—you and I and several million of our closest friends—are beginning to face our deepest resistance. We are facing and naming our cocoon of fears, womb of matter, shadow self, fallen angel, fission power of splitting atoms, particle physics, magnetic meltdown of entropy, great adversary. And in the naming, we disidentify from the fears, and lift upward. Among the 6 billion of us, a critical mass is ready to lift upward as the *soul of humanity*—as fearless butterfly, spirit baby born of matter, light-body self, tangible angel, fusion power, unified field physics, magnetic melt-up of syntropy, great reunion. In that transformation, initiated at the identity level, we form a critical biomass that blossoms steadily and inevitably. The great Yes to life has begun.

That blossoming was glimpsed in a recent acute phase in 1989 as the nations in Eastern Europe said Yes! to democracy. The tidal wave for liberation came through hundreds of thousands of people, gathering in the capitals of imperial totalitarian states — and the Berlin Wall fell. No one person, no dozens of persons, no hundreds of persons could have done that. It took a critical mass of hundreds of thousands to express an early seed of the unified field of will of humanity. The potent heart of the planet was lifting and finding its voice.

After 40,000 years of spoken language, this is where the climax of culture has led us: to a planetary moment when a nucleus of humanity deliberately (rationally and lovingly) answers evolution's summons. And by our response to that summons, we — humans and the planet together — bring forth the leap that we have dreamt of and yet dared not bring forth into the risky realms of "daily life." How many of you have had the experience of hiding a beautiful ability or a beam of wisdom deep inside you because it wouldn't be safe to bring it into the light of day? As we learn to speak a new language, in the truest response to the freedom and creativity that are at our core, nothing can stop us. The full birth of our heart language in the 21st century will be an exact, higher analog to the blossoming of spoken language 40 millennia ago, and of cities blossoming 10 millennia ago.

Through the steady growth of identity beyond human, we can learn to govern and dilute the poisons, the fission, the violence, the fears, and the ignorance. Our strategy is to energize the glass half-full, to pour life juice liberally and generously, and literally to dilute the dregs at the bottom. As the radiation of our greater identity percolates down through the unified will of millions of people, the innovations will accelerate, the negotiations will become positive, and the win-win approach can become realistic and nurturing instead of a cynical selling point. We can and will bring the next major shift of identity into Earth's life.

And as we lift upward, a great proportion of humanity will lift with us. We as pioneers are the helium to their oxygen, and both gases are lifting together. The shift in identity, from human to beyond-human, is functioning as a natural mental mutation, an adaptive change in our genome. This adaptive change will produce survival advantages comparable to the development of spoken language 40,000 years ago. We are stepping forward and upward, just as our ancestors did. They developed spoken language and became world explorers with creative powers that brought wagon wheels, violins, penicillin, novels, and cell phones, and everything in between!

The 10,000-year journey has been a success in many ways, yet has reached clear limitations. Much of the current turmoil and suffering exists because we are ready to make a gigantic, quantum leap step hop skip jump upward to a soul-identified planet. That is what living from the planetary throat center will be about: Living in and as awake cells of a beloved friend-planet, indeed, a sacred planet. A planet whose heart center, *Homo sapiens*, has learned from the newcomers, the creative ones called *Homo deva*, how to be truly peaceable together.

The changes I am discussing are fully as scientific as they are mystical. The shift upward in identity, on a planetary basis, is another way of describing the practical harnessing of solar energy and the development of cold fusion for everyday applications. Solar energy will be an intimate and potent expression of Earth's throat. The shift will eventually involve the use of *Homo deva* vision to guide laser surgery, expanding the diagnostic techniques that medical intuitives have begun to use in the therapeutic repertoire of research hospitals. And these are just a few examples. Clearly the practical applications of our new journey will keep us busy for several centuries to come!

≈

Chapter 3

Who Are "We" in a
Subject-object Unified Field

After the scientific revolution of 400 years ago, it was generally agreed that we as "subjects" observe "objects." In other words, the scientist observes nature from a detached, objective perspective, thereby coming to know the truth as it really exists. This detachment, however, has been challenged by recent developments in physics that teach us (1) we and all the world can just as validly be understood as wave patterns, and (2) the presence of the observer affects the location and conditions in timespace of the object. This brief digression into a physics concept is needed because both pre-humans (such as your family dog) and beyond-humans (such as your *Homo deva* children) can see patterns that we cannot see. Our seeing-knowing is evolving. What the *Homo deva*s will see utilizes wavelengths from human visual range, and amplitude from deva vision (that is an oversimplification, but it helps us move forward). In this hybrid perception, the boundary between self and other can be more or less permeable, as the persons involved mutually wish it to be.

In the new epoch that we are entering, a unified field is created by the permeable interface between *Homo sapiens* and *Homo deva*. The previously solid subject-object boundary is becoming much more interactive. This species interface will produce some strange results until we understand it better. For example, our identification with parts of the world (e.g., "I am a Californian," as distinct from being an Iowan) is steadily merging with a larger identity with the whole. For example, the relationship between the USA and the collective of humanity as represented at the U.N. is increasingly complex because it is not clear who is the greater whole. The heated visceral reactions on both sides of the debate are testimony to the "self-other" boundary becoming murky. The interface is interpenetrating and growing.

As the identification with the planet increases for thousands of our young people, they are resonating deeply with the changes in the planetary biomass, particularly between the heart center and throat center. As we will discuss in later chapters, the significantly increased incidence of chronic illnesses such as hyperactivity or autism among our children in the past decade is, I believe, partially caused by stresses at the growing edge of our species. We haven't yet learned how to help our children deal with the accelerated inflow of species energy—mentally, emotionally, and physically.

Through natural maturation, most children learn to empathize with the "other" and to identify with larger entities. That is, they develop compassion, the capacity to suffer with (com-passion) the other-as-self. In Figure 2 (page xii), we can see that the growth and development of the human capacity for compassion has gone through comparable phases. Humans feel with others more than animals do. Higher animals, such as chimps and dogs, feel with the other much more than primitive animals or plants do.

Current crises in the world reflect two concurrent wave patterns that result from the developmental step we are traversing: (1) the dregs of humanity's heart wounds or limitations are finally bubbling to the surface, and (2) the early seeds of humanity's (and the planet's) full throat energies are becoming active. Deep distortions of willfulness are one temporary result, until the natural dampening of the wave collision. In other words, our human capacity to *suffer with* (highly developed heart center) is being distorted so that its expression has overlays of violence and hostility. And very twisted, partial, terribly wounded aspects of our species' capacity to create (the next major level) are being expressed.

The prominent case in point from a few years ago in 2001: Nineteen terrorists take control of four airplanes, intentionally and synchronously crash into several buildings, and massacre over 3,000 innocent people. That is a terrible and *awesome* (fear-full) example of *lack of empathy*, of de-personalizing and objectivizing one's fellow human beings. And it is an equally awesome example of planning, logistics, and execution of plan. It is tremendous dedication for a very limited and de-humanized purpose. In other words, that action demonstrated (a) deep dedication of feelings, (b) coherent rational planning, (c) unified field of will at group level, but all this in service to a (d) very narrow self-identity. It is the (d) that needs to shift upward, asap, because the identity level is the governing point, the leverage from which the lower three levels will naturally align and nurture the whole. Unfortunately, our current national leaders of both major parties (and those of other nations) are working from the same narrow self-identity as the perpetrators; they are fighting at the (c) level, which is force of will. This is bringing tremendous clashes and vociferous debate without long-term resolution, until a shift occurs in identity for a critical mass of human beings.

The events of September 11, 2001 illustrate a *breaking of the waves* at the level of our species: A developmental wave crashes at its peak against the shore with everything it has left (in this case, the dregs of humanity's heart wounds). In the same breath, the tremendous energies of the succeeding wave that is just beginning to come in are co-opted or perverted. Creativity is warped into the robes of destruction, self-other is blurred into Shiva destroying the illusions without mercy. In a word, the heart is raped. Rather than expressing *empathy for the other person* in front of them, the terrorists (whether in Middle East, Iraq, Rwanda, Chicago, or Oakland) are caught in *empathy for All*, for which they are courageously willing to die. They are literally caught in the gap between microcosm and macrocosm. They have fallen into a terrible confusion of levels, in which any visible "other" becomes nothing, a barrier to smash in defense of All. They believe that All is to be protected and defended, at any cost, even at the cost of annihilating every particular manifestation in front of them. Personal self becomes a willful instrument of All, a messenger of a vengeful deity, rather than a life-giving candle within the radiant embrace of unified field. This is species-will without the redemptive power and inclusion of agapé, Krishna, Christ-ness.

Are you with me on this crucial point? The past 10,000 years of developing human civilizations have come down to a very narrow, razor's edge decade of decision. A critical mass of people needs to recognize other-as-self and self-as-all, held within the unified field of humanity itself. To say that in more psychodynamic terms, the heart and head of humanity need to move into alignment with each other and express through the throat. And this is indeed happening. However, the residue of resistance between head and heart, at the level of civilizations (e.g., economics, survival techniques of corporations and ethnic groups, and violence between genders as archetypes of head and heart), produces all the traumas and atrocities that we see in the daily news. The dregs of our *Homo sapiens* wounds and limitations are not a pretty sight, nor a gentle one.

We need to energize the greater wave that is emerging, the throat wave of expressing will-through-love. It is the field of I-Thou (first described by Martin Buber in relation to people), now expanding to express the creative power of humans, nature, and all of Earth as family. That is why the re-orientation toward the whole human family is occurring.

Evolution and revelation are indeed partners, in a deep and thoroughly interpenetrating and intimate way. The goal now is to allow that partnership to emerge at a pace that dissolves the subject-object boundary (interactive interface instead of rigid "us vs. them") without destroying humanity.

This decade of decision is a biological and spiritual crisis. It has been described as a global "turning point" (Macy), a physical and planetary "jump time" (Houston) that defies rational explication. We are called to engage in the "great work" (T. Berry) of bringing humanity's impact into harmony with our planet-habitat, and we are in process of lifting even toward the "universal human" (Hubbard) beyond the planet. We as a species are riding a wave that is beginning to curl as it approaches the shore. Now we must learn, quickly, how to ride that wave all the way to the beach of daily life, and to teach others to do so as well. If we do not teach enough people by 2020, many will crash into the pounding surf and be rendered literally extinct.

Life will continue to send pulsing streams of energy to that shore whether *Homo sapiens* survive or not. It would clearly be better, for Earth as well as humanity, if we do survive. *Homo sapiens* is a product of over 1 million years of careful planetary evolution, and we will not be given up easily. Remember that *Homo sapiens* are the planet's heart center. The heart is completing a major wave, which is beginning to stabilize as the next major wave is starting to come in. The next wave is vitalizing the planetary throat center. Throat energy helps us attune to the *we* of unified field, because the throat partakes of both reason and passion. The throat bridges head and heart in an intimate, breathing-with process, sending out the lyrics and melody and rhythm of our life's song. The very nature of throat energy is life-affirming. From the perspective of the throat, neither the head nor heart is the "bad guy." Neither the yin or yang, the him or her, the particles or waves will be left out. The throat expresses the best of both.

Put your hand on your neck for a moment. Feel the living pulse of your lifeblood as it carries oxygen and other nutrients to the brain. Listen to your breath helping nurture your brain and caress your heart. Your breath is the fusion medium between life and consciousness. We as a world community are learning to synchromesh human breath and mind at ever-higher mental velocities. Here is a brief graphic view of this acceleration across several major steps of growth.

≈

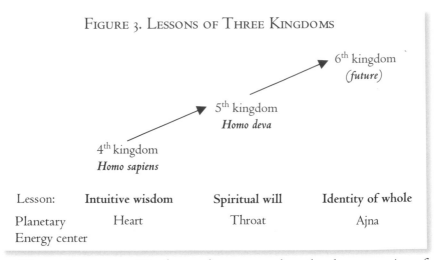

FIGURE 3. LESSONS OF THREE KINGDOMS

Figure 4, on page 29, shows these same three levels as a series of growth steps. In the first phase, a person (or group) lifts upward from rational, analytic mind to the intuitive abstract mind. This does not imply that the person leaves the analytic mind behind. In fact, the analytic functions will be strengthened by the greater knowledge that is available.

Likewise, the second and third phases reflect a process of greater and greater fusion. The mind becomes like a very coherent fusion laser, able to focus and illuminate. By its intimate bond with the heart, the head can bring both clarity of focus and deep caring.

There are three major phases in the mental development of early *Homo deva*. As the transition progresses, these phases move in both directions, ascending and descending. As you learn to recognize this movement in your own life and that of your colleagues and friends, you will be able to open your eyes to the physical reality that wants to incarnate among us. That which seeks to birth through humanity is divine energy seeking our hearts and heads as its literal grounding point. This is an evolutionary fact, as well as a re-mythologizing of our own creation. It is the story of a new species emerging through the wisdom tradition of 21st century physics and biology, which are already being shown to be consistent with many of the world's classical traditions. (see the work of Arrien, 1993; Borysenko, 1999; Chopra, 1993; and Friedman & Moon, 1997 as doorways into the large body of work in this area.)

I am sometimes using the term "waves" of evolution, which refers to a longitudinal sense, across time. For example, there is a wave of greater cross-cultural empathy that emerged during the past fifty years, as people heard and viewed on television the suffering of people in other parts of the world whom they had never met. The term "phases" in the context of this book means a greater developmental capacity, a learning that is demonstrated by an individual, group, or nation. For example, the worldwide waves of increased literacy for women over the past century have produced many benefits for children's well-being. The particular phases involved in reinforcing the literacy varied a great deal, depending on which nation we are looking at. We will examine this in more detail in Part Three of this book.

While the three primary phases of species emergence occur in each human being, they have particularly strong effects within the mental and physical bodies of certain children. Think about young people you know who may be experiencing various crises as a consequence of the following:

Phase 1

Intuition awakening: This is the major developmental task of Phase 1, to make a link upward from the analytic skills to seeing larger patterns, recognizing new kinds of order even in chaos, and looking at the holographic relationships between parts in complex networks (as exemplified in current research on fractals). Linking rational mind to intuitive wisdom, spiritual insights; dreams linked to world events and planetary energies, including the higher senses such as precognition. There is extensive research literature on abilities in children for all of these aspects of Phase 1.

Phase 2

Intention awakening: The developmental task of Phase 2 is linking spiritual will all the way down through human emotions. Phase 1 is a prerequisite for this step; if a person has not gone through Phase 1, there is greater risk of emotional / chemical capture, such as addictions, in which the direction of alignment is reversed (see the downward arrow in Figure 4) as the personality is captured by the magnetic field of physical matter. The best and most effective forms of recovery and rehab programs train people to link their own will to an inclusive divine will ("higher power") that wishes good for all beings. By such deliberate alignment with a greater force for good, they can learn to lift up to a strong, skillful, and creative expression of personal will that identifies with the greater whole (humanity, and planet).

Phase 3

Identity awakening: The developmental task is linking the level of being all the way down through human physical functioning. Eventually this will include greater coherence of the human immune system, longevity, and healing by focused radiatory attention (e.g., touch, song, music, thought). This later phase includes learning to express right relations between the part and the whole. As young people enter this phase, they need careful mentoring to discriminate between experiences of species and planetary identity, and their own individuated incarnation of that energy. As this phase becomes better understood, some of the creative young people who now languish behind bars for nonviolent but "antisocial" behavior can be helped to re-enter the culture and contribute to the world's healing as well as their own.

I expect that many of you recognize yourselves in the "cultural creatives" (Ray and Anderson, 2000). Ray and his colleagues did extensive survey research over a period of seven years, and found a highly consistent cluster of values and lifestyle issues that fully 24 percent of American adults said were their concerns. This is a large shift from similar research done twenty years earlier.

Here in capsule form are the core values of the 44 million cultural creatives in the United States, as shown by Ray and Anderson's data. By extrapolation we would expect that approximately 300 million people worldwide are supportive of these values as central in their life at this time.

"Our research indicates that the people at the center of the general movement for change are the Cultural Creatives. They are the shared constituency of the social and consciousness movements.... Cultural Creatives have shared what they believe, what they feel, what they have

FIGURE 4.
THE ASCENT WAVE: PHASES OF
INTUITION, INTENTION, AND IDENTITY

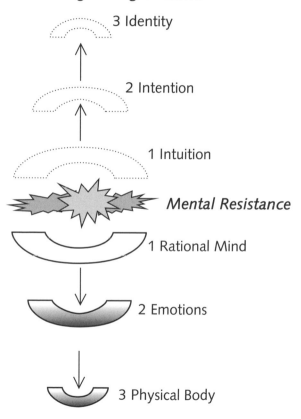

**Human wavefront on the ascent:
transmuting into higher matter.**

3 Identity

2 Intention

1 Intuition

Mental Resistance

1 Rational Mind

2 Emotions

3 Physical Body

Binary-laser grows in coherence

**Wavefront on the descent:
incarnating into denser matter.**

read and are thinking about, and most of all, their moral concerns." (Ray and Anderson, 2000, p. 217)

Here are five of the realms of meaning or social movements that the Cultural Creatives describe themselves as deeply involved in:

• The ecology movement (as distinguished from conventional environmentalism)
• Feminism
• Alternative health care
• Self-actualization psychology
• Spirituality with a psychological (as opposed to traditional religious) focus. (Ray and Anderson, p. 217)

In Loye's (1998) very useful discussion of Ray and Anderson's work, he emphasizes that the desire to rebuild community and heal society is being increasingly related to healing ourselves, physically and spiritually. This is indeed a core message from Ray and Anderson's data. The macrocosm and microcosm of impetus for change are increasingly linked through such areas as health education for individuals, a renewed sense of the sacred and community, and ecological sustainability and stewardship.

Paul Ray's description of this important and growing subset of our nation's population corresponds with what I am calling Phase 1: the transition from rational mind to intuitive wisdom, greater inclusiveness, more ecologic values, more political tolerance for and support of diversity, and enhanced individual creativity and optimism in both the professional and personal life. It is pertinent to note that Phase 1 encounters the point of tightest resistance. The threshold to enter Phase 1 and claim the creative / ecologic / nurturing values as your own has a very steep slope. Once people have taken that step, the succeeding ones, although difficult, provide increasing support and rejuvenation because there are fellow travelers to share the journey with.

Figure 5, on page 32, is a graphic version of the progression from intuition to intention to identity, showing the dual wavefront. The "three I's" of intuition, intention, and identity are crucial components in the phases of *Homo deva*'s emergence.

Of course, the phases are not separate events but a series of energy flows. These energy patterns build through the many daily choices of our lives. Notice that there is a wavefront moving up and another wavefront moving down, simultaneously, during all the phases.

My best guesstimate is that most people who find this book will be experiencing the shift into Phase 1, and will be exploring issues and new commitments related to the value clusters that Ray and Anderson describe. Then, about 10 percent will already be putting these concepts into specific action in their daily lives and service to local community. This is Phase 2, which I am calling the phase of spiritual intention. These people are grappling with the nitty-gritty issues of spiritual will. For example, do we continue using a gas-guzzling vehicle, or does our family choose to walk the walk and convert to a combination of smaller cars, public transit, bicycling, walking, and car-sharing? Do we continue to consume three times the necessary calories, including dense meats and enriched sugars, or do we actively implement our intention to live a more healthy food-lifestyle, for our sake and that of our children? Do we send messages of complaint and outrage about the violence and seduction demonstrated in TV and magazine ads; and in a related vein, do we support boycotts of certain products that violate our beliefs and values?

Phase 2 is a crucial turning point upward in the growth spiral for individuals, families, and groups. This phase aligns personal lifestyle choices over a longer timeframe, with intention to heal the larger whole. That larger whole starts with our families and friends. Phase 2 involves the fusion energy coming through the second aspect of the personality, the emotions, and aligns our individual emotional-desire energy all the way up to the purpose of life itself. In later chapters, we will look at some well-known people whom I believe are expressing the transition at Phase 2.

It's amazing to think that one's choice of morning coffee with two lumps has planetary significance, isn't it? At Phase 2, we are taking aligned action in many daily choices, not just brain-tripping about it, and the focus shifts to community engagement more than individual development. I believe that the number of persons at this phase will increase steadily over the next decade. In fact, I estimate that Phase 2 will be the fastest growing segment of the population by the second decade

FIGURE 5. DUAL WAVEFRONT OF UNIFIED FIELD

Incarnation is happening: The width of the waves represents the number of people who have reached this phase of soul precipitation into human realms.

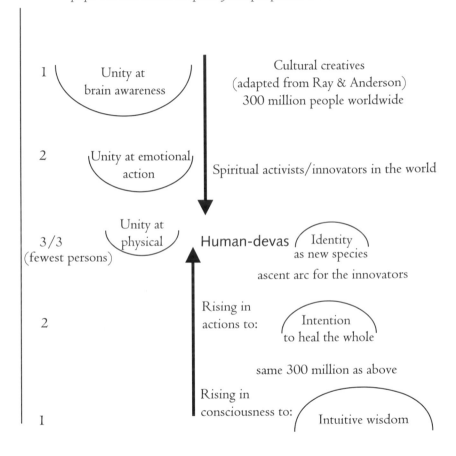

Both waves are real. Their fusion cannot ever be taken away because they are the lifethread of Earth itself.

Transmutation is also happening, as the other end of the fusion reaction. In scientific terms, transmutation is the reference beam.

of the 21ˢᵗ century. We will discuss this in more depth in later chapters.

Next, there will be a smaller nucleus of people reaching Phase 3. Among every 100 people who are now actualizing the steps of Phase 2, about two persons (2 percent of the 10 percent in Phase 2) are sensing some strange and unfamiliar issues having to do with sensory skills beyond rational human. They are beginning to approach Phase 3, and will fully enter this phase by around 2020. These are people who have grown, along with family and friends, beyond the value-changes of Phase 1, and have begun to ground in daily life the changes of Phase 2. Still, something new seeks to emerge, but they usually don't have words to describe it. They may be experiencing new bursts of creative energy and yet are unclear how to focus it. They may be finding that their need for sleep at night significantly decreases as their life's work becomes more focused and manifested in their community. They may experience unexpected openings of artistic, mathematical, or spiritual capacities, a degree of opening that leads them to seek out others and discuss what is going on. They may have psychic moments of knowing what their friends are going to say before they say it. In diverse ways, these persons realize that they have crossed a threshold, are reaching a new sense of who they are in the world. The concepts of this book will be pivotal for this group.

Who they are has yet to be recognized (let alone accepted) by the larger culture. This will take time. There will very likely be stresses and strains in the process of acceptance, even more so for this smaller cohort than for the creatives in Phase 1 and for the innovators in Phase 2. We are talking about a new species, all the way to physiological, perceptual, immunological, and mental functioning.

The persons who will enter Phase 3 by 2020 are generally younger than 20 to 25 years at this time. They are truly pioneer members of a new branch of the human family. They are creating a branch that will lead the rest of humanity from the era of *Homo sapiens'* intelligence and innovation into a new era of creativity. Among the courageous pioneers, those who survive this decade will be the pilots for shifting our species' locus of identity upward to the next major level of life on Earth. The step is from fission to fusion, from aggression / dominance to radiating healing, from fear and self-doubt to the release of joyful will, and from entropy of matter to the syntropy of Life birthing life. If any of these concepts touch a chord along your spine, please keep reading.

In order to ground all these high concepts, we can also describe the step as a movement from a consumer-driven economy to a healing and artist-driven economy. Humanity is ready to learn the creative powers of life as an art form, a cornucopia of art forms that can be self-sustaining in the marketplace as well as support the ecosystem of our world.

Chapter 4

OUR LEGACY AND DESTINY:
VISION AND LANGUAGE

In this chapter, I would like to introduce the idea that we are bringing an evolutionary legacy from our past, in terms of our senses, into a future destiny that will include significantly enhanced senses.

To present a capsule summary of this idea: Our legacy as *Homo sapiens* is binocular vision and verbal language. Our destiny as *Homo deva* is bifocal vision and intuitive language.

One of the more intriguing components of the emergence of *Homo deva* involves the perception of space and time. A primary legacy of *Homo sapiens* on the sensory level involves the perception of spatial dimensions. Humans and other higher animals use the conjunction of left and right vision. Our two eyes integrate different angles of perception from the left and right sides of our face. Through that hybrid view our brain makes inferences and interpretations about the spatial dimension of depth, and constructs an image of where we as viewer are located. This is the physiological origin of self-image. Thus, the intersection between the focal-angles of our eyes gives us depth perception across space. The *Homo deva* sensory organs are evolving to include more degrees of freedom because of their greater perceptive acuity across time. The ability to sense *now* meaningfully within very long timeframes, while keeping our *Homo sapiens* spatial skills, will give us a deeply different mental perspective.

Even as our perceptual vision has given us the ability to perceive depth, so our verbal language has facilitated tremendous flexibility in communication across great distances and physical conditions even in the depths of the sea or on the surface of the moon. The past 1 million years have brought great physiological growth and cultural development for our species. In a closer turn of the spiral, the past 30,000 to 40,000 years since the dawn of spoken language and diverse art forms has resulted in hundreds of human languages and other forms of expression, including music, dance, ceramics, photography, computers, and telecommunications. In this era of cell phones and PDAs, it is literally true that distance is no longer a barrier for us.

All of these innovations were made possible, in large measure, because of our binocular vision and our languages, both spoken and written. The crucial issue now is whether the expanded vision of *Homo deva* through time will facilitate concomitant growth in ways of wisdom. It is my belief that this new development will bring extraordinary new kinds of innovations to support human life, innovations that will be based on both external technology and internal knowing. These innovations will inevitably, by their nature, bring expanded possibilities for harmony and peace. A person who sees hundreds of years ahead knows how to wage peace effectively. The very nature of a unified field linking now and the *long now* (see Brand, 1999) guarantees that the purposes of these innovations will be peaceful.

How will this new perception work? Our eyes will integrate different angles of perception from "above" and "below" a line that relates to time itself. Here is an introductory description of these steps.

One of the central characteristics of higher animals is that they have depth perception. Humans have developed depth to an acute degree, through our mechanical extensions, such as eyeglasses, microscopes, telescopes, and satellites, all of which expand the sensitivity and focus of our distance-seeing. In the new step beyond *Homo sapiens*, we are learning to develop deep-time perception, for both past and future.

FIGURE 6. SENSES IN THREE KINGDOMS

Animals	Homo sapiens	Homo deva
Five physical senses (brain talk)	Words (brain and heart talk) Five senses	Song (throat talk) Words Five senses
Breathe air	Speak lyrics Breathe air	Sing melody Speak lyrics Breathe air
Instinct Width dimension Vision very local	Reason and I-Thou Depth of binocular vision across space	self-in-All as unity Reason and I-Thou Height of bifocal vision across time

Figure 6 indicates that the third kingdom (animals) uses the five physical senses: vision, hearing, smell, taste, and tactile touch. These are the language of brain talk, with quite varying degrees of specialization among the animals for hearing, smell, etc., which are all mediated by the brain. In the fourth kingdom, *Homo sapiens* uses words and conceptual mediation, or spoken language, as well as the five direct senses. These are the language of heart talk, produced by the deep passions and identifications of which humans are capable. In the new step, the fifth kingdom of *Homo deva* will continue to use brain senses and heart words, but will add song. The new species will be masters of the language of the planetary throat; they will be releasing through their activities in daily life the deeper tones of the song of Gaia. The term *song* here means more than we usually imply by that word. The modes of *Homo deva* communication will extend beyond our usual categories. This doesn't mean, of course, that *Homo deva* will be a continually singing species! For now, think of the relation of song to words as an apt metaphor for the relationship of *Homo deva* language to *Homo sapiens* language. We will all learn more about this in the coming decades.

As humans living through the transition from *Homo sapiens* to the new species, you and I and our friends have the amazing destiny to know both worlds. We will retain the capacity to use binocular vision all our lives. In addition, many of us are developing the ability to use bifocal vision, the ability to see instantly the short-term and long-term consequences of specific choices. This vision allows us to perceive the above and below aspects of a situation, a place, a thing. We will be able to recognize and assess the general abstract pattern and all its related specifics, all the myriad contingencies of potential choices across time — as easily as we now scan a busy street for traffic before starting across a crosswalk. As another example, rudimentary bifocal vision allows parents to respond maturely and compassionately to a child's loud entreaties at the checkout stand of a store. We "see" and know that the short-term desire for a gift or toy needs to be balanced with the longer-term view of what the child needs and what the budget will allow. We stand steady from that perspective and are able to be gentle and firm with the child at the same time. You can do the extrapolation from that example, to such species-wide issues as negotiating regulatory policies for storage of nuclear wastes, or for logging in national forests.

The balancing of short-term and long-term views is well researched in the business community, where people look ahead with five-year strategic plans. Likewise, in health education we conduct epidemiological studies of disease patterns in communities over decades, and in meditative practices we learn ways of detachment from the desire nature. Now, we are learning to expand this capacity, in an organic way. That is, a five-year plan for our family or community would include priorities and goals, such as helping a teenager in high school start thinking about possible options for later, the necessary courses that are prerequisites. As bifocal vision moves to the next major level, it will allow a broader horizon. For example, our city and regional planners will be able to anticipate more coherently and effectively the trends and needs of various constituencies at five-, ten-, and fifteen-year horizons. This will be achieved through projects that include some thorough analytic work, as is done now. In addition, the synergies of intuitive knowledge, analytic information, and larger identification with regions or nations will allow the *Homo devas* in specific agencies or corporate departments to optimize their efforts. In effect, they are breathing the longer timeframe context for planning in whatever specific task they are doing.

∿

Here is a brief exercise to practice your legacy and your destiny: Visualize three living beings, one from each kingdom, all trying to get some attention. For instance, imagine that the three beings are your favorite family dog, your *Homo sapiens* son, and his daughter (your granddaughter), who at age six is beginning to express some abilities and sensitivities of early *Homo deva*.

Now, imagine these three having an interaction at one of the following venues:

- A neighborhood picnic at the park
- At a local bus stop with traffic going by

How do these three beings communicate with each other? How do you respond to each? (Be aware of your heart rate, your breathing, and your smile factor as you look at each of the three.) How would you describe the unique wisdom of each?

Next, to stretch the exercise a step beyond the familiar, imagine the following trio: a young wolf, an executive director from your local utilities company, and a *Homo deva* who works as a medical intuitive in the surgery recovery room of an acute-care hospital. Again, imagine the interaction, this time at:

- A city council meeting
- On the 11:00 PM TV news, after a large snowstorm

Take a moment, and consider these questions to clarify your responses to the scene:

1. In imagining the interaction among these representatives of the three kingdoms, which senses do you see being used among them? How do the animal–*Homo sapiens* bonds differ from the animal–*Homo deva* bonds?

2. Which of the three kingdom ambassadors (the young wolf, the corporate executive, the medical intuitive) did you most identify with?

Why? Do you think your responses have changed from what they would have been a year or two ago?

3. Do you harbor any fears toward these three kingdom ambassadors? The fears are probably quite different, yet looking closely enough to touch each fear by describing it is a very useful act of healing—and courage—for who you see yourself to be.

You may want to share this exercise with a family member or friend and see what interactions they describe. Through exercises such as this, we are practicing a greater perception and recognition of the kingdom parts of our family on Earth—from the past, in the present, for the future.

This kind of exercise can also help you move back and forth between the abstract principles explained in this book and their flesh-and-blood reality, which is the interaction between the kingdoms as we learn to live and breathe and move through daily life together. Seeing a deva in a medieval painting and recognizing a ten-year-old *Homo deva* neighbor at your local bus stop are two radically different experiences! Yet those experiences are both happening to someone, today. We are learning to catch up with the reality that is already happening in our world.

The link between children and devas, and children and nature has been documented for centuries. For hundreds of years spiritual traditions in several cultures have written of devas, the divine or good spirits. Often these messengers have been recognized by children, before our analytic mind develops and tells us such beings are "not real." The descriptions of encountering devas often refer to the beneficent spirit of a tree, a lake, or a community consecrated to peace. In many cases, these descriptions match the modern physics descriptions of "organized wave patterns." We will discuss in a later chapter how such organized patterns will become the norm as our perceptions open to both longer timeframes (amplitude), and greater I-Thou identification with others (wavelength). It was necessary for us, in our evolutionary journey, to go through the stage of scientific reality, in which we focused primarily on "facts," "data," "mitigating circumstances," "proximate causes," and "risk management." That was what life on Earth needed us to do. Now, the needs have changed, and we are being called to bring our beautiful analytic capacities into harmony with larger morphological fields (Sheldrake) and ecological truths (T. Berry) that underlie the millions of years of our legacy-destiny. That term is hyphenated because we are opening our "visual lens" to include the far past and far future, in a single unified perceptual field.

While we as *Homo sapiens* have definitely lived in relationship with Nature, during the past 10,000 years the relationship has been largely characterized by relatively short-range vision. We developed a human "command and control" mentality toward Nature, thus leaving us estranged from both the spirit and the matter. Our agricultural revolution enabled us to break away from the terrible survival threats that accompany the hunter-gatherer existence; yet that same revolution separated us from the healing rhythms and exigencies of the biosphere within which we live and move and have our being. Many excellent texts of the past two decades have documented the psychological, political, and physiologic estrangement from Nature that our cultures have brought in the past 10 millennia. The basic reality in the new era is that as we become *Homo deva*, we become Nature; and in that becoming, we are partners with both the smaller ("younger") humans and the younger devas who are embodied in the lakes, the trees, the animals and plants that nurture and sustain us. Regardless of which gender we embody or the human ethnic culture from which we arise, there is an intimate unity between our personal identity, our "I," and the All around us. The developmental shift is one from relationship to identity.

This shift will still incorporate our cultural legacy of analytic reason and compassion, our legacy of binocular vision and verbal language. We can take the best of human culture with us into the future! As one door closes, another opens. The historic chapter of *Homo sapiens* as Earth's dominant life-form is coming to a close, and a better chapter is dawning. Our destiny in the 21st century is to belong to both chapters, the one from the past and one from the future. We are an integral part of the transition from both sides.

Chapter 5

EARTH IS HAVING A HEART ATTACK

Another way to describe the deep underlying pressures in this decade of human cultural climax is to say that Earth is having a heart attack. Our species is a central member of the ecosystem of the planet; in fact, we are right in the middle, with three levels below us and three levels above (more on this later in this chapter). Humanity's position in the morphologic field of Earth is exactly analogous to the heart in the human body. The next planetary wave of evolution is inexorably lapping at the sand castles that *Homo sapiens* have built, both those in our mind and those in our cities. Sometimes the wave is gentle, but because of human resistance, the impact is becoming both louder and more violent. We have only to glance at the evening news to have this truth brutally emphasized. The fourth kingdom ways, *Homo sapiens* ways, of perceiving and thinking have carried us a long way, but have now reached a blind alley. Only those who learn how to see over the walls, to help each other climb them, will find a way out—which is a metaphoric way of suggesting that new ways of perceiving and of acting will both be involved. Without developing new ways of perceiving and thinking, the heart attack will progress to full cultural fibrillation and possible death.

It is accurate to say that Earth's dominant life-form is currently a bipedal group we can call Adam, Eve, and their relatives. These hominids have become mentally-identified, have developed thousands of languages, and are now on the verge of destroying themselves if they don't learn to ask "Who are we?" and "Why are we here?" Adam, Eve, and their kin are members of a highly endangered species called *Homo sapiens sapiens* (the scientific name of all humans living today). Our mutual task, you and I and all our friends, is to help this species uplift to the next step of evolution. We are not talking hundreds of years here. The pace of crises stacking up in the daily news tells us that we are talking about the next step occurring within your lifetime.

Look again at Figure 2 (p. xii). In order to understand *Homo deva* as the throat energy center of the world, we need to see clearly what preceded it. One of the central premises of this book is that Earth is a dynamic ecosystem, with its own planetary chakras that function on a necessarily deeper level and wider scope than the chakras of individuals, groups, or nations. Earth's chakras are expressed through large aggregates of living beings. Remember the basic childhood game of naming something as animal, vegetable, or mineral ? That commonsense demarcation of the three basic kingdoms of physical creatures on our home planet is where the story begins.

The mineral kingdom is Earth's base-of-spine, the first among the seven major chakras traditionally known in healing and spiritual traditions. The base-of-spine (BOS) is where the *will-to-exist* is called forth from elementary chemicals, crystalline formations, salts, and acids. Through our own BOS energy center, we express ourselves through physical organization, the drive to endure and keep going through adversity and to keep physical stability and integrity when outside forces press against us. The Earth's force of gravity holds all minerals in existence, stabilizes our movements upon the Earth, and thus holds together relationships between crystals, plants, and animals as well.

The plant kingdom is the second chakra of Earth, her sacral center. Within plant matter, sexual differentiation first began. The fertilization process between plant-organs lays down the pattern for all subsequent elaborations on the theme. Through the sacral center evolves the *will-to-procreate*, to ensure the survival of one's species and, on higher levels, the *will-to-create*. This energy generally infuses our creative efforts, projects, and dissemination of our thoughts, friendships, and other bonds that are important to us; the quest to outlive our physical body and link to something "immortal" begins at the sacral level. The generic pattern of sacral energy is something we share with all animals and all plants. The plant kingdom is the earliest version of Earth's sensual nature and the obvious foundation of her fecundity.

The animal kingdom is Earth's third major chakra, the planetary solar plexus center. Here evolves the *will-to-achieve*, which is expressed in myriad ways as the will to take action. From this center also emerges the urge to dominate, to establish oneself in the pecking order—whether that is in a family of toads, prairie dogs, moose, lions, horses, chimps, or college students. The emotional nature individuates and becomes very active through the solar plexus. Animals express and indeed are the quintessential solar plexus on this planet: They roar, bleat, whinny, and hoot their various emotion-desires. We often call these emotion-desires, which we share with the third kingdom, "basic animal urges"—those behaviors of driving away or killing off the competition, hoarding the food, stealing someone else's mate, chasing others away from our territory. How can we help being that way, when it is part of our "animal nature"?

These animal inclinations, which we all express to some degree in childhood, are ones we inherited from our roots several million years ago in the animal kingdom. Because the animal kingdom has been around for several billion years, there is a large legacy of impulses coming through the planetary solar plexus, affecting us and influencing our cultural upbringing on all continents. Through those several billion years, the animal kingdom brought the focused energy-circuits of the planet through Earth's emotional body, so that the rudimentary chakras in the millions of microcosms (each animal species) directly expressed and reflected for the first time the greater macrocosm of the planet.

∼

The human kingdom, as a whole, is the fourth major chakra of Earth, the planetary heart center. *Homo sapiens* has been an anatomically modern species for about 200,000 years, and it has been considered "modern" in cultural terms for 35,000–40,000 years. You can see from Figures 1 and 2 (pp. x and xii) that the shift upward from animal to human was gradual, with higher animals such as chimps and gorillas sharing some of our emotional sensitivities, careful child-rearing practices, and the capacity to feel concern and affection for another.

The human intellect and compassion are two poles of *Homo sapiens'* binary laser—the beam of life energy with two ends that characterizes our capacities and propensities. In other words, our ability to reason and also to feel deeply with (com-passion) another person are two main characteristics that differentiate us from the third kingdom. Earth's heart chakra, as it has evolved through humanity, expresses a *will-to-harmony* and unity. This is the universal desire for peace that is spoken of and sung about in innumerable human statements. Thus far, the behavioral expression of harmony and peace has been neither stable nor global. That is not, however, due to a lack of heart devotion or stamina on the part of human beings. It is because the heart cannot govern the entire living organism, whether we are speaking of an individual or a planet. The next higher level needs to help us.

It is important to note that these kingdoms, or planetary quantum energy levels, are very deeply interpenetrating each other. The minerals of the sea float and circulate in the veins of all animals and humans; we and the ocean are intimately linked in our well-being. Plant elements are digested in our bodies every day and support our body's repair and maintenance. The higher levels partake of all the levels below them in the evolutionary scheme. The coherence of the whole depends on healthy interactions, reciprocal relationships, and dynamic balance between all the kingdoms.

Humans are Earth's heart energy and expression. This might sound outrageous. We—the bipedal primates with abilities to write emails and launch intercontinental missiles—are the heart of Earth? It seemed more likely, especially during the past century, that we were the parasites come to trash the host planet. How can this be? Our populations crowd across all continents, while broken good intentions and fragmentation seem to be our impact on Earth's flesh. Here is a crucial clue about the role of humanity at this pivotal time: *The heart governs the lower three chakras, and it responds to the higher three.* Within this dual function as the center of the seven centers, the heart holds and manages the most stress. You might say, in a metaphoric sense (and for too many individuals, quite literally), humanity is right now in the middle of a heart attack.

As *Homo sapiens*, we have learned to control—to explore and often dominate—the lower three kingdoms. We are masters of the physical plane, especially when our analytic mind teams up with our solar plexus to "have it all" or in the alternative to "die with the most toys." Yet that impulse for total conquest and acquisition has made us out-of-tune with the whole. We are out of balance, not because we are inherently bad (as some religions would have us believe) but because we, in our strong, vigorous, and passionate *Homo sapiens* identity, are "only" the fourth kingdom. We are not the whole. We are the fourth level in a life-field of quantum steps. The stress of attempting to govern all four levels is making us spin out of control, into incoherence, depletion of resources, and toward blind chaos and violence. Are you surprised?

The heart of Earth is out of tune with itself, trying to handle too much. Large sectors of humanity, particularly the wealthiest 5 percent, are trying to spin the planet by holding tightly to their assets and using the force of human will alone. Many of our fellow humans see no need for mysticism, "soft values," eternal verities, or transcendent qualities. In contrast, many of the mystics see no need for business values, long-range planning, or development of cutting-edge technologies. Both camps say, in effect, we can do it all ourselves! Just leave us alone! The resulting entropy, constriction, and self-split are ignored until something goes "boom," whether that is a myocardial infarction for the individual, high homicide rates for the community, bankruptcies and high unemployment in our major industries, or escalating species extinction and resource depletion in our bioregions. So much for *Homo sapiens* trying to be the Lone Ranger.

The heart of Earth is out of tune with the higher identity that comes from the three higher kingdoms, above the now-visible planes. We of *Homo sapiens* are attempting to govern the lower three, yet we are being spun with centrifugal force into greater and greater fission: violence in our schools and cities, our nations, our bodies. We at the planet's heart level are trying to do it all, and we can't! By the laws of physics and metaphysics, we are not the whole. We are not all seven major energy centers. We live, move, and have our being within the fourth kingdom. In planetary terms, humanity is the pivotal part — literally the pivot and central kingdom of seven — but it is not the whole.

Hearing this is important for reassuring ourselves and our exhausted co-workers at a deep level: The violence now erupting in many areas of our world culture is not an intrinsic failing of our species. True, the violence entails crimes committed by individuals and small groups, and they should bear the consequences and be held accountable. Yet on the species level, we are not bad, or crazy, or stupid. We are just human beings, reaching the "end of our rope" as a separate life-form. We are stuck at an impasse, functioning as the fourth kingdom having an attack of separation anxiety. The internal voices keep yelling, "What happens if we can't do it all?? What happens if we're all alone, if we let go and nothing is above us??" We are attempting to hold the whole planet to-gether when we were never meant to do that. No one expected us to do that. Humanity has been doing a good job, but we have reached a critical blindspot in our species' perception and development.

You may justly ask: If this is true, what do we do next? What is needed for a rebirth of stability, for the peaceable and viable self-governance of humanity? Clearly, the heart needs a greater something to help stabilize the system from above. The heart needs a guide ... force ... gear ... reg-ulator ... locus of gravity ... center of identity .... These several words all fit here because the energy dynamic adapts to the diverse worldviews that humans are now using. Whether you are living within a scientific or religious, high-tech or hip-hop worldview, the truth remains: This stabilization is critically needed.

As you may have realized, such stabilization is essential in order to protect the heart's wounds (limitations) from destroying the lower three kingdoms and, in that process, bringing self-destruction to the heart. To state this in blunt, legalistic terms, we of *Homo sapiens* have in the past couple decades become an imminent danger to ourselves. We need to find help, ASAP. Or, alternatively, if we don't know how to ask for help, the help needs to approach and hold us closely.

The planetary heart has gone as far as he can go by himself. The "lord of the heart," as it is called in some spiritual traditions, needs an ally and nurturer from the next great energy center, the *throat*. The ally is ready, willing, and able to serve as a partner. It is time for the planetary throat to emerge into physical incarnation. The throat energy center embodies the fifth chakra and expresses the *will of self-expression*, which manifests in artistic and creative forms. The throat wants to open and bring forth songs of life, healing, redemption, intuitive knowing, creativity, and peaceableness.

What does this mean for you and me? The bridge that humans, as the fourth kingdom, were designed to make links the planetary heart with both the three lower kingdoms, and those above. We are the living link from the planetary caring, the agapé, expressed through Earth's attractive powers, upward to the planet's creative urges of mind and heart as one.

Now, holding that beautiful thought, take a moment and carefully look around your local business district or shopping mall. You will be immediately reminded that we have a tremendous challenge ahead of us. The millions of high-functioning *Homo sapiens*, in a "give me more stuff" mentality and "kill the competition" attitude, would have only dim notions of what an epoch of planetary creativity might look like. (And of course, in my most tired and uncharitable moments, there is a voice that says, "Should we even tell them?" But that discussion is for another time.)

The epoch of Earth's throat will be tangibly dawning during the next 10 to 20 years. It will be a surprise to a lot of people. Mission impossible? The mission will become not only possible but also guaranteed and exciting, as we understand much more about the nature of the transition.

Here is another exercise: Imagine what it would be like to sit down together with an intelligent Cro-Magnon from 30,000 years ago and teach him or her how to use your cell phone. He or she is very interested in your handheld tool, and has recently developed the ability to count. Yes, it is an amazing conversation. Then, as if the technical part isn't mind-bending enough, try to explain what it means in terms of geography, travel, family relations, and human longevity that you are talking on the cell phone with an 85-year-old family member who is right now four time zones away. Whoa! That is just a simple example of the magnitude of leap that we have come through, and now are anticipating again in the next half-century. But this time, we in our *Homo sapiens* identity are in the learner role like Cro-Magnon, and the visitors from the future are our cousins, the *Homo devas*.

As another example for those of you with historical interests, imagine Leonardo da Vinci attempting to describe his diagrams for submarines to his contemporaries of 400 years ago. Some of our children who are now in elementary school or junior high are having analogous difficulties in communicating their creative visions with their peers, their teachers, and perhaps even their parents. The programs in our schools and communities for gifted children will need somehow to incorporate a much wider definition of "gifted" as the *Homo deva* young people bring their own unique vision of what education is all about. The trade-offs in upgrading our programs to help all children and providing specific enhancement to nurture these particular species pioneers will be a challenge, yet one that we can and will navigate through.

We need to help each other in making this bridge from the "been there, done that" attitude to a receptiveness to new ideas that haven't been conceived before. A sample newspaper ad for finding our companions on this journey (with gratitude to Daniel Quinn) might say:

"Pioneers wanted for new species.

Must have caring, intellect, and sense of humor intact. Inquire within."

Millions of people already recognize a definite impulse to move upward to another plateau of human functioning, a place that respects peace, trust, nurturance, and creativity rather than dominance, pillage, revenge, and intimidation. We know what our best looks like (for some inspiring examples, see Appendix 6, "*Homo sapiens* Associations"). We now need to recognize the quantum step in identity that is involved. From the steady energizing of this identity through our daily choices and actions, the qualities of *Homo deva* will be nurtured to blossom. The throat of the planet will become manifest.

Figure 7 below presents a simple map of the two-step process that can help lead our species and Earth itself beyond the current heart attack. The first step was from animal to human, the evolution from planetary solar plexus to heart. The second step, which is now emerging, is from *Homo sapiens* to *Homo deva*, bridging from planetary heart to throat.

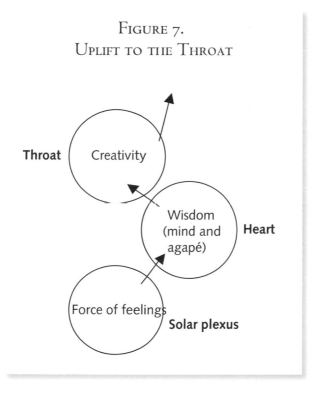

FIGURE 7.
UPLIFT TO THE THROAT

A primary source-point for this step, beyond what is generally known as human knowledge, is spiritual intuition. In later chapters, we will explore in more detail the three phases of the bridge to *Homo deva*. The first of the three phases is helping the higher intuition to unfold. Many excellent books are widely available on this topic.

The mainstream *Homo sapiens*, the million-year-old species that has been here long enough to take over the planetary neighborhood, is now threatening our own children and other species with final extinction—all this without fully realizing how deeply our fates are intertwined. In Part Two we will look at some of our *Homo sapiens* children and how their suffering is an early warning sign about the health crisis of our species and planet.

≈

PART TWO

OUR *Homo sapiens* CHILDREN

Chapter 6

Individual Children Are Embodying The Pain of Species Transition

This chapter is a clinical bulletin from the trenches of species transition. Those of you who are more accustomed to discussing cultural transformation over latte and rainbow crystals may need to take a long, steady breath. We are going to be dealing with painful issues here. In fact, the painful issues have names and faces.

When we speak of a species transition bringing stresses and pains, whom are we talking about? Who are our children? Among the several billion young people alive today, many are physically or emotionally hurting. Based on twenty-five years' experience as an educator, administrator in juvenile justice, and supervisor in emergency social services, I believe that many of the diseases and dysfunctions now ravaging our younger generation are being intensified by, if not proximately caused by, the species transition we are discussing. The suffering of young people stems in part from a cultural dissonance, a gap between what we preach as our cultural beliefs and what many adults live in their daily actions. The suffering is also caused, in part, by the stretching that we are doing as a species. It is a natural consequence of rapid acceleration in our collective mental functioning. Whether we speak of the dissonance as a cultural gap or natural pain of species stretching, it is contributing to making many of our young people sick, hungry, terrified, confused, cynical, violent, or all of the above. In order to heal, they need the presence of truth—integrity—the wisdom of the whole—the touch of a unified field. Within the context of today's world, they need assurance that tomorrow will provide them with safety, shelter, food, a friendly face, and support for their own dreams and aspirations. These are simple needs, but far from easy to fulfill.

The cure is not something magical or ineffable. In colloquial terms, we adults need to get better as role models, for talking the Talk, walking the Walk, and living the best that we know is inside us. One part of the difficulty lies in our own paucity of role models at the local, regional, and national levels. In later chapters, we will look more directly at what this implies for adults' well-being.

Figure 8 introduces some young individuals (all in the U.S.A.) who are suffering as our species enters the threshold of evolutionary transition. Each of these young people was in crisis at the time I either worked with them and their families, or heard directly about their situation from colleagues. The year in parentheses indicates when I met them.

FIGURE 8. OUR CHILDREN ARE HURTING

Name (Pseudonym)	Age (Year met)	Imbalance within Personality/Culture/Life
Alyce	8 (1985)	Cancer—Alyce is one of seven small ones with head turbans, holding hands with each other and walking in a line of "seven dwarves" at Emory University Hospital, on their way to receive radiation therapy.
Bert	10 (1973)	Refugee with malnutrition—Bert is suffering severe dental decay and bone conditions caused by experiences he and his family suffered during several years as "boat people" refugees. He has never seen a toothbrush.

Carrie	12 (1999)	Homelessness—Carrie is living with her mother and a younger sibling in a city-sponsored homeless shelter, while her mother recovers from wounds due to spousal abuse and assault.
David	14 (1988)	Delinquency—David is serving two years in a Youth Development Center, charged with burglary and arson in a hardware store. He reads at a third-grade level and has a shy smile.
Emily	16 (1990)	Autism—Emily is severely autistic, unable to speak or feed herself, and has frequent tantrums; her family is struggling with the related emotional and financial stresses and the choice whether to institutionalize her.
Frank	18 (1987)	Alcoholism—Frank is in a university teaching hospital with end-stage alcoholism. He is a good student and an athlete, but he will die one month after his eighteenth birthday.
George	20 (1992)	Isolation—George is an engineering and programming major at a state college; socially withdrawn, he has recently joined a hacker club and frequently changes his residence address.
Henry	22 (1989)	Gang—Henry is a high school dropout and member of a gang. He has no arrest record, but recently totaled his car and has been seen harassing high school boys at the city's basketball courts.
Isabel	24 (1980)	Asthma—Isabel has severe asthma and is unable to run or climb stairs without respiratory distress; she drives by freeway to work. She and her sister are thinking of moving out of southern California.

Jerry	26 (2000)	Political violence—Jerry recently enrolled in a job training program sponsored by a faith-based organization; the teacher worries about his new friends who may have domestic terrorist connections.
Karen	28 (2001)	Attention Deficit Disorder—Karen was diagnosed with ADD when she was a teenager; the syndrome didn't slow her down when she lived with her parents, but now she is having trouble remembering tasks in her own apartment.
Larry	30 (2002)	Depression—Larry is a former investment banker who earned $100K / year right out of college. Then he was laid off in the economic downturn of 2001. He has now been diagnosed with clinical depression and severe eczema.

These crises clearly do not exhaust the list; you could add others for our consideration. The goal here is to step back and recognize new patterns. We are going to take a risk and make three generalizations about this diverse group of young people in crisis.

The patterns that we are working with include the following:

1. These young people, ages 8 to 30, are under significant stress. Stress is experienced when any of the three primary levels of a child's functioning (physical, emotional, mental) is out of balance, overstimulated, or overburdened.

2. The stress is being expressed at a wide spectrum of wavelengths (physical, chemical, emotional, mental, behavioral, social), and these young people are having difficulty keeping their own stress from being amplified by the stresses they encounter in their daily lives. Their illness or dysfunction is a reflection and interaction of patterns on other levels—some in genetics, some in individual feelings and beliefs, some in family patterns, some in the culture, and some in the interactions between these levels.

3. Note this fact: The best treatment and prevention approaches now known for all twelve of these conditions are not preventing a steady increase in incidence and severity, across all socioeconomic levels and all regions of the country (and for several of these conditions, internationally). Read that sentence again. It is a very difficult fact to accept.

Something that *Homo sapiens* culture is doing is making its children sick—not just sick in one or two ways, but in multiple ways that are growing and interacting. And this clinical sample group is from an affluent country without overt warfare. In many nations, the stresses are even more intense at the physical level of bombardment and widespread malnutrition. It is very hard to look at this, but look at it we must, and soon. The primary reason that we haven't looked all the way before relates to the deep vein of despair and hopelessness involved in seeing how many of our children are embodying the stresses. Until we know in our hearts and minds that there is hope for these young ones, it is literally impossible to look. Without such hope, we couldn't withstand the species shock and pain.

Autism Rate Doubles

Concern over rising autism rates has been growing since the late 1990s as parents, educators and pediatricians began reporting increasing numbers of affected children across the country. In a 1999 report, the state found a 273 percent increase in the number of children treated for autism in California between 1987 and 1998. Thirty-one out of every 10,000 children born in 1997 have been diagnosed with autism, up from 9 per 10,000 for those born in 1987.... The legislature added $17 million to the budget to cope with the increasing numbers now being served at the network of centers around the state....Steep increases have also been documented in other industrialized countries such as Japan and Israel.

— *San Francisco Chronicle*, May 14, 2003

Another area that has seen sharply increasing numbers is eating disorders among teenagers:

> To treat eating disorders in America is to treat our culture. We need a revolution in our values and behavior. We need to define attractiveness with much broader parameters, so that most women, not an infinitesimal few, can feel good about their appearance.... The professional literature suggested that the incidence rate for bulimia among college-age women was as high as 25 percent. The average person sees between 400 and 600 ads per day. Most of these ads show women who are pencil-thin, even anorexic. The average model is now 5 feet 10 inches tall, and weighs 111 pounds.... When you overvalue the packaging, it's easy to undervalue the woman inside.
>
> — Mary Pipher, Ph.D., *Hunger Pains* (1995, p. 5, 20)

For the reasons discussed above, I believe that the study of *Homo deva* and the steps toward understanding and welcoming their skills and innovative ideas is critical for the health of the next generation. The good news is that there will be increasingly effective ways to approach the healing of children such as those described above. We can't expect immediate results or easy answers; the stresses on humanity have been increased manyfold during the collective birth process of the next species. But hope is alive and well. The alternative to looking directly at our children's suffering, dear reader, is ignoring it. And we ignore it at our peril. If we persist in ignoring the interactive nature of their suffering, a great number of our children will go the way of cousin Neanderthal within 30 to 50 years. That is neither necessary nor, heaven knows, desirable. The choice is before us, as individuals and as a species.

∼

Chapter 7

Knots In Our Energy

Each of the children described in chapter 6 is suffering. Some are "acting out" their suffering, while others are silent in their trauma. In either case, their suffering is the result of a knot somewhere in their life energy. Society views some of these young people as the good victim and others as the bad perpetrator. I agree with that judgment when it is limited to the choices that they as persons have made. Some of these youth made wrong behavioral choices and need to live through the consequences. And yet, in a majority of the case studies described, the children's and youth's choices are a subset of society's larger choices that are putting incredible pressures on the individual young people.

Beyond the level of the individual, a lack of cultural wholeness is continuing to breed and accelerate these varied dis-eases. These cases represent the diverse ways in which we are not at ease with ourselves, and with the whole body of humanity. Diagnostics at the start of the 21st century is a highly difficult task, because on top of the levels that we have been trained to observe, the pressures from the species transition are also present—and interacting with all the other factors. However, the converse is also true: As the pressures from the species transition are lifted, a lot of the negative effects will also be reduced. As Dr. Deepak Chopra has taught us, "Life at its source is creation . . . In the old paradigm, control of life was assigned to DNA, an enormously complex molecule that has revealed less than 1 percent of its secrets to geneticists" (Chopra, 1993, p. 36). Now, in the emerging paradigm, control of life results from wider consciousness blended with disciplined focus. The greater awareness and greater focus are both essential. From young children who can shift their own growth hormone to meditators who can regulate their heartbeat, the list of bodily processes that now respond to human mind grows longer each year. At the same time, an increasing number of children and adolescents are not able to control their tantrums and aggression in the schools. One way to describe the dilemma is that many people were born into a world that does not nurture or stimulate the best in young humans. Thus, how can we now seek to pass on a positive world to the next generation, a world that we ourselves never knew? It has also been difficult because we did not see the next step of where we were going. Those of us working as teachers, social workers, therapists, nurses, or change agents in public or private agencies have grown increasingly frustrated in the past decade. Often, our diagnosis of the individual child's or family's issues has needed to include recognition that the larger culture seems to be "falling apart" and failing to support this child, this family. Yet the literature in our professional field seems to be talking from the other side of a gap, where the answers do not acknowledge this limitation of culture.

Tomorrow morning, we need to face our clients, patients, and friends. From where do we draw hope and inspiration for the short-term, in the midst of longer-term crisis?

Here are three hypotheses for us to consider as we move forward in this decade of decision. I happen to believe that these hypotheses are true.

The most selfish humans ever to live on the planet are alive today. These people explicitly seek energy that feeds their own personality, at the cost of energy to others. These people actively and intentionally seek only that which feeds their own needs and desires and strengthens their sense of self, their locus of identity, however that is described. They are supersaturated with fear.

The most giving and generous humans ever to live on the planet are alive today. They share, recycle, and create new energy to radiate to others, and feed their own personality last. These people actively and intentionally seek ways to feed the needs of their community and the larger world, strengthening their sense of unified Self with all life on Earth. Two examples of people who radiate energy of hope to others are Betty Burkes and John Hatch. Betty serves with the Hague Appeal for Peace (HAP), begun in 1999 at the largest peace conference in history. She collaborates with people in several countries to establish locally driven peace education programs for schoolchildren. John is founder of the Village Banking network, a program of FINCA International. Village Banking now has projects in 20 countries, helping clients build financial and social stability for their families and community, through microfinance loans and education that break the cycle of intergenerational poverty.

The contrast between those supersaturated with fear and those serving as universal donors of life energy is one of timeframe. And one's timeframe is an expression of one's deepest identity.

The contrast between fear-driven selfishness and love-generated altruism has never been more extreme and pervasive on our planet. This is true, in my opinion, because *Homo sapiens* have mobilized tremendous resources in the short term and yet remain conflicted about the long-term priorities for using them. We as the "sapient," rational species are literally at the end of our rope. Truly looking at the long term (e.g., next day beyond the food / alcohol / drug / work addiction, next month beyond the luxury vacation or unemployment check, next year beyond tax-cuts or state services cuts, next decade beyond the deforestation, next century beyond the nuclear stockpiles) is becoming impossible from the *Homo sapiens* perspective. We extract unbelievable energy from the mineral / plant / animal kingdoms, and from each other—and yet we are not able to teach our young people how to feed the energy back into the social and biological ecosystem, to recycle plastic and love on a species-wide scale.

Humans in the industrialized nations have become parasites on the rest of Earth's life-forms, both human and nonhuman. The lack of respect for our home-friend, the Earth, is exacerbating our evolutionary crisis. Even people with the best of intentions are left with ecological dilemmas that seem to have no answer: Should we drill for oil in particular wilderness areas to help immediate energy needs, or shouldn't we? Should we keep our immigration policies tolerant in order to welcome more people fleeing oppressive regimes, or should we tighten the policies considerably in the wake of terrorist acts? Should we limit pollution controls to save jobs, or increase them to save air quality? And how do we weigh these either / or decisions from the perspective of the greatest good?

Most of our mass media, and our legal system, are built around the question: Is the particular problem really more in the individual or the culture? Right there, we need to say "stop!" and ask ourselves a new question: What if it is both? In the midst of our mainstream culture's either / or thinking, *Homo deva* is both a source of hope and a child to protect. These newest members of our world are both strong and vulnerable, because their life experience comes from a deep identification with the larger whole. They are rising from the midst of the intuitive cultural creatives (Ray and Anderson's data, 2000) in many nations. They will continue to increase in number and creative presence during this decade leading to 2020. They are often more sensitive than the norm for *Homo sapiens*, and they sometimes lack support from their immediate family for their gifts and capacities. We need to help all children in this crisis, and we need especially to help those who are our trailblazers for the next era. They are depending on our trust and support.

The crisis point is rapidly approaching, probably between now and 2020, when the incoming impulse from *Homo deva* will meet the maximum resistance from *Homo sapiens*. The waves from the past and the future will meet head-on. The interface between them, called the present, will suddenly be very full of electromagnetic energy. This may not be visible to the general public, but the crash of waves will be noticed by you, me, and most of our friends. [Note: This chapter was drafted in the summer of 2000, prior to events of September 2001. It appears that the waves of collision have begun, and are proceeding through human culture.]

Will we, as a nation and a larger world culture, respond with a warm welcome to young *Homo deva*s as our new family members? Or will we reject the wisdom that is attempting to grow within our own neighborhoods? A diagnosis of "stresses of new species" for an individual child would be a complex one to make, and actually would be a partial truth. We as adults don't yet have guidelines to follow. Yet, if we continue to see only the external factors and ignore the deeper reality that is struggling to emerge, these children will experience further rejection. Rejection and self-hatred cause a deep wound. These young people will find the wound in their identity difficult to overcome if they do not have at least one trusted friend or mentor who supports them at their own level of development.

As we have seen, the interaction of cultural stresses, individuals' knots between emotions and mind, and environmental stressors is causing quite specific illnesses. In my view, some of the illnesses are produced quite directly by the knots in our collective mental functioning, as we move from *Homo sapiens* to *Homo deva*. Figure 9 illustrates four illnesses, as examples, that are increasing in incidence and severity among children and teens. These trends are based on reports across several countries.

The width of the line below each knot illustrates the capacity for an individual to function in daily life in spite of the disease; the thinner the line, the greater the disability. The size of each arrow tip likewise indicates the degree to which people with the disease are generally able to function as human beings, although their daily life may have much struggle. For example, a person with asthma can generally be employed, get married, have children, and participate in other normal human activities to a much greater degree than some persons with anorexia and most persons with autism. Each of the four can be fatal. When the knot or occlusion in the lifethread is closer to the ground of daily life (e.g., asthma), the person has severe block in physical breath. In contrast, when the knot or occlusion in the lifethread is closer to the top of the personality, at the mind-soul interface (e.g., some forms of autism), the person has severe block in "mental breath," and as a result cannot speak, although they may have comprehension of what other persons are saying to them. All four of these diseases have increased in incidence during the 1990s.

Treatment / educational objectives, which need research to verify:

Figure 9.
Four Terrible A's: asthma, alcoholism, anorexia, autism

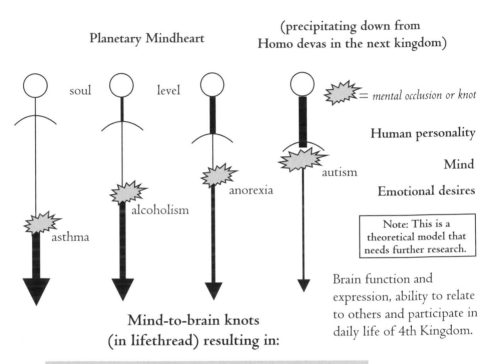

**Mind-to-brain knots
(in lifethread) resulting in:**

Asthma	Alcoholism	Anorexia	Autism
breath	*emotions*	*stomach*	*speech*
blocked	blocked	blocked	blocked

The hypothesis is that as the individual learns to reorient upward and breathe in synch with the larger community, species, planet (at whatever levels that involves), the knot can dissolve. In many cases the knot has multiple causal factors, produced by interactions of environmental toxins, emotional stressors, mind-body beliefs, as well as genetic factors. All these are part of the species mind; as these toxins are reduced and the mind-to-brain link made coherent, the individual can learn to ingest energy from our species mind (i.e., a *higher power*) by group patterning, individual coaching, peer support, and other methods that provide meaning. This will help the individual increase their capacity for breath at whatever level they need, even when moving against the tide of their local group's mental / spiritual inertia. The significant interaction effects of genetics, beliefs, and identity will become more widely understood in the next decade as the species mind level emerges through thousands of people.

The unorthodox view that I want to communicate here is that these four illnesses involve knots in the life energy of these children. Each illness is the physical and behavioral expression of a knot in the life flow through these children as a system. They are starving for life energy at various levels, and are drowning in energy at other levels. Even though they as souls (or as higher intuitives) are radiating positive energy, the culture is not yet receptive to their gift. Thus, the social and physical environment is not giving back to them positive energy in exchange. Their energy exchange is badly skewed, with the individual child pouring out positive energy like a universal donor on the higher planes, and receiving relatively little energy into their personalities on the mental, emotional, and physical planes. The term "planetary mindheart" at the top of the figure refers to the level of mental functioning where a person experiences directly the unity of life. In several spiritual traditions, this realm is where a person has direct knowing of how all living creatures are intimately related, and how the universe is nurturing all of us, that truly "God is love" and that love is made manifest through life on Earth. The evolutionary step from *Homo sapiens* to *Homo deva* is bringing us into closer relationship with that planetary energy, but the process of opening that connection across the world is bringing some serious knots, both individually and collectively. In the examples of knots shown in Figure 9, we can infer by the nature of the physical illnesses that the level at which the knot exists differs among the four diseases. Because of the introductory purpose of this book, I am not going to discuss specific treatment approaches for these four illnesses. Much good work is being done on all four; and the Resources section and your link to Internet can provide much material for any of the four that you are especially interested in.

Our focus here is on the pattern of energy knots that are causing our children to become ill. One image may be helpful: Imagine a garden hose that is steadily being turned on above us, bringing life waters for the parched cultures and institutions that are currently pinched in fragmentation, fears, material greed, and dwindling resources. The garden hose comes from the next evolutionary level, and will continue to open towards us more and more. The stream will increase in width and velocity. That is Nature's way. However, the hose is, in many instances, pressed against a brick wall. In these places, the receptivity to life waters is quite low. The image of a wall represents *Homo sapiens'* diverse ways of rejecting or repressing the universal; the wall is our human terror at welcoming the planetary spirit or deva energy into our lives. What might happen? We might not be in control. Our sapiency, our very species-identity, is at stake. Will we stand and fight our higher nature to the edge of extinction over "who is in charge" of this planet? Yes, I'm afraid that some of us will, including several current national political leaders. But you and I, and our children and friends, still have choices. Free will exists.

Anyone who is standing at the interface between that hose and the brick wall is going to be experiencing a lot of pressure per square inch—from both sides. For a child who is receiving high-velocity energy from higher levels, their family or community may be a kind of brick wall in terms of acceptance, or even recognition, of more inclusive intellect / intuitive powers. For a child who has opened at a young age to significant artistic, mathematical, or musical abilities, or spiritual experiences, there may be instances of other people grasping at them for energy. Other people sense the connection to the planetary energy, and their own relative starvation can produce a habit of grasping even though this is not their conscious intention.

There needs to be an opening—a receptive channel of human organizations, agencies, schools, communities, linked families—if the life energy (water in our metaphor) is to come into healthy contact with *Homo sapiens*. We need to help each other, and help the children with illnesses, to recognize that there is plenty of energy but we haven't learned how to share it yet. We are like plants after a drought. We need to open carefully to the wisdom, creativity, and innovation that the life water can bring. We need to have coherent pathways to bring the juice of the future into our communities, into our daily lives, and into the bodies of our children.

Otherwise, the velocity of the incoming flow will scatter across the parched ground and become a run-off, a flash flood of consciousness. Without sufficient percolation into the ground, the energy will be lost among the eroded soil and rocks of the concrete human mind. And the individual children who have *Homo deva* sensitivities will continue to be blocked, ripped apart, crumpled, and withdrawn. Some will continue to escape the overstimulation, self-rejection, and dissonance through the numbness of alcohol, overeating, other drugs, or other activities designed to crash their nervous system and bring temporary relief. Several polls in recent years have found that the average home has a television turned on eight hours a day.

Why are we seeking such diverse and widespread numbness? And why does it take many people linking together to bring a few of these children out of their violent habits and / or addictions? Because the rational mind alone cannot handle the velocity and volume of the energy that is beginning to reach our species. Logical, epidemiological studies can take us a long way (and I still read them), but the health crises that are now accelerating will not be resolved by our traditional approaches. This is key: Medical drugs, genetic studies, positive affirmations, support groups, and asking a higher power for help will not be sufficient to heal us and our world, as long as we stay stuck at the level of *Homo sapiens* identity. Neither the chemical, nor the genetic, nor the affective-cognitive, nor the social solutions are sufficient. We have outgrown our culture's analytic mind / emotional empathy, and we need to move upward ... to evolve ... to learn to move through "gentle chaos" ... to bootstrap ourselves to, link up in prayer with, choose to align with the next level. We name it, and it will come to find us. This is true in a way that we can only glimpse at this time.

In the previous rapid leap of evolution, about 40,000 years ago, the cultural edge took over from the biological. This of course did not mean that we stopped having a body with its physiological processes! Now, the spiritual / intuitive edge of evolution is taking over from the cultural. This does not mean the "end of culture." Our culture will adapt to support the new species that is birthing. However, as long as we stay in ignorance and / or denial about this higher shift, our children will continue to suffer deeply, as they attempt to handle within their bodies the pressures of the species reorientation toward longer timeframes.

The quantum step upward will eventually involve physiological changes. These changes will bring significant steps for improved health, such as changes in our genetic / physiological responses to food and our relationship to sleep. The current U.S. epidemic in overeating and obesity is, in my view, a key example of the brain being hard-wired with redundant defenses against starvation, which were beneficial 10,000 years ago but are actually harmful to us now. Today, most of us have plenty of food, but the regulatory systems in the body haven't caught up with the environmental realities. And as noted earlier in this section, the environmental realities of marketing are giving us very distorted messages, saying that we will literally die or be unattractive or lonely, whichever is worse, if we don't have the sugar-coated cereals. A reorientation is clearly needed.

However, the reorientation does not start with physiology alone. The many research studies on the four terrible A's have given us very useful information. For example, the recent data on high levels of concentrated heavy metals and metal imbalances in the bodies of some children with autism can provide clues for individual treatment approaches (Marohn, 2002); that clue involves environmental factors in many communities, as well as family incidence patterns. Next, that information needs to be incorporated into a wider view that looks at species identity, and why are thousands of children suddenly having trouble with heavy metals. In the 1980s, we learned a great deal about plant-human interactions, and the complexities of food allergies; and in the 1990s, we have begun learning more about mineral-human interactions, and how that interface is expressing in physical imbalances in our children's bodies. The path of descent, of incarnating spiritual humanity in right relations with the lower three kingdoms (animals, plants, minerals), is proceeding. Now, the healing arts need to include a greater perspective on the interactions among five kingdoms, not just us and the lower three. It starts with species identity, at a very high and at the same time very molecular level. There will be more on this in the next several chapters.

~

Chapter 8

FAMILY AND COMMUNITY EMPOWERMENT

An old adage frequently cited in recent years is, "It takes a village" to help a child grow up healthy. I would extend that folk wisdom about a nurturing community to include the support we can provide from future realms. The new era of *Homo deva* will provide a context of caring, a habitat of nurturance and creativity. As such, the world village will bring much solace, healing, and inspiration to our young people.

Our children need a nest of caring to shelter from the outside. And likewise, they need an infusion of higher energy to nurture the intuition and creativity that are each child's birthright. In this new decade, the teachers, parents, counselors, and even employers among us will look higher ... deeper ... wider ... at the patterns that are emerging among the younger generation. From that greater vision of who we are and what we can be, a more nurturing and life-affirming (e.g., long-lived as well as peaceable) existence will become possible.

In some ways we can serve as beacons for our children, and in other ways they are the beacons for us. Together, the beacons of family and community can point the way. "Think globally—Act locally" has been a popular slogan for bumper stickers and posters during the past few years. A new one that I saw recently said, "Think globally—Act neighborly." That will continue to be one of the best slogans around for this new decade. In order to empower families to help heal the children, particularly in cases like the four A's and the other circumstances described in chapter 6, the families must be able to have hope in the future. Seeing the global patterns in child illnesses can empower researchers to coordinate their efforts and share their results. Community resources and a network of support will be a crucial healing force, especially with the children (of all ages, nationalities, and ethnic groups) who begin to manifest the greater sensitivities of *Homo deva*.

The goal is to hold these children in our collective mental field of light, love, and creative power—in essence, in a prayer field through both heart and head. With this field as a medium of receptiveness, we can develop practical and effective programs to welcome these strong souls into our midst. Some of the individual children described in the past chapter may be able to make definite steps of improved health. In many cases, this may not be possible. But the children's interaction with the community can be a powerful force for integrating the capacities that they do have, which helps them be more effectively engaged in the healing process. Beyond the known realms of head-and-heart, we anticipate that greater circuits of Earth's unified field will bring much energy into human daily life. This unified field is both a physics development and a spiritual development, and will open up dimensions of healing that we don't yet have words for. Some excellent references to learn about this work are included in the Resources (e.g., Capra & Steindl-Rast, 1991; Hirshberg, 1995; Kabat-Zinn, 1990; Marohn, 2002; Myss, 1996; and Wolf, 1999).

For example, if mind-heart integration has brought a wealth of treatment options in pain management since 1970 (e.g., meditation and guided imagery for chronic pain), what further options will result from the integration of intuition and abstract mind to the brain? Or the integration of spiritual will and genetics? Or even further up the trail, the integration of species identity and the electromagnetic level of atoms? In each of these steps of developing options for our children, the presence and support of the family and immediate community will be key factors.

It is important to acknowledge that effective approaches do exist for the four conditions mentioned in the prior chapter. Many very dedicated health professionals are working in these areas. For example, even now, the family and community are being specifically mobilized in new treatment approaches to anorexia. According to Dr. James Lock of the Stanford School of Medicine, anorexia carries the highest mortality rate of any psychiatric condition. Incorporating the family as an integral player in the treatment is showing some preliminary positive results. From the perspective of the model we are developing, such family involvement could provide crucial support for children who are vulnerable to such illnesses because of their *Homo deva* characteristics. For instance, family involvement might help children with a highly permeable boundary between self and non-self learn to recognize when and how to safely "ingest energy" from their surroundings.

I am not talking about miracle cures here. I am talking about shifting the lens from a life half empty to a life half full. This shift in perspective comes when we recognize each person we meet as an early pioneer for a new species, and when we can identify the specific problems that entails. Whether the global shift will occur in the lifetime of the young people now hurting with these illnesses is not possible to know for sure; my personal opinion is that it will. But the shift must occur. The alternative would be to keep our blinders on and not recognize these larger patterns. That would be worse.

Look beyond the external symptoms of the four terrible A's described above. Beyond the chemical or behavioral changes, there is a deeper truth. Recall the dynamics from Figure 6, Knowing in Three Kingdoms. Whereas *Homo sapiens'* communication pattern is in words, the communication of *Homo deva* will be more like a song. What is happening in the song, the melody of life that these children are tuned to? What has happened to their song to produce a block in their expression—a block in their will-to-speak, their will-to-digest, their will-to-breathe, or their will-to-emote? As one of the clues that are already appearing, it is intriguing to note: Medical science has recognized that many children suffering with autism seem to have perfect pitch. They are naturally tuned to higher harmonics.

As we have seen (look again at Figure 9), blocks in energy flow generally occur in two instances: Using the hydrodynamic metaphor, the "pipe" is too narrow for the inflow, or the "soil" is too hard to receive the waters. Both of these conditions can be seen happening, in environmental and behavioral and genetic combinations, in the terrible A's. We can learn how to help these children even more and prevent future children from having these blocks, if we understand more fully the nature of each occlusion or knot in their ability to receive and metabolize energy.

Figure 10 examines in more detail the proposed species mind dynamics that contribute to the conditions of asthma and autism. These two of the four A's are quite different. The child with autism may have no visible dysfunction or problem in physiology (unless there are other conditions present such as hearing loss from premature birth, etc.). The child with asthma has visible respiratory system dysfunction. Our theory, however, suggests that both children are having difficulty in processing the boundary between self and other. That boundary is what "understanding words" or "ingesting food" or "taking in breath" is all about, on the higher mental level.

Figure 10.
Points of Resistance: Autism and Asthma

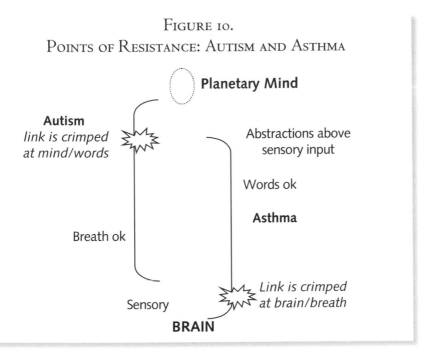

Hypothesis: The points of resistance in these two illnesses are types of mental-electric knots. The knots are "inverses," in the sense that the child with autism has a crimp in the mind-brain connection quite close to the mind end. The child with asthma has a crimp in the mind-brain connection quite close to the brain end. There are also gender-differences that will be important for further investigation, in terms of growth and development; i.e., the majority of children with autism are boys, while the distribution of asthma between boys and girls is more evenly spread. The multiple genetic studies on both illnesses clearly show family patterns, which in itself does not invalidate the model. The genetic configurations can be dense matter reflections of these higher knots.

Figure 10 illustrates how autism and asthma function to "block" a child's energy flow when another level in the personality becomes saturated. In asthma, when the brain perceives an irritant, the physical reaction ensues. Several studies confirm this process, showing that a child's asthma attack can be triggered by watching TV ads with pollen blowing in a field. When the brain visually perceives an irritant ("anti-self"), the physical reaction ensues, as the body attempts to fight off the "other." In such examples, the child's self-other permeability is too high at the brain-body interface.

Autism follows a similar process of the body attempting to keep the child's organism intact, to maintain integrity in the face of sensory assault. However, in autism the interface where the child is caught in knots is between higher mind (realm of soul) and the concrete mind (through brain). It is a different interface from that involved in asthma, yet the result has commonalities in that the child attempts to "fight off" the inundation of stimuli in order to maintain physical, emotional, mental integrity. For example, consider this scene:

> In a school playground, "[Sam] walks by himself to a lone tree, retreating far away from the mad dash to recess. He starts dancing, his legs jerking from side to side in an awkward dash, almost as though the 7-year-old is trying to get rid of fire ants climbing up and down his pants. He kicks and hops, his face crunched in concentration, trying to shake off frustrations he can't put into words."
>
> — *San Francisco Chronicle*, June 9, 2002; p.1A

The model of a developing *Homo deva* suggests that Sam cannot grasp spoken language. He literally cannot get a grip on it with his mind; it is like you or me trying to pick up grains of sand with our toes. Our hypothesis is that the concrete language is too fragmented, too linear (i.e., too short in wavelength) for his mind to process and recognize patterns in. Language is, above all, a medium for finding patterns and sound-meaning associations, so you can recognize that "dog," DOG, and d.o.g. all mean the same thing. Like trying to make a sand painting by picking up individual grains of sand, this process of pattern-recognition is an awesome skill for which *Homo sapiens* have developed a considerable capacity. Yet beings with a natural time-horizon of centuries rather than months will, most likely, have initial difficulty in following the linear nature of human speech, with its limited degrees of freedom. Some children with autism may be groping to find meaningful patterns while they are bombarded by mental and emotional stimuli, extremely high time-amplitudes and even from dimensions that we don't yet have names for.

This diagnostic framework is still speculative, based on anecdotal reports, and has not been explored clinically. However, the model has grown in credibility during the past 20 years. Persons from our future who are incarnating into our midst with much higher-voltage brain / mind connections will initially have severe problems in "gearing down" to comprehend the speech of *Homo sapiens* spoken around them. At any of the several centers currently doing research with autistic children, these concepts could be explored further with the goal of helping individuals at their specific level of language acquisition. For those interested in exploring this field, I highly recommend the approaches described by Kaufman (1994) and his associates at The Options Institute; Marohn (2002); and Rocha (1995). There is also preliminary work on clinical treatment of some autistic children who have severe copper / zinc imbalance. Such chemical distortions in their electromagnetic systems may eventually be found to be direct expression of higher imbalance between abstract (universal mind) and concrete (brain) conceptual functioning. In other words, children are manifesting in their bodies our species gap between "Now" with all its particulars (all the way to metals), and "Eternal time" of beyond-human realms.

Children such as this are suffering from isolation, blocked speech, and an absence of mutual interaction with their family or peers. Their families are suffering as well. One possible factor contributing to the condition is that the child's mind (wave pattern) may be moving at too high an octave, or too fast a frequency, to un-zip the meaning of language and bring their comprehension back through linear expression into sentences. Our model leads to the hypothesis that many autistic children may be suffering from a lack of synchronization between the wavelength of their brainwaves and the greater amplitude of their mind, which participates in the collective universal mind of our species. We could describe this circumstance as the child's mind "participating in" the universal mind. Thus the child's locus of identity may be at the universal mind, while his brain is spinning at the individuated human-being level. The lack of bridge, synchronizing gear, or patch (to use a term from computer software) between his mind and his brain is producing a highly dysfunctional child.

There are two possible ways to describe the situation for some of these children, given our premise of a gap in electromagnetic transmission between the mind and the brain: (1) He is living within an "energy sink" inside his own mind, unable to gather enough momentum to push across the event horizon and "emit" light (to use words expressively); (2) He is working hard to emit a tremendous voltage of mental light, and knows how to step down the light into words, and yet he has incarnated within a very great black hole (the boundary of *Homo sapiens* species). The boundary limits of our culture are not allowing his light to be perceived by the rest of us. My work leads me to suspect that both (1) and (2) are occurring in some children who express autistic behaviors. These potential interaction effects need to be explored.

Whichever scenario makes more sense to you, the experiential result of the gap between the mind and brain levels is painful. Some autistic children are locked inside a silence that no treatment approaches developed thus far can touch; some others are being reached and are unfolding their expression, but with exhaustive investment of time that many families are not able to arrange. Perhaps this prognosis can improve as we understand more deeply the nature of the threshold between the *Homo sapiens* brain and the *Homo deva* brain. Perhaps their futures will look more hopeful if we can diagnose and describe the boundary between these individuals and the mental field they are touching—the universal field that is non-local, everywhere, everywhen.

Some creative clinicians have begun using approaches that are more supportive of the child's mental and community context. These health professionals are, with great intuition and dedication, moving toward the issue of identity in their clients' lives (e.g., Chopra's description of preliminary work; the approach developed by Barry & Samahria Kaufman, and documented in his several books). Eventually, they will help us all understand more about this and other related illnesses. Our responsibility as parents, counselors, and health educators for the 21st century is to push beyond the current research and therapeutic models. We need to create ways of exploring these brain and mind wave patterns and helping individuals bring the patterns into alignment, into synchronous motion, to support the expanding identity of the next generation.

One way of thinking about this boundary is to consider how human children learn to differentiate between "inside" and "outside," how they learn to own their issues and identity. As young children, many of us learned to "get tough" in order to prevent some kinds of hurts from "getting to us." As adults, we learn to be selective about what we share and what we keep inside. We individuate, and that process is a natural process of becoming mature. Our boundaries between self and other are not impervious, but they are relatively stable. In contrast, children born with *Homo deva* sensitivities are breathing in a higher identity-space. Their sense of self does not stop with their own personal identity, and they naturally breathe-with all elements (chemical, physical, emotional, mental) in their environment. Thus, they may have trouble recognizing the cues for how "permeable" to be and when to put up a personal boundary. They may be absorbing tremendous amounts of electromagnetic friction from the emotional and social space around them, and yet have no skills for decreasing the saturation by passing that friction upward. They may be lashing out in tantrums or destructive acts partly because they have no means of diffusing the electrical chaos that they are naturally ingesting every day. (Think for a moment of the repetitive behaviors, such as hand-flapping, that some children with autism exhibit; one hypothesis is that they are attempting to "shed" the overdose of electromagnetic energy, as well as attempting to pacify themselves in a frightening and chaotic world.)

In some situations, their self / other boundary is too permeable. At those times, the child takes in too many "foreign'" particles. Toxicity results — with breathing difficulties, allergic reactions, drug-induced unconsciousness, screaming tantrums, or repetitive rocking motions. In other cases, the self / other boundary is not permeable enough. What do you suppose this would look like?

The recent second book by Temple Grandin (1995) is a remarkable personal description of her almost five decades of life with autism. She has persevered through internal chaos and external rejections by people in her social world; and has developed considerable professional standing as a designer of facilities for managing livestock. Her experience is serving as an invaluable map for teachers and researchers who are exploring more integral approaches to helping children who have autism.

The increased sensitivity that Grandin documents is very much consistent with the view I have of autistic children's attempts to limit and manage an unbearable velocity and volume of stimuli. They have no idea about self/other boundaries, and therefore are swamped by the chaos of the universal sensory world. Grandin also comments on the two primary types of autism, those whose continuous mental associations express as cognitive disorders, and those with sensory processing disorders. The former may demonstrate highly eccentric skills in mathematics or memory (e.g., quoting any page of the phonebook), while the latter may have extreme disabilities such as self-assault or biting themselves. These two types might correspond to the higher and lower ends of the mental field shown in Figure 10. Those autistic persons with cognitive disorder quite often are visual thinkers, to a degree that is difficult for the rest of us to comprehend. Grandin states quite clearly, "When I invent things, I do not use language. . . . When I read, I translate written words into color movies or I simply store a photo of the written page to be read later. When I retrieve the material, I see a photocopy of the page in my imagination. I can then read it like a TelePrompter. Pulling facts up quickly is sometimes difficult, because I have to play bits of different videos until I find the right tape. This takes time." (Grandin, 1995; p. 27, 31)

Perhaps after reading this personal account you too, as I did, have a quiet sense of awe and gratitude for our fellow human beings, like Temple Grandin and Raun Kaufman, who have struggled up out of the silence. From their courage and perseverance, and that of their family members, they are giving us clues about a critical aspect of our mutual family. To Temple Grandin, the idea that language must have preceded tool use is ridiculous. The idea is absurd to her because her mind works from the universals, and her brain works from the particulars, and there is a massive disconnect in between. She doesn't have the "middle range," where affect and empathy (and spontaneous language) are born. She remarked to Oliver Sacks, who had interviewed her for his book, *An Anthropologist on Mars*, that she could never understand Romeo and Juliet. She just couldn't follow "what they were up to." Temple Grandin, in my view, was born with early threads of our future-mind, one that isn't fully incarnated through the human personality (yet). She thinks in whole pictures, has great caring for the animals that she deals with in her work, and has visuals of all the specific incarnations of life—ALL the specifics she has ever met in her life, including all the dogs, the lines in a phonebook, etc.

Her visual mind and her brain language are not synchronized, because we as a species mind have not previously built or evolved the continuity all the way from planetary amplitude to individual persons (more on this in Part Three). That is the developmental task of the next 20-30 years for all of us, to synchromesh the mind-and-brain from the *Homo deva* level all the way to daily life of human children in physical matter, and to express that integrated functioning as kinetic souls—as *Homo deva*s who have personalities and live in the world. And yes, to do it with visuals and with language, with song, dance, and all the other human art forms that have been part of our heritage these past 40,000 years.

Raun Kaufman was a sophomore in college when he wrote the following lines, as Foreword to his father's book, *Son-Rise: The Miracle Continues* (Barry Kaufman, 1994):

> When I was diagnosed as autistic (and also severely mentally retarded, with a below-30 IQ), my parents were given ample opportunity to treat the event as a tragedy.... Sometimes it dawns on me how close I came to spending my life encapsulated inside my own head, lacking the tools to interact with the rest of the world.... You don't have to "cure" your special child in order for his or her specialness to have meaning and value. The value lies not in "results" but in how you treat your situation and your child.

Personally, I see autistic children as possessing a unique talent and ability, not a deficiency. When this talent and ability are embraced instead of viewed with horror, some amazing things can happen. Kids can make leaps people never thought possible. (p. xiv)

How should we balance the realism and optimism that Raun describes? The increased sensitivity of children (with autism, asthma, and other conditions) is, in several ways, related to the condition that all *Homo sapiens* have as infants, except on a higher level of species growth. The notion that human babies have an undifferentiated sense of self and that we learn to become an individual (and that this is a good thing) is fairly old and widespread. What we are proposing now is that the development of an individual, with a stable ego, naturally moves upward to a mental-emotional-physical identification with all of humanity and eventually with the planet.

Our children and youth, whether they have asthma, autism, anorexia, alcoholism, or other illnesses, will eventually be able to respond to the rhythm of *Homo deva*'s higher song. As with other areas at the frontier of science and health, such exploratory work needs input and cross-fertilization from many people. The most important step we each can take now is to get involved, to act as family and community members to further explore possibilities for helping our children. If you are interested in this area of research, I encourage you to contact your local university or teaching hospital and to discuss these ideas with some of the staff. Or look on the Internet for groups that have similar interests. The step of pioneers is to bridge the gap between defining healthcare as a matter of "fighting the germs and conquering disease," and defining it as a matter of "breathing on all planes and being true to thyself." Bridging that gap is a big step, a giant leap for some. You may wish to look at some names from the past, those who attempted to introduce cutting-edge concepts in health and well-being (see Appendix 3, "*Homo sapiens* Hall of Fame" as a starting point). We recommend that you follow your own best intuition about who is ready for this dialogue.

Each person who takes this step has their own unique experiences; yet a core commonality is that the self/other boundary becomes a Self-self link. There is no "other." We are one family. And the Self-self link becomes a wonderful healing force for our family in the world, because each individual who reaches this level serves as a fusion generator, to provide new energy and to cleanse the toxicities out of our immediate environment. (A friend remarked recently that perhaps *Homo devas* could be described as "universal garbage disposals," and in a sense that is exactly what is happening. But the "garbage" is also being fully recycled as life energy!) In historical times, there have been many groups such as the monastics in western Europe during the Middle Ages, who consciously served that function and helped lift the culture upward during periods of chaos and trauma. Those individuals and groups served as beacons of coherent mind to retain the wisdom of the culture and cleanse out the violence and other toxicities. You and I and the thousands of young people now incarnating as *Homo devas* are being called to do likewise for the species and planet as a whole.

∼

Chapter 9

GREATER SENTIENCY AT SPECIES CLIMAX

We turn now to some recent research on sensitivity from other angles. Rupert Sheldrake has researched the sensitivity between pets
and their beloved human companions. His book, *Dogs Who Know When
Their Owners Are Coming Home*, describes the quite amazing results of
some very innovative research. In one project, the research team set up
one video camera in the person's office at work, and a second camera
in their living room at home. Several animals in the study (generally
dogs and cats) responded at the very moment the owner got out their
car keys, miles away at the office, and prepared to start home. The pet's
response was vivid, observable, and perfectly in synch with the timing of
the owner. This research has several implications for hypotheses about
human sensitivities that may be affecting health.

For instance, in the case of autism: One of the current hypotheses,
with which I concur, is that autistic children are more sentient, more
sensitive and receptive to mental stimuli than other children, and certainly
more than domesticated pets. In other words, this hypothesis considers
the possibility that some autistic children "hear" (are sentient to the
vibrations of) the wave patterns of thoughts in their general proximity—both the angry, hurtful, or scornful thoughts and the gentle, happy,

or trusting thoughts. They are bombarded with mental stimuli, with no clues about how to manage the data overload.

Their mental field is developed beyond the norm for *Homo sapiens,* but their environment does not give them ways to interpret and respond to all the inflowing data (wave patterns that they experience viscerally). Some of them may, in fact, be processing conversations with a parent on a cognitive level, but because of the bombardment they cannot bring coherence through to the brain / speech level. The normal *Homo sapiens* brain organizes the mental patterns into categories; for example, I may wake with a nightmare and be terrified until I say the word "earthquake," and then I recognize that I am processing a memory. If the brain of *Homo deva* children is processing memories from the species (and even planetary) level, they don't yet have a way to articulate that level into words. As we discussed in an earlier chapter, spoken speech, mediated through the brain, is a relatively recent development in our history. To articulate one's experience through words is to have a "self," and to express the miracle of individuation. Now, we are working on the next major level of miracle: to articulate one's experience as Self in the world, a member of the unity-of-life-on-Earth. In some cases, it involves painstaking translation from an inner life expressed in vivid imagery and "thought pictures" into the more restricted realm of linear words — words that continually emphasize "me" and "other," and the subtle demarcations between "inside" and "outside" in social life. The anecdotal reports of several adults who have become more functional after a childhood of autism, and related reports of children who suddenly start talking in complete sentences after being silent for the first six or seven years of their lives, do seem to support this model (see reports in Marohn, 2002; Grandin, 1995).

This theoretical framework suggests that the sheer quantity of the thought-and-emotion waves and the extreme difficulty of filtering through the onslaught renders many of the children mute. They don't have guidelines to decipher what someone is actually saying because they perceive far more than most people; in addition to the spoken words they also perceive the wave patterns of the speaker's emotions and thoughts, all of which can contradict each other. This hypothesis will benefit from further research.

The international increases in incidence for anorexia, autism, alcoholism, and asthma during the past decade are, I believe, directly related to our species' mind-body link. As Figure 9 suggested, these illnesses involve different levels of "knot" in the greater mind-to-individual-brain connection, and there are also interactions between emotions and beliefs. The children who are bombarded with stimuli at their knot level seek various ways to relieve the pressure and pain. These attempts at self-healing are as divergent as bingeing on cupcakes, stealing amphetamines, drinking, retreating into silence, banging one's head on a table, having a tantrum, or choking from lack of breath. Our society — through family, school, community, and law enforcement — needs to provide appropriately supportive and firm consequences in each case. In addition, the alignment of brain to mind to species necessarily involves environmental and genetic factors, as well as the factor of individual brain receptivity to our species' current propensity to violence.

Although this hypothesis may eventually be shown to be correct, the treatment options will not change overnight. Much exploratory work needs to be done, with great sensitivity to the family issues and concerns surrounding these and other illnesses. I definitely am of the view that as our collective mind becomes more coherent and sensitive to higher octaves during the next decade, the isolated suffering of children will diminish. As teachers and parents more fully understand these higher causation factors and when to include them in our causal attributions and clinical workups, we will discover new directions for therapeutic programs.

Another example of how we might re-vision treatment for these illnesses is found in rehabilitation programs. The low success rates with most rehab programs for drug or alcohol addiction might be re-examined in terms of the identity level at which the interventions are offered. In other words, if the gap between the patient's brain and mind exists at the level of spiritual will (for those who are familiar with the seven major levels, this is above the analytic mind and above the superconscious or buddha mind), then offering a series of positive affirmations will help align their feelings with their mind, but it will not affect the root of the gap. It will not touch the source of the addiction, which is where the asynchronicity between mind and body lies. The person will still lack what we might term "psychospiritual leverage" and will not be able to maintain long-term commitment to their choices to be clean and sober. They are fighting a fire of desire in a six-story building, while standing on the third story. The relative success of 12-step programs, for various kinds of addictions, appears to be a function of the emphasis on aligning with a higher power, of admitting that one's "self" alone cannot conquer the addiction. Together with a support group, a respected mentor, and a daily living link to one's spiritual source, the higher Will can govern the desire nature and govern the addiction. As treatment approaches become modified specifically to target the spiritual will and then the identity levels, the person's ability to get leverage will increase significantly. And the leverage will be in the name of wholeness, of an integrated approach of healing oneself, one's family, and community.

The recovery programs that are showing the most success (the least recidivism) at one year are those that emphasize aligning one's daily choices with a Higher Power. This is a behaviorally developed version of bringing personal will into alignment with the species-wide spiritual will, the divine Will. Eventually, sometime in the future, this alignment will expand from our species to the planetary will and beyond. I definitely agree with the approach offered by 12-step programs that are grounded in daily life and have well-trained teachers. The crucial reorientation from negative addiction into positive addiction through various behaviors such as meditation, journaling, and talking with peers and mentors is truly a 180-degree shift in will.

A further aspect of the emergence of *Homo deva* is that the will is expressed down to the level of mental molecules. Our model predicts that future research will show an atomic reorientation in cases of successful recovery from addiction. For instance, there will be a change in the angle of rotation, the L- and R-handed spin of molecules. People who are maintaining their recovery program after physical dependency are literally bringing their body's atoms into an upward spin, toward the spiritual will and away from the "lesser will" (magnetism) of physical/chemical matter.

It is no accident, dear reader, that the spiritual will has been identified in ancient writings as the Great Attractor. Here is an area that is ripe for medical programs utilizing imagery—work to help people learn to visualize the reorientation of their physiology upward toward the planetary will and universal will, the truly unified field of healing. On the mystic side of recovery programs, this has already begun with meditative exercises and prayer circles (see for example, Borysenko, 1999; Kabat-Zinn, 1990; Chopra, 1993; Ram Dass, 2000).

It is important to remember that this is not a fast-track process. The force of attraction at the molecular level (upward to monad mind, if viewed from ascent development of humanity) needs to be reoriented upward by gradual, cumulative, and steadfast acts of will, over days and months and years. Chemical and physical dependency cannot be reversed overnight, or even over months. Many young people today are accustomed to speedy lives, with cell phone instant-talk, computer instant-tickets, TV instant-replay, sugarfoods instant-high, and so on. From this approach to life, within a chronic short time context, they try to yank themselves out of dependency on drugs or alcohol, and the fast track does not serve them any longer. Taking the time to relearn habits learned over years is something they are not accustomed to doing.

In Figure 11, you can see in schematic form the realignment of personal will with higher Will. This process benefits from focus on beliefs and affect, such as through positive affirmations. Yet that alone has not been shown to be as effective as incorporating the exercises for focusing intention or will on a greater healing, being part of a greater community, and entering a wider circle of identification.

In both orientations, with negative or positive addictions, the Great Attractor is life energy. In negative addiction, the person is being pulled downward to a source of energy below their identity level: for example, the significant numbers of health professionals who have battled or are battling with drug or alcohol addiction. When they can learn to make the reorientation to something "greater than self," and make daily commitments to serving that greater wholeness, the addiction can gradually be reversed. It is a difficult task, but can be done.

FIGURE 11.   REORIENTATION OF AN ADDICTION

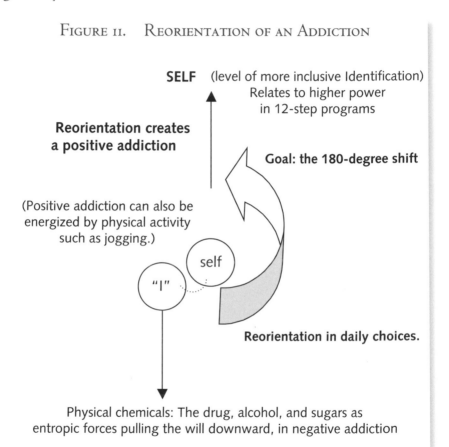

I imagine that many of you have also experienced the "pull downward" on occasion, perhaps when you faced a piece of chocolate cake at a dinner party. The concentrated and refined sugars act to stimulate the brain in the short term, and then cause depression (experiential separation-from-Self). This, in a microcosm, is what negative addiction is about: seeking Self (fulfillment, peace, nirvana) in the short-term fix, a kind of wholeness-through-oblivion, with no regard for the longer time horizon because the immediate pain is too great. We can reverse that process by choosing what we ingest at all levels (even choosing the chocolate cake or, in my case, choosing the peanut butter), and recognizing that our choices need to come from the wisest part of ourself. That part can celebrate the present moment and enjoy a dinner party, as well as the years and decades ahead.

Training in daily choices for greater wholeness (greater identity, at whatever the next step is for the individual) can help a person's recovery process, regardless of their educational level. I have seen this process bring small steady steps of progress for persons residing in homeless shelters, persons who often have very few outside sources of support. Making that commitment to a higher source of wholeness, having one or two peers for support, and a guide who has been through the recovery process is a powerful force for healing.

In positive addiction, the person allows him-or herself to be pulled "upward" in some way that includes receptivity to life energy above their identity level. For example, the positive addiction of walking or jogging several times a week has been shown to have multiple health benefits, including lowering blood pressure and improving cardiopulmonary function. The beneficial effects are greater when the person is doing the activity joyfully, with an attitude of lovingkindness to oneself, rather than being a drill sergeant and rigid taskmaster to oneself. The attitude of gentle guiding of oneself to greater wholeness is part of the orienting to higher identity, to realize truly that compassion begins at home.

The Great Attractor is neutral, but how we relate to life itself makes the difference in orientation. As *Homo deva* emerges through the culture in the next decades, we will understand more fully what life energy involves. One clue is the energy link from head to heart to base of spine—which are the three involved in the activities of most successful rehab programs. That is, the mental, the affective, and the action components are all emphasized, with the will of the person increasingly engaged in making choices for better health.

Those who begin a rehab program with lower sense of personal power, stemming either from sociocultural factors such as abuse based on gender or race or age or from familial trauma or other life-experience, often have more difficulty in choosing the positive addiction. They have not had much life experience in the potency of making their own choices. Without that baseline experience, they have fewer "hooks" to pull themselves upward toward the positive addiction of healthy choices. Having hope, knowing the power of making your own choices, is about having a clear stream of life energy through the head to the base-of-spine. As the old maxim goes, "where there is hope, there is life."

The brief descriptions of treatment approaches that we have explored in this chapter indicate why I believe that the evolutionary threshold that has come to our culture is also contributing to our various health and family crises. Next we must learn more about the specific dynamics at each phase: the quantum step from intellect to intuition, from intuition to spiritual will, and from spiritual will to species identity.

∼

Chapter 10

OUR CHILDREN ARE CANARIES IN A MINE SHAFT

For those who don't see the species horizon we are heading toward, the spiral of hopelessness is understandably getting thick. There are many reasons to buy into that spiral. You and I both know adults who have done so. What amazes and heartens me is that most of the younger generation, in the midst of extraordinary pressures, is not succumbing to that hopelessness. When children and youth are given a clear choice, they usually know what is more healthy, even when the options may look desolate to us adults.

Here is an example from my recent experience: Two young brothers who lived with their mother in a city-sponsored homeless shelter in San Francisco told a staff member in spring 2000 that they did not want to leave the shelter. In their own words, "It's the best place we've ever been." Children know when caring and safety are being offered to them. They know when a habitat is a nurturing spot, and when it is a toxic mine shaft of danger. Even with years of barren soil and little support in their lives, these vulnerable young members of our species sense the difference.

Animals who are more sensitive to toxicities and pollutants in the air can serve as a preventative buffer for humans. In this sense, canaries have been used for several centuries as early-warning signals for miners.

When the air in mines becomes toxic, the canaries demonstrate their distress, and some of them begin to die. When the miners see that some canaries are distressed, the miners leave the mine quickly. This has saved countless lives.

Our children are now serving in that sacrificial role. As our most sensitive citizens, young children are getting sick, dysfunctional, and violent, and they are dying in unprecedented numbers. The work of diverse teachers and health professionals in the past 20 years suggests strongly that many of the unhealthy conditions experienced by children are related to toxicities, many related to the concept of materialism as the path to health and "good life" that our culture forces us to breathe. The toxicities are in some cases chemical in the environment, some are emotional, some are behavioral in the children's social world, and some are mental from the larger culture. We have considered a few of them in these chapters about *Homo sapiens* children.

I am not saying that ideas are directly causing disease. That is too simplistic, and it doesn't fit the physical reality. We are dealing with a puzzle of multiple causation that also exists on multiple planes and manifests to human senses with multiple patterns of perception (some of which have not yet been named). All the levels of *Homo sapiens* functioning are contributing to a gross imbalance. The imbalance leads to a build-up of toxicities, or to the starvation of physical / emotional / mental bodies, or both. As parents and teachers, we feel at times an understandable impulse to flee in order to get our children beyond the toxicities. Yet, where would we go? How we move through that escape impulse is a challenge that each of us has to face for ourselves. How we face the boundary-wall of *Homo sapiens* culture will affect how we can help the children we love.

A parent or teacher might naturally ask, What will it take to galvanize our society into action on behalf of the children? How do we move these issues higher on the list of county and municipal priorities in the midst of severe and even emergency budget crises for schools and social services? The answer, in my opinion, is to share our concerns directly with those people who are cultural change-agents at the local level. Talk with them about the path that we see ahead of us for this decade. The path exists, and it is leading to a wider view of our choices for life . . . health . . . unified will . . . and our species identity. As the understanding of this path grows, teachers and parents will join forces, and from their renewed hope and enthusiasm the children will gain strength. Breaking the cycle of hopelessness only takes a few, the critical mass of persons who are willing to lift upward in an act of spiritual will. If our local leaders don't know what is needed, if they don't know what to call it, then they won't do it—even with all the best intentions in the world. Intentions don't work if one doesn't have a clear vision of the future's scope and direction.

As we have seen in the chapters of Part Two, there are many factors currently leading to illness and dysfunction in our culture. Many of our children who are particularly sensitive are suffering the most—for they are serving in a deep way like canaries in a mine shaft—warning others of toxic conditions by their own chronic or sudden illness and, at times, their tragic death. Take a moment and look again at the 12 brief case studies with which we began chapter 6. Multiply each child's experience by 1,000, or 10,000, or by 1 million. You would still fall short of the real numbers. Clearly we can't afford to ignore the cries for help.

The next step is to understand more fully what the disintegration conditions (e.g., illness of blocked breath, illness of blocked words, delinquency, isolation) are symptoms of. What is the positive that is buried within the negative? What is the seed that is being smothered and not fed? The seed within one child will have reverberations to many other children.

To explore this question, in Part Three we turn to the biophysics of our imminent divinity.

∾

PART THREE

THE BIOPHYSICS OF
OUR IMMINENT* DIVINITY

---

* The word imminent implies that which is likely to occur soon, at any time. The word immanent, in contrast, means that which remains within, or indwelling. The meaning that we intend here is that *Homo devas* are imminent.

Chapter 11

BIRTH OF A SPECIES

The species that is emerging will look like us because it is born from us. It will be divine in that *divinity* implies more whole, more advanced, than we are now. At the start of the 21ˢᵗ century, the next level of Earth life is coming into direct manifestation through physical human lives. The biophysics of the transition from *Homo sapiens* to *Homo deva* will be studied, investigated, learned about, and eventually taught to our young people. Whether your own background and inclinations are more scientific or spiritual / religious, you will find familiar elements in a thorough study of tangible divinity. You may not be accustomed, however, to seeing the elements *together*. The biology and physics of species transition need to be explored and discussed just as much, if not more, than the spirituality. What we know now is a mere thimbleful of what we will need to know in order to deal with cutting-edge issues during the transition decades.

When we realize that our view has been accurate but our perspective has been relatively narrow, there is an "aha!" experience, perhaps several "aha!" experiences in a cascade. We then readily recognize that the emergence of *Homo deva* is a further phase of our own growth and development. Of course, parts of the path look very familiar. We realize, with a nod of gratitude, that this view of the species threshold is a natural and logical extrapolation from the recent writings of authors such as Quinn *(Ishmael; Beyond Civilization)*; Ray and Anderson *(Cultural Creatives)*; Klein *(Dawn of Culture)*; Keck *(Sacred Eyes)*; T. Berry *(The Great Work)*; Capra *(Hidden Connections)*; Houston *(Jump Time)*; Pearce *(The Biology of Transcendence)*; Macy *(World as Lover, World as Self)*; Sheldrake et al. *(Chaos, Creativity, and Cosmic Consciousness)*; and Hubbard *(Conscious Evolution)*.

Let's briefly put our current transition in context: By 100,000 years ago, *Homo sapiens* had evolved a modern anatomy and a brain size comparable to ours, but their behavior was still premodern. As work by Klein (2002), Diamond (1992), Tattersall (1998), and others has shown us, physically modern humans produced the cultural big bang of 40,000 years ago. The remains of their tribal habitats and village sites provide distinct evidence of innovation and many modern behaviors, including living and hunting in groups, making and wearing climate-resistant garments, constructing sturdy huts, and creating intricate jewelry and other art forms. This Stone Age Renaissance was possibly triggered by the impetus of spoken language, which enabled early humans to transmit ideas as well as to react to direct sensory input to the brain.

Between 40,000 and 35,000 years ago, we went through a huge and sustained wave of migration as well as cultural distribution. Physically modern humans moved outward from Africa, the Near East, and Asia into Europe and Australia. Later, by about 13,000 to 11,000 years ago, our ancestors had reached the Americas. The several pre-modern hominid species that these early *Homo sapiens* encountered, such as *Homo neanderthalensis* in Europe and the Middle East, died out within a very few thousand years, a remarkably quick replacement of the alpha species across two continents.

Then about 10,000 years ago, the agricultural revolution introduced widespread cultivation of plants and herding of animals to all continents (see Keck; Arsuaga; Eldredge). This is what Robert Keck describes as *Epoch II*, the full domestication of plant and animal kingdoms in service of human growth. By the time of the agricultural revolution of Epoch II, the fourth kingdom called humanity was vitally alive and growing.

We had established ourselves as the dominant force on the planet. We have remained in this position for the last 10,000 years.

Eventually, the first major cities appeared around 6,000 years ago, and the historic record emerged. By 5,000 years ago, complex human civilizations had emerged in early Egypt, Mesopotamia and the Indus Valley, and China (Leslie, 2002, p. 59). This was the beginning of historical time, at least according to your college history textbooks.

What is crucial for our discussion is the fact that our ancestors of 30 millennia ago had basically the same biological anatomy and physiology as we do now. Their brains were significantly more evolved than the other, early species of genus *Homo* (e.g., *Homo habilis*), thereby making them much more adaptable to change. They rapidly developed an ingenuity that has served us well over the past 30 millennia.

When the surge in neurological brain-organization occurred during that pivotal time, an abundance of totally new cultural developments followed: body garments to withstand harsh climates; sturdy, well-heated shelter; weapons to hunt larger animals; successful sheltering in caves even against competition from large animals; sophisticated equipment for fishing, and water canteens for travel; and diverse art forms and ornamentation, some with symbolic significance. The accelerated pace of this development guaranteed that *cultural* advancement rather than *biological* evolution would emerge as the central force shaping humanity's progress. That is a quick review of our story (see Appendix 1 for a description of the technical names for the major species in our hominid family history).

We are now entering a comparable great leap in the course of life on Earth. This time it will be a very interdependent cross-fertilization between the same three levels as before, yet on a greater scale: (1) physiological change, (2) brain function development, and (3) cultural evolution. The leap will be more than a quantum step in brain-organization (as the sensory matrix for all consciousness). It will involve some further physiological maturation of the species, but generally as a corollary effect of the brain-mind integration. The primary shift will be within human mental function and will produce totally new areas of cultural innovation, such as are already nascent in the recent advances of nanotechnology; the worldwide use of the Internet for research, learning, and communication; and the participation of medical intuitives in clinical diagnosis and healing.

This time the species uplift will involve a synergistic enhancement of those three levels of our functioning: The human physiology (physical), the brain (consciousness / heart), and objective innovations (mind's effect on matter). The latter aspect of tangible innovation will primarily be expressed through the focused will of the whole—which at this time reflects the human and planetary level. This triad of physiology / consciousness / will functioning as one *(at-onement)* will bring creative powers that we can barely conceive of at this time. In later chapters, we will consider these in more depth.

What does such a major shift look like? To get a few clues, we might look to our past. Imagine for a moment what it would be like to have a conversation with a *Homo sapiens* family of 30,000 years ago. What would happen if you attempt to describe to them your day of driving on the freeway, entering a large city stadium, and watching a major league baseball game with 25,000 other people? That would be totally inconceivable to the tribal members from the savanna who spend their time hiding in the bushes to escape large predators, perhaps taking food from smaller mammals, and existing in a band of fewer than a dozen individuals, each with a life expectancy of less than 35 years.

A crucial dialogue will occur in our own time between the *Homo sapiens* of the 21st century who are on the old side of the current transition and those who are on the new, *Homo deva* side. The dialogue will require compassion from all of us, because this great shift will feel more welcome to some people than others. Within our individual families, yours and mine, some will accept this transition with open arms; others may resist, and this is an opportunity to bring our authentic selves to the dialogue. We need to listen and hear the reasons why this message may not be welcome to some friends and relatives, and what they are truly hearing. Part of the lesson of this transition is to share what we see, truly listen with compassion to our friend, and then let go to respect and accept someone else's timing.

Consider the digital divide, a term that describes the gap between those people who can converse about computer issues and controversies, and those who can't. As an extrapolation of that phenomenon, I believe that by 2020 there may be a comparable *species divide* between those who welcome the very concept of a new species and all its creative potential, and those who feel threatened. Be gentle with both groups, for you have both voices within. We all do. That ambivalence is part of being the pivot generation at the threshold between kingdoms. We have the unique gift and the responsibility to live both as humans and as early versions of kinetic devas. In the course of this dialogue, we will come to realize quite viscerally that whatever side we are on, we are all one family. All the children of Earth are going to learn to recognize each other as family and to celebrate our diverse interests and skills. In fact, the threshold into the *Homo deva* era will be in some respects a joyful reunion.

In terms of the biophysics of this threshold time, we can view the three aspects of human life (physiology / consciousness / will) as reflections at slower octaves of the triad of matter / soul / spirit. All three are intimately involved in the leap of species identity. The participation and interaction of these three aspects have been variously described as echo patterns (Wolf), as morphic resonance (Sheldrake), as the dance of a Master of Play (Swimme), as our entering the Ecozoic Age (T. Berry), and other exquisite word songs about the reorientation of humanity into a deeper interaction with the planet. The role of humanity is now to help the interactive nature be heard, to literally voice the sound of planet-human-spirit evolving together. Through *Homo deva*, the three-as-one voice of wisdom about preserving and nurturing our world will be heard among all Earth's peoples.

One of my favorite examples of this interaction is the alignment of overtones or harmonics in music. When any level becomes a rounder musical seed-tone, the overtones likewise become rounder as well. Just as overtones combine with the fundamental to produce a rounder, more complex tone, so the human body, brain, and will are interacting to produce a new, more complex being. Or, to use the image of a dance of atoms: In the context of wave function, the three dimensions of amplitude (light), wavelength (love), and frequency (creative power) shift in relation to each other. They move in an ever-changing dance in relation to each other's wave pattern, with synergistic fusion effects.

In the biophysics of our imminent divinity, the levels are calling to each other—not just across space but, now more than ever, across time. The biology of higher instincts across time is a fertile area for further research (see Pearce, 2002, for fascinating development of biological models). As we tune more deliberately and coherently to the unified field of physics, the great Dreaming Mind becomes increasingly accessible, approachable, familiar, playful, and beloved. In another kind of metaphor, we can say: The mind of God is a library with open stacks. All we need to do is learn how to stand up straight so we can see what is on the higher shelves.

Homo sapiens, all 6.3 billion of us, are the present self. *Homo deva* is our future self—the soul of humanity—emerging from the planetary mind and incarnating among us and through us. Our future is incarnating as an international group of people who will become friends, real people with residence addresses, favorite movies, and Social Security numbers (or the equivalent in other nations). In their presence, we will all become closer to our best selves and will be able to reach out to help many people who are now suffering. And, according to my reasoned estimate, the *Homo deva*s will number in the tens of thousands by the year 2020. This is not your father's version of enlightenment.

∼

In order to comprehend with our analytic mind what imminent divinity will bring to our world, we need to explore how the levels of functioning and their links are changing. What we have described for many centuries as the heart is clearly a central aspect of living beings on earth. The lifethread is the energy connection that anchors in the heart, and as long as the lifethread is intact, a person (or animal) is alive even if knocked unconscious or held in a fever. The heart is a breathing-bridge between the fourth and fifth kingdoms. Think of the lifethread as the energy connection between a microcosm and its larger hologram, its corresponding macrocosm. Having the lifethread intact keeps us incarnate within our physical bodies. When the lifethread is "broken" or the circuit between microcosm and macrocosm is closed, our physical body returns to the atoms of Earth from which it came; and our essence likewise returns to the energetic realms from which we came, however we each conceive of that realm.

Regardless of language skills, or life experience, level of education, or any other dimension of consciousness, as long as the heart is beating, a person is alive; and the breath is the medium through which the heart receives oxygenation to maintain its incredibly efficient circulatory action for years and decades. In the past couple of centuries, we have traditionally believed that the head is the locus for thought, for consciousness. From the frontiers of neurocardiology come reports of the relationship between the brain-in-our-head and a newly discovered brain-in-our-heart. As a brief summary of the work reported in great detail by Joseph Chilton Pearce (2002), the neurological structures in our brain-in-head correspond to the past evolution of life from the reptilian, old mammalian, and human levels of development. Now, the new biological fact is that another kind of neurological organizing structure has been found in the human heart. Pearce calls it, logically, the fifth brain in our system. He postulates that the great saints and spiritual leaders in history were representing or embodying hints of our next evolutionary step, by utilizing the interactive effects of the head brain and heart brain. This proposal fits quite consistently with the model that I am developing. Although I am not familiar enough with the biologic detail to assess its role in learning disorders, eating disorders, or other syndromes with which I have worked, the disconnect between people's mental functioning and their feelings would quite naturally have a neurological correlate. We can see this kind of problem in the compulsive behavior that surrounds some addictions, and in the blocks that make learning to read very difficult for some children even when they very much want to make the step of pattern recognition.

There are fertile areas for further research here, in exploring how the heart brain has a role in our learning to think with our caring. This may be analogous to our head brain becoming more sensitized to empathy. These two aspects of a polarity are beginning to share and cross-fertilize, and in the process are becoming more integrated as a larger energy system. The growth of mind-heart as an integrated system is the cause, and one of its effects is the lifethread shifting upward to anchor in the head rather than the heart. On a very tangible basis, we can see this shift in the growing incidence of human beings who have had open-heart surgery, or even a heart transplant. Their heart is literally stopped; they are kept alive (by the combined mental understanding, physical surgery skills, electronic and mechanical technology designed and built by humans, and compassionate caring of other human beings) until their own heart is either repaired or replaced. This is an evolutionary miracle. It is an act of skillful will by the macrocosm in dedication to saving the individual human. And its corollary on an individual level is mental-governance of lifethread. In effect, the person says, "I choose to die temporarily in order that I live longer." On a higher turn of the spiral, that is what humanity needs to choose during the process of species transition.

These are some preliminary comments about the transition from our old view of head-heart to the new view, and its effect on the lifethread. Our intent is to help get the concept visible, and then trust that other writers, researchers, and teachers will join in contributing to our collective understanding.

The next core concept about imminent divinity involves the electromagnetic field, both yours that reaches a few yards around you, and the larger ones that reach for miles. Imagine a planet-size field of energy. There is a pair of arcs, one vibrating down and the other vibrating up. The arcs are curving fields that go across all of spacetime. We (humans and animals and all other objects) manifest as visible beings by the coming together of an electromagnet with two poles. The poles are like the energy zones at the North and South poles of the Earth, where electromagnetic energy comes together and flows outward in great bands. In the model I am presenting, the arcs of energy flowing between the poles get stronger as humanity learns to focus our attention more and more. Giving attention directly gives energy. Energy is matter. Matter is ultra-slow-motion spirit. The two poles of the magnet, which for purposes of this discussion we name *matter* and *spirit*, get more interactive as we include feedback, that is, as we are receptive to our daily life experience, and as we radiate or emit our own thoughts and feeling nature.

To ground this physics commentary a notch closer to our lives: As Spangler (2001) beautifully reminds us, we can learn the art of blessing as a form of radiation to others in our lives. That example, in fact, fits quite well in our consideration of the physical nature of divinity. To gently give blessing to someone or some place is to share one's essence in gratitude. The energy of gratitude concentrates our awareness of who we are, our will in opening in vulnerability to the other, and our recognition of a shared identity between self and that other. Precisely, in gratitude we acknowledge receiving energy from other; we are a part of a larger whole called self-and-other. And in blessing we share energy of our identity with other. In such acts of spiritual energy-exchange, we inevitably bring more coherence to the arcs of energy in our own life, in our personal energy field.

Then, you may ask, what is coherence? Here is the scientific meaning first, and then I will give an example: Coherence in terms of light means that the electromagnetic waves that are emitted have a fixed-phase relationship over time. Waves with high coherence keep their electrons bouncing at extremely regular and rhythmic vibration rates; there is an overall harmony in their orbits and frequencies. The waves that have less coherence spread or get diffused over time, as they propagate outward through space; they don't keep a fixed-phase relationship. In everyday language, they get a little bit messy after a while. That is the nature of a world that has inertia. That introduction of inefficiency into the wave-pattern is why things wear out, break down, and don't work as efficiently. That is why a regular flashlight that you shine into the sky will not illuminate the surface of the moon; the light has too much refraction, which decreases the coherence of the beam. If a beam of totally coherent light were to shine into the sky, it would illuminate all the stars in that path for many miles out.

To summarize the implication of this model, we are seeing that humans are learning to govern the various electromagnetic arcs that make up our personalities. Each pair of arcs is a different level of polarity. Here are just a couple of them that will be familiar to you in other contexts:

FIGURE 12. POLARITIES ON THE PATH

Polarity or Feedback Loop	Brief Example of Human Activity
Feelings Body	Relieving emotional pressures that contribute to and intensify physical illness and pain perception
Mind Feelings	Relationship counseling; grief work
Mind Body	Meditative practices and imagery for pain management in chronic illness; for joyful childbirth; clarifying beliefs that may contribute to eating disorders.
Soul Personality	Dealing with species despair over the environmental crises facing humanity and the planet; unlocking the barrier between abstract mind (soul level) and concrete mind that may prevent spoken language in some autistic children.
Spirit Matter	Choosing to re-embody after a near-death experience (NDE); the dissolution of past traumas held in the physical body; the choice to consciously withdraw from the body at the moment of death. Emerging creative powers of *Homo deva;* opening relationship between sentient humans and the planet; precognition regarding "acts of God" such as earthquakes, avalanches, and other natural catastrophes.

Each of these polarities clearly has different dynamics, and there is extensive research and clinical literature on each of them. The specific question we are focusing on is the pattern made by the progression of these polarities, and what does the pattern imply about human divinity. The pattern formed by all of them together is of progressively larger loops of a magnetic field becoming more integrated at each step by the *higher pole* in each dyad. The two poles where the energy streams from are in closer "dialogue" or interplay at each step; and at each step the higher pole learns to govern the lower pole in a coherent way. For example, the healing of eating disorders involves a person's mind and feelings learning to govern the physical body's reactions to food. That governing is in complex ways supported or sabotaged by messages from mass media, cultural institutions (e.g., school), and family.

When the polarities are all brought into coherent energy fields, i.e., when the loops are harmonized all the way through the soul and personality arcs, and then the spirit and matter arcs, the individual person can live and move with minimal friction, minimal dissonance. What we describe as "imminent divinity" in the first decade of the 21st century will probably look like a children's storybook to people in the year 2050. Yet right now, this is what the mind and heart of humanity needs to hear—that there is a progression, and our helping several thousand people move to the completion of this progression in the next couple of decades will dramatically reduce the violence on Earth. As we increase our understanding of the progression of polarities, this itself brings more energy into coherent expression—reducing dissonance (friction / entropy / fragmentation / violence) and establishing a higher equilibrium. As recent research suggests, the greater creative balance emerges even when expressed in chaos and other patterns (e.g., fractals) that are difficult for our dedicated linear-mind to recognize.

The shift upward in locus of identity, from feelings—to mind—to personality—to spiritual consciousness—to spiritual will—to identity, is a long process. The process takes years for individual humans, without exception. Now, for the first time, we are able to see that the same threads of this greater-identification process are happening in the *species as a whole.* The good news is that our individual progress—yours, mine, and our friends—has an increasingly direct and immediate impact on the progress of the species as a whole. That is the nature of *coherent light*, reflecting the patterns exactly, with fewer distortions or refractions. There are fewer distortions, and more degrees of freedom.

The bad news is that quite a few humans who are capable of functioning at the level of spiritual will are currently caught in illusions about who they are. To be precise, they are handling tremendous energies from the plane of spiritual will (atmic level), but have a fragmented or partial sense of identity (monadic level). You may wish to refer back to Figure 4 regarding these terms. The significant degree of coherence they have built up is not yet focused in support of the whole identity of humanity, let alone the planetary field. Their energy is dedicated to *saving the good guys*; that is, those of their particular nationality, ethnicity, industry, religion, brand name, gender, age group, urban tribe, or the like. Therefore, they function as open pipelines for fission energies (e.g., greed, hate, revenge, envy, contempt), which in turn reinforce and indeed amplify the viciousness of the "we vs. they" mentality. Dissonance in the electromagnetic loops, and suffering in human lives, results.

Pick up the evening newspaper, and you can find several articles about some of these persons. Let's call them the Screaming Suicide Squirrels, or the Omnivorous Oligarchy. While you are smiling at the labels, just remember that you and I also have these evolutionarily regressive voices deep inside us.

How do we get rid of them or, to phrase that question more politely, how do we lessen their impact on all of Earth's children? The feedback loops or polarities such as soul-to-personality, and spirit-to-matter, are each becoming more integrated. The process is happening all over the planet, as individuals steadily connect to a larger identity. The three phases of this process have historically been characterized by terms of respect. In ancient texts and mystical teachings, they have been called the *teachers*, *sages*, and *saints*. Although these titles of respect refer to personages, they can also be metaphors for the phases of life-energy becoming more coherent, more sacred. You may have met one or two persons whom you would nominate for those respected categories. You may even recognize yourself. In 21st century terminology, we are naming these three phases of development the *creatives*, the *innovators* of wise action, and the *lifeseeds* of fusion power and spiritual grace. As I mentioned earlier, I have adopted Ray and Anderson's term "creatives" here because their description from survey data matches considerably with my research in social services, regarding the characteristics of Phase 1. All three groups are growing quite steadily, although the first and second groups are the only ones publicly visible at this time.

These three phases of growth and development from human-to-beyond-human will be described in more detail in later chapters. What is important to understand is that you can be of immense help right now, today, by recognizing that you are part of this blossoming of a new species. The hopefulness, trust, and networking that you express on a daily basis will have many positive effects far beyond your localized time and space. The nature of these enhanced feedback loops guarantees that each of us can be of direct help to our fellow humans and, to some degree, the whole species by serving as amplifiers of coherent life-energy. We do this by being *aware of our identity as a new global species* and by making many daily choices from that dedicated place. One of the first dynamic loops to start linking us to the larger species mind was created in the past twenty years. That is the Internet itself.

There is no longer any reason for wringing our hands and saying, "But what can *I* do about this problem . . . I'm *only one person!*" That is a correct premise, but a wrong conclusion. Here is a promise that the future now gives to each of us:

- Everyone who reads this page and thinks about it for more than 10 minutes will have greater coherence in their brain, and that coherence will be *in synch with* our species' coherence. As a result, we will help hundreds of other persons reach more coherence in their lives.
- Everyone who recognizes and accepts themselves as a *creative* (Phase 1 of the transition) will help thousands of other persons to reach

that phase. Their mind and feelings are becoming an integrated system, a large polarity that is being bridged and healed in their daily lives.

- Everyone who recognizes and accepts themselves as an *innovator* (Phase 2 of the transition) will help hundreds of thousands of persons to reach their own unique next steps. Their soul and personality are becoming an integrated system, a much larger polarity that is being bridged and healed across the energy field of humanity.

- And everyone who recognizes and accepts themselves as a *lifeseed* (Phase 3 of the transition) will help millions of persons to breathe more gently in their daily lives. They are breathing as an integrated system of spirit and matter, the highest polarity that our human physical bodies can currently bridge while remaining incarnate.

Be reassured that if you make affirmations for a level that you haven't tangibly reached yet, there is no harm done. It is a totally self-regulating and self-healing process. The phrase used above, "recognize and accept," is designed to remind us that the process is freely chosen and is self-sustaining from the planetary level. We can do no wrong here. Humans can only radiate identity energy from the level where we have *physically actualized* our own unity with Earth.

Here is one of the basic rules for the biophysics of *Homo devas*: Amplification of positive coherence is highly contagious. Your positive energy is highly contagious! First, the positive coherence of a person is just like a laser beam that amplifies light. Second, the amplification of coherent electric energy is like the process of *falling in love* in that it amplifies trust and goodwill and can actually aid the healing process. We have known about some of the scientific attributes of these two processes (light and love) in human development for almost a century. Now, we are beginning to learn about the next process: amplifying power—the *creative powers* that are released within our soul and germinate in our personalities, in the same manner that the *future* is birthed through the present moment. The power of attraction between light / love / power as a triad, working synergistically together, is contagious. Indeed, it is highly contagious.

Let's spread the good news. Our neighbors and friends need some good news that is juicy and weighty enough to chew on for a while and to discuss vociferously. Some of your friends, let's admit it, always welcome an idea that is debatable, and this one surely is! In addition, we as a culture need to deepen our mental diet to include concepts that bridge into ideas and can generate program innovations, and thus last much longer than mass media sound bites. The concept of *Homo deva* fits all these parameters.

A Prescription for Our New Species Identity

How exactly *are* we going to make life on Earth better for our children and grandchildren? What could your home videos of the next 10 to 15 years show our successors in year 2025 about the choices we made during this critical transition? We would probably want to illustrate for them the shift that we have been reading and talking and thinking about for several decades—and are now actually living through.

To clarify one item from the discussion above: The change in identity that we are approaching is not merely a mental statement, as in "I affirm that I am 5'11" and weigh 130 pounds." (In physical fact I am not that tall and weigh more than that.) The *power of positive thinking*, as commonly understood, will not by itself get us to *Homo deva* and a peaceable world. That kind of affirmation is indeed effective, but limited to the level of affect-and-intellect, because that is where most people are living.

The full transition we need is beyond our rational, linear mind. The species birth comes in three phases (look again at Figure 5), and the particular timing and combination of sub-phases will be different for every individual. As with any discussion of development and maturation, the exact patterns vary significantly among different groups. Yet, based on 20 years of research, observation, and reflection, I will say the following: The first phase of *Homo deva* emerging is the quantum step *beyond intellect to higher intuition*. Then the second phase is *beyond consciousness to spiritual will.* And the third phase is lifting *beyond unified will to identity.* This last is at the level of being-energy, or "be-ness." It involves the relationship between humanity and the planet; for if "we" collectively are the heart of the world today, we aspire to embody and express the throat of the world by the year 2025. And the planet *inspires* us to lift upward and become, truly, the creative 6-billion-member unified voice of our world.

The third phase grounds the transformation all the way through our hominid bodies to the level of biological and genetic function. Of course, in each phase the "lower" level from which we start each step is not abandoned. It continues to be an integral part of the living entity (whether that entity is a person, a family, a community, or a nation). The energy-circuit becomes more integrated and the pacemaker of the higher level governs the lower level. For example, the creative intuition as a pacemaker governs the analytic mind, and together they serve as partners and beloved co-creators.

The *identity* of which we speak in the third phase is at the level of the *lifethread.* For many centuries and in different cultures, wise ones have spoken of this phase as one in which the person is awake to the choice to incarnate, and also to the choice to discarnate at the end of a lifetime (called in some teachings the *process of abstraction*). Based on research as well as anecdotal evidence, the behavioral indicators for early Phase 3 might include capacities such as waking easily after three to four hours sleep at night and having enough physical stamina to work a double shift, with enough energy left over to help your children with a science project. These examples both have to do with energy levels, because they refer to *early* Phase 3. The further reaches of Phase 3 relate to the processes of birthing and dying, and the conscious choices for timing of each. The third phase of the transition is a finely differentiated physical change that grounds the high level (*be-ness mind*) down to the lowest (actual fusion of *consciousness thread* and *lifethread*), producing the ability to govern the breath of beginning and ending life. We will examine these three phases in more depth in Part Four.

How have we come this far without seeing the imminent change in our species? The brief answer is that we received plenty of clues, but we didn't know how to connect the dots in a line reaching upward to our future self. We didn't realize fully that *raising consciousness* would lead us to transcend the wounds of consciousness itself. We didn't realize in the 1960s or 1970s that the cutting edge of humanity would eventually reach a level of functioning within the unified spiritual will of the whole species, and from there to the level of planetary identity. Here are just a few of the primary footprints that have provided clues in the past decade (refer to Resources for others):

- Daniel Quinn, in his spiritual novels *Ishmael* and *My Ishmael*, calls us the *Leavers*, the ones who stay linked to life's rhythmic pulses while the *Takers* are off looting and pillaging, collecting trophy-spouses, trophy-mansions, trophy-vehicles, huge stock options, and corporate perks. The *Leavers* are willing to "leave life *in the hands of the gods*"; while they do not presume to be masters of the universe, they affirm their trust and intimate partnership in life's patterns and synchronicities.
- Paul Ray and Sherry Anderson call us the *cultural creatives.* They have documented in their impressive blend of sociological and psychological data the journey we have been on these past three or four decades. In thorough detail and with extensive anecdotal reports, they describe the shifts in values, interests, and activities that 50 million pioneering creatives in the United States (and approximately 300 million worldwide) have chosen on an intriguing variety of dimensions.
- Jean Houston suggests that we as humans are facing challenges of the "jump time," and that we can learn to anticipate the optimal responses for our own *jump* and that of our loved ones.
- David Spangler describes the process of encountering our "co-incarnational self," the greater being that *is us* in higher dimensions and who wants to approach and partner with us.
- Robert Keck presents a wonderful panorama of humans learning to open their "sacred eyes" into the start of Epoch III, just as the

earlier Epoch II of 10,000 years ago led us through the agricultural revolution.

- Joanna Macy calls us the pioneers who have consecrated our life work to the preservation of the "eco-self," in which the planet's mind as no-separate-mind learns to express through humanity.
- Barbara Marx Hubbard regards us as standing at a threshold from earth-bound species to a much wider evolutionary horizon, in which we will explore the solar system and beyond, and eventually become truly "homo universalis."
- Wes Nisker reminds us that one of the core ways to discover our place in the world is through our *buddha's nature*, the relationship of buddhic-within ("abstract mind") and buddhic-outward, the manifest world of cosmic mind that is everywhere immanent.
- Michael Lerner speaks to the yearning in all human hearts for a peaceable world, and describes how a quest for "emancipatory spirituality" can infuse our society with new meaning and joy.
- Joseph Chilton Pearce gathers for us a bouquet of new research in fields such as neurocardiology, describing how a "fifth brain" within our hearts is helping guide us through the species transformation. He is a dedicated pioneer whose current work is deeply infused with the creativity of early *Homo deva*.
- James Redfield inspires us to live our individual versions of the *celestine vision*, and to approach each other through the lens of integrity, creativity, imagination, and synchronicity.
- John Robbins presents finely articulated steps for us to support the *food revolution*, for our health and greater well-being. The food revolution is a focused expression of the higher identity beyond dominator *Homo sapiens* and into early *Homo deva*, using spiritual will to choose physical nourishment that is more aligned with all Earth's beings in the web of life.
- Michael Toms opens and consecrates our *dialogues about democracy* and the deepening sense of sacred mission that we seek to express, a sense of mission that we sometimes hesitate to bring forth because of self-doubts at the community and national level.

- Robert Thurman invites us to look deeply at the *inner revolution* of our times, where the practices of Buddhism meet counterparts in our best democratic principles.
- Matthew Fox reminds us of the cornucopia of blessings from many human traditions, the "one river and many wells" that nourish our thirst for wisdom and truth in times of peril.

The next time that one of your friends laments the lack of encouraging signs of the times, you can refer them to this couple of pages — or to any of the authors and artists in the Resources list. These are a sampling from among the writings in many languages that are blending into a song of renewal — the reunion of the soul and the physical plane.

Do We Have Time?

Will these enhanced moments of transcendence be sufficient? Will the steps of reorientation of will, realignment of identity, synergistic movement of part-and-whole be enough to heal our world? To the mystics among you, this may seem a strange and rude question. Of course we have time, don't we?

Yet the question must be raised. Is the widespread spiritual awakening that we have described thus far actually going to be sufficient for what humanity needs? The grounding of beautiful insights in the most dense levels of human life reveals some painful realities. Many wise elders have discussed potential solutions, but each solution is premised on a limit to the self-destruction of our species.

Given the model we are developing, time is of the essence. Through *time itself*, the power of eternity is on the homestretch to birth within Earth's planes. The shift from "conqueror" of matter to *beloved partner* is a major change. Can we befriend matter, so that our very bodies vibrate with hopefulness, and thereby access the life breath of Earth? What I have called *bifocal vision and knowing* of spacetime is actually the experience of *Homo deva time.* This knowing has the potential to help transfigure life on Earth, because a person living in *Homo deva time* both nourishes and is vitalized by the life of the planet. There is literally no separation "in thought, word, or deed" (to use the scouting phrase). From this greater angle of spacetime, my reply to the question above is a resounding YES—we can face the crises, and find ways and the time to move through them.

This is both a hopeful and a serious message. There are critical issues demanding the attention of our wisest and most dedicated leaders. To be specific, the fusion of *Homo sapiens time* and *Homo deva time* will only be successful if it can assist us in facing and dealing with the following, for starters:

- Save South America from financial and social disaster, with particular reference to Argentina, Brazil, and Colombia, as their economies reach the turning point toward either healing or collapse into entropy.
- Halt explosion fishing and a dozen other commercial practices across the globe that have very short-term vision and are now destroying fragile and vital underpinnings of the planetary ecosystem that our species and many others literally depend on.
- Defuse the armed threats in several major *Homo sapiens* political face-offs, including the Middle East, Iraq, that between the atomic weapon nations of India and Pakistan, and China and Korea.
- Save West African nations, Russia, and other countries from disintegrating politically and sliding into anarchy as greater than 25 percent of their populations become objectively symptomatic with AIDS.

You can supply other hot issues to add to the list. The birth of a new species is imminent, but the infant's head is a little stuck in the birth canal. As you are probably well aware, a birthing is no time to lose your cool and start yelling hysterically. It is a time to keep focus, trust in the wisdom of the evolutionary process, and use all of the emotional, physical, mental, and friendship resources at hand. In a very real sense, we are the birthing parents, we are the midwife, and we are the *future-child* being born. A species birth is a sacred time, as well as a time to use all the analytic knowledge, pragmatic skills, intuitive wisdom, and courage that we can muster.

That is what you and I and all our friends need to do, and we need to sustain this effort over the next 10 years. It is really not as complicated as it sounds. As with most important tasks, it is simple, but not easy. In the next chapter, we will look at some characteristics of a fusion beam, and how this can help us recognize the steps of birthing the future into our own daily lives.

Chapter 12

EACH FUSION LASER HAS TWO FOCI

In our discussion in Chapter 11 about a new species, I spoke of an upward arc and a downward arc. These arcs or movements of energy have been known and described for thousands of years. One of the deepest sets of arcs is what we call in human language the *path of evolution* (moving upward), and the *path of revelation* (moving downward). Now these paths, also known as the ascent of matter and the descent of spirit, are in their final era of blending and, eventually, fusion.

One way to think of this process is in terms of nuclear fusion, which occurs when atoms are compressed under extreme pressures until they fuse together. Tremendous amounts of nuclear energy are released. An approach that several national labs are experimenting with in an attempt to produce safe nuclear energy involves multiple laser beams. Between 50 and 200 laser beams are simultaneously aimed at hydrogen molecules from many directions. The goal is to create a fusion reaction that generates more power than it consumes. The same dynamics of self-heating or self-generation are involved in the *fusion reaction* between the two planetary arcs, evolution and revelation.

In this chapter, we will examine briefly another way of describing the two arcs, namely as *two foci*. In many growth patterns in nature, two foci are needed. The first is a *reference beam*, and the second is its *partner.* In the field of genetics, scientists have described the two foci through the beautiful model of the double helix of chromosomes. The two helices are, indeed, a reference beam and its partner. In my looking at future possibilities, I believe that research will reveal important dynamics embedded in the relationship between the two helices at the electromagnetic and nuclear levels. The two strands function very much like a binary star, a dyad system that produces nuclear energy. In a metaphoric sense, we might say that the two foci serve to "inspire" each other, providing life breath to their partner, the other beam of energy. Some future scientific investigations will look particularly at what this means for "curing" human health dysfunctions, including the conditions associated with aging, with the immune system, with specific eye conditions, and in prenatal healing.

⁓⁓

Heroes Come in Dyads of Many Shapes

The concept of *two foci* working together for healing can also apply at the level of mind, in healing work on behalf of regional or national populations. Recall the three phases of our transition to *Homo deva.* These can be referred to, from another angle, as affecting the body / emotions / mind of humanity. Phase 1 affects the physical body. Phase 2 affects the emotions / consciousness of humanity; and Phase 3 affects the mind and will of humanity. We each have parts of our lives at these three phases. However, we will have our primary identification with one or another of the three. The dynamics of species transition include more than movement from one phase to another. For example, on the following page in Figure 13 is a table with six names of sample heroes whose work is helping humanity's transition. These six people are diverse in their professional calling and in their personal background. Each of the six is a hero of our species. The future self of humanity is infusing each of these six individuals and their life's work.

The purpose of this table is to indicate how our pioneers manifest divinity in several different paths, each of which expresses the best qualities of our species. Each of the six people is an example of the focus, dedication, and caring toward human beings that characterize early *Homo deva* on world scale. (We will look more thoroughly at the transition from early *Homo deva* to mid–*Homo deva* in subsequent chapters.) Notice that the six are paired at the levels of Civilization, Culture, and Unified Field. These refer to the general visibility of their work within the "eye" of humanity; the heroes at the level of civilization are the most visible in initiating changes for the species. But all three levels are infusing our world with compassionate and potent pulses of divine-human energy. Each pair illustrates several important dynamics of our collective healing. For instance, each pair involves a reference beam and partner (the two foci) relationship. The two partners' work cross-fertilizes, counterbalances the other within the polarity that they are expressing, and benefits from the other's presence, even if the persons have not actually met.

FIGURE 13. SAMPLE HEROES OF HOMO SAPIENS' TRANSITION

Fusion Level For Humanity	Heroes Among Us	Chosen Path
Civilization	Bishop Desmond Tutu Aung San Suu Kyi	Path of forgiveness, *the divine Yes* Path of protest, *the divine No*
Culture	James Redfield Rupert Sheldrake	Path of storyteller Path of science
Unified Field	David Spangler Ken Wilber	Path of mystic union Path of pure reason

In the model I am presenting, each of the six people above is an early divine human. They are helping to uplift all of us together, beyond basic *Homo sapiens*. Their steps are along different paths of the healing of our collective heart. Yet they are all heading in one direction—that of energizing the *unified field of humanity*. In addition, all persons who read or hear of these heroes' work then participate in that uplift. It is true that the angle of divinity varies among them according to the energy configuration of their words and actions. The primary focal-length of their wisdom varies across the three levels of fusion. All six people participate in all three levels in their lives, of course, yet their primary focus is through one of the three. Thank goodness this is true, because we need wisdom and creative power at all three levels of humanity in order to heal our world.

It is intriguing to reflect on the interactions that each of the pairs involves on the mental level. Their work has mutually stimulated each other and has brought greater hope and clarity for many people who are also taking steps along those paths. That is a principal dynamic of the *two foci*, acting as reference beams for each other, to amplify the power (as a laser does with light) and then send it out to others. I have a conjecture that similar processes are going on in biology, with each strand of the double helix eliciting creativity for the other. In a very real sense, these six individuals (and many other people in similar dyads) assist each other in stimulating new innovation and in recharging their batteries over the long term.

In the next two decades, educators and health professionals will be able to investigate the hypothesis that the physiological brain-waves of *Homo deva* pioneers are distinctive in various ways. These distinct patterns will have both generic commonalities, such as voltage, and some unique individual characteristics. For such dyads of two foci, the greater resonance that their mental fields can generate when they voluntarily interact and amplify each other's work will be another useful area of healing and study.

As Joseph Campbell and others have taught us, the hero's journey often involves slaying dragons as well as bringing healing gifts for our loved ones back home. Our dragons exist on many levels, and humanity has been battling them for quite some time. Each of these dragons has a signature mental pattern by which it can be recognized. Just as the two strands of a double helix have their signature pattern, the dragons of the human mind have unique signatures, or footprints. If this pattern is seen quickly enough, the dragon can be fully captured and governed. This will be one of the deeper gifts that *Homo devas* bring to our lives.

The names of the dark dragons that our wise heroes have successfully battled include: fear, hatred, greed, scorn, contempt, jealousy, envy, pride, deceit, revenge, fragmentation / fission, doubt, and entropy. One of the reasons that the *Homo deva* heroes will be highly potent in destroying these dragons is that *Homo devas* never travel alone. They always travel (incarnate) as partners—functioning as fusion lasers or, to use another metaphor, as binary stars. They face the dragons as teams.

Thus, in the early 21st century, the dark dragons are being hunted and herded by pairs or groups of spiritual warriors who serve wisdom, love, and creative power. In a sense, the four functions that Arrien (1993) elaborates so beautifully—of warrior, teacher, healer, and visionary—are skills that thousands of heroes are calling on to help in battling the dragons. We need experience with all these qualities in order to survive the journey and reach our goal. In scientific terms, such patterns of mindheart coherence can help maximize the coherence of our laser beam. During the next decade, researchers and educators in several fields will learn to understand more deeply the energy dynamics of these dragons. We can then cut them off at the root. Once cut at the base of their root in humanity as a whole, they will not be able to grow back. The dragons pretend to be agents of infinity and eternity, but they are not. The dragon wounds of fission are finite, and thus will be steadily defused, diluted, and dissipated.

In the past three decades, the healing work of human heroes at the levels of civilization, culture, and unified field have become more *in tune* with each other. Their messages are becoming more related, more synchronous in tone and strength. The dragons have had to increase the intensity of their dark fire in response. Dark dragons are an endangered species. Although they are fighting hard, they will inevitably lose. Here is another view of sample pioneers, this time showing four individuals at each level of visibility in humanity's mind:

Pioneers and Early *Homo deva*

Unified field: *David Spangler, Ken Wilber, Jean Houston, Joanna Macy*

Culture: *James Redfield, Rupert Sheldrake, Fritjof Capra, Joseph C. Pearce*

Civilization: *Aung San Suu Kyi, Desmond Tutu, Bill Moyers, Jane Goodall*

The people named above are selected as examples of visible pioneers working in different fields, all contributing to our understanding of the best in human nature. You might also know people in your local community who are leading the campaigns for better public services, more disclosure of financial donors, programs to develop more affordable housing, to provide after-school programs. In Parts Four and Five, we will discuss more specifically how current organizations (e.g., Friends of Foster Kids, Grey Panthers, Habitat for Humanity, Students for a New Direction, Rural Cancer Care Association, Grandparents Raising Grandchildren, Friends Outside) are helping in the global battle to slay the dark dragons. The many thousands of people who are involved in these efforts are participating as part of a massive upwelling of commitment to help people whom we have never met but whom we wish to aid. These sample pioneers are helping lead the way as wise elders in a wonderful turning of the great wheel, the blossoming of a great flower, the ignition of a great healing, the radiation of a joyful creative fire.

You and I are also participating in the great work of healing Earth and her children. Each time we infuse our day with *goodness, truth*, and *beauty*, we are part of the healing. At some moments we breathe the work through love, in others, through faith, through analytic thought, through intuitive insight, through right relations with those we meet, and through steadfast goodwill. In the next chapter, we look at a specific aspect of *Homo deva* that takes us beyond the traditional realm of "living by faith." For now, let's call this step *vulnerable knowing*.

∾

Chapter 13

Beyond Faith to "Vulnerable Knowing"

As we discussed in earlier chapters, humans are the fourth of seven kingdoms and devas are the fifth major kingdom (refer again to Figures 2 and 6). There were evolutionary transition species between the animal and human kingdoms; we call them *Australopithecus*, *Homo habilis*, and *Homo erectus* (see Pieg; Lewin; Arsuaga). The scientific teams of the 20th century characterized the steps of the prehuman transition primarily in terms of braincase size, teeth placement, legbone angle (indicating how upright they walked). These transitional hominids are scientifically accepted, widely known, and are called "prehuman" and "early human" by many respected researchers.

We are now on the verge of the next major transitional step, from *Homo sapiens* to the species and kingdom beyond. Will researchers 100 or 500 years from now call this transitional form "posthuman," "prede-va," "creatorlings," "earth-angels," or some wiser terms that we cannot yet imagine? For now, I and others who have considered the process are proposing that we stay within the scientific nomenclature developed by Linneaus in the 18th century. According to this nomenclature, the new species should have two names: first, the genus, and second, the species: *Homo deva*. The upright, walking hominid-deva, the species who embodies spirit-and-matter fusion, the Earth species who lives fully on both sides of the veil. The name is offered in the manner of *vulnerable knowing*, an intuitive recognition of a deeper truth. (Also, see Appendix 7, regarding development of the H.D. Newsletter.)

What will be the identifying characteristics of our new sibling species? Surely not brain size, for larger average head volume is not physically possible to birth through the female *Homo sapiens* pelvis. Nor will it be teeth, or legbone angle. If not these, then what? Perhaps you have ideas on this issue to offer as hypotheses.

Here are some preliminary suggestions for your reflection, and possible inspiration:

Advanced *Homo sapiens* and Early *Homo deva*

- Awareness of all sentient beings as kin, including people, animals, and plants; visceral awareness of other beings' states of feeling, of mind. Many young children coming into incarnation in this decade have this capacity and will feel increasingly trusting enough to mention it to older friends (see Sinetar; Carroll & Tober). There have been anecdotal reports from every continent in the past decade, describing children with varying degrees of remote-viewing, "reading by color," and other capacities.
- Creativity with a wide variety of media—visual, literary, musical—and increased facility with multiple languages and with computer technology and graphics.
- Active participation in and advocacy for their community at a young age, whether local, regional, or national; heightened ability to stimulate dialogue, commit acts of redemption and generosity, build trust, and initiate community bonding.

Middle *Homo deva*—All of the above, plus...

- Innovation mentally across several major disciplines; their interdisciplinary collaboration is a deeply natural and synergistic impulse.
- Conscious healing when they become ill; naturally responsive and effective immune system.
- Awareness of links between mental states and physical illness; medical

intuitives, music therapists, recovery coaches, and mentors, among others, are beginning to express these capacities.

- High receptivity to synchronicity (see Satori, 1999), awareness of macro / micro links between world events and groups of people; and ability to govern reactions that help defuse the negative "fission-reactions" of others, both in physical proximity and at a distance.
- Heightened ability to think in terms of very long timeframes, and ability to communicate this in layperson's language to other people.

High *Homo deva*—**All of the above, plus...**

- Full governance of lifethread, with continuity of consciousness at both birth and death.
- Receptivity and responsiveness to other kingdoms, as human-deva hybrid species.
- Healing presence by touch of the five regular senses, the breath, the mind.
- Permeability of mind / body / will, with capacity to withdraw into a body-of-light at will.
- Many other capacities that we cannot see yet.

This description is meant to imply stages of development, a natural progression. The *Homo devas* will look at their *Homo sapiens* kin and friends in much the same way as a mature eleventh-grader looks at a seventh-grade student: *They remember totally what it is like to be there*, and they respond with generous compassion. They relate to the younger student with kindness and companionship. They clearly remember the struggles and suffering, the daily pressures and moments of happiness. And they want to help their friend-sibling to grow upward to a place of greater self-expression and confidence. This maturation is a *bio-psycho-spiritual progression* that all persons will experience, some sooner than others. The *Homo deva* children will realize all this from a deep inner knowing.

Here is an example: A successful business person in the year 2030 will demonstrate several skills and capacities that today are considered to be on the mystic edge or perhaps aberrations of what is normal. These include enhanced creativity, reliable and detailed intuitive knowing, the need for only a few hours sleep per night, an excellent immune system, the experience of work and life as a synergistic whole, greater longevity by choice, a diet that includes less meat, although food habits will still vary greatly with cultural and regional favorites, a tendency to practice green policies in their business and residential community, and enjoyment of a variety of artistic media for self-expression. Stress management methods will be as commonplace and routine as washing one's hands before eating.

Another example: What do you imagine that *Homo devas* trained as scientists will be able to accomplish in the following fields in the next 20 years? Gene therapy, nanotechnology, robotics, geriatric medicine, prenatal care, aqua-agriculture (from oceans and lakes), female and male contraception, chemical processes for much of manufacturing and processing, and transportation.

The shift will be a quantum step with big magnitude, in many fields. If hearing specific predictions in quantitative statements is helpful to you, here is an estimate: By 2030, there will be 10 times the level of innovation we see today. And the great majority of innovations will be dedicated to helping people live more lightly and peaceably on the planet.

A major reason that such innovation will be possible is that the soul and personality of humanity (as two great foci themselves) are steadily coming into greater alignment. As the soul-personality system becomes integrated throughout our species, the next level of spirit shines through. Thus, *Homo deva* is both a catalyst for the fusion of the soul-personality of humanity, and it also emerges as *the child* of that union.

Religious traditions have helped humanity through many issues on the basis of *faith*. In general, a central aspect of religious promises has been that there will be a *positive future*, even though this future is "ineffable," impossible to understand, and far in the distant future. Now, without taking away life's mystery, we are being called as a species to move beyond faith as our highest doorway to reach a positive future. This step of greater wholeness celebrates life through the *vulnerable knowing* that an innocent child brings—the intuitive and yet empirical knowing that simply recognizes when someone is telling us the truth.

In order for this blossoming of the *Homo deva* creativity and innocence to emerge, we as a species must pass through a "dark night of the soul," the last struggle in the birth of our future self. The next 10 to 15 years will be the climax of that struggle. It is a biological climax—it is a spiritual threshold—and it will be a series of political, financial, scientific, and artistic happenings. All levels and fields of human endeavor will be touched by this struggle. Many of the authors listed in the Resources section have explored this struggle from various angles.

Another way to describe this turning point is to say that the *lifethread of Earth* is beginning to be expressed directly through human beings. In the next chapter, we will look at the dynamics of the lifethread in more detail. As the 21st century begins, the fourth planetary center or kingdom, humanity, is facing its ecological climax. This is the maturing crisis for humans, while at the same time the fifth energy center or kingdom emerges as a new babe.

The heart of humanity has been expanding steadily since the cultural big bang of 30,000 years ago. The heart of the planet went through a major expansion at that time, and then again in the past 400 years, since the Renaissance, and yet again in the past 40 years. Each time, the heart's expansion became more deeply incarnated, more focused through the individual humans as arteries of the planetary heart. In electromagnetic terms, humanity has been ramping up its voltage over the past 400 years, until we are now ready to *synchromesh* our electromagnetic energy with the actual energy field of the planet.

At the same time, humanity's heart energy has grown weary and fragmented, torn by wounds of partial identification and self-doubt. Those wounds are allowing severe violence/fission/entropy to destabilize the heart's rhythm. When a heart's rhythm weakens, it is a danger signal for the organism. It is time for the full *throat energy of humanity* to emerge and, through that birth, to vivify and incarnate the throat of the planet. The throat of Earth will bring an abundance of energy and healing presence for the heart as well. They will work in tandem. They will be biophysical and spiritual partners in the highest and best sense of the term.

In the next chapter, we will consider several of the wisdom traditions that can assist us in our acceleration into the greater release of Earth's creative energy.

∾

Chapter 14

WISDOM OF OUR ELDERS

Much of the vulnerable knowing that we discussed in the last chapter has to do with the integration of the *lifethread* and the *consciousness* thread. This integration has been described through the centuries as the wisdom of our elders. Those of our species who age gracefully and share their life experience often seem to have a twinkle in their eye. They are deeply alive in the sense of the sages—their mind and their life are at peace with one another. Even when their physical steps have slowed, their hearts and heads are still pulsing steadily and coherently (see Roszak, 2001 for a good review of current trends in creativity and health among elders).

In this chapter, we will examine several areas from which we can discover renewed wisdom for the task ahead of us. Evolution is in its nature a blend of scientific and artistic pursuit. The same intelligence, love, and creative power that designs the wildflowers in a meadow also produces an NT-based computer and the Hubble Telescope. The wisdom of our elders in the era of *Homo deva* will come through *all* branches of human endeavor. This is a commonsense idea, but also an immensely important one. We are not generally accustomed to receiving wisdom from people who are different from us, even if that difference is as slight as that between a sales department and an accounting department in the same corporation. One of the invitations that *Homo deva* offers us is to recognize the wisdom that is close by.

I wish to introduce three concepts in this chapter to present a wide-spectrum view of what "wisdom" is all about. The first has to do with lifethread and consciousness thread. These two energy templates or patterns of *becoming incarnate* have been described in spiritual traditions for several centuries. We do not presume to present their intricacies here. Our purpose is limited to suggesting that these two templates are in the final steps of becoming one. When you understand this idea, you will realize why our wonderful species is hurting so much right now. The full birthing of *Homo deva* will bring forth persons who are themselves embodied strands of the lifethread of our species and, beyond, the life-thread of our planet.

Let us start with a basic description of how the two templates differ.

The Lifethread as a Link to the Planetary Life

The *lifethread* is the connection to being alive, to being incarnate. You can imagine it as a vibrant thread, a fiery cord, a pulsating link that keeps us "here on Earth." Lifethread is basically our link to the greater planetary life; Earth is our womb, and the lifethread is our placenta, giving us nourishment and the oxygen that is essential to life. Lifethread, in psychospiritual terms, is the analog to *amplitude* in wavepattern models of energy—it expresses the *up and down wave*. As the "height" of the wave can be thought of as how far an individual's energy resonates directly with the larger whole, so the height of the lifethread expresses the relationship between the part and the whole (see Figure 14 below).

Each individual expresses varying degrees of focused purpose. There is a relative focus in how each of us dives through the entropy of matter and connects the resonance of our purpose to our physical daily life. The intensity of our lifethread helps us keep a vibrant *life-link* to purpose and thereby prevents us from succumbing to weariness—to the seduction of boredom, frustration, the classic ennui of either old age, or of satiation in our consumer culture. Our lifethread prevents us from succumbing, that is, until the time is right for a conscious choice to die and pass on to the next cycle. This last phase could be physical death, but it could also be an existential death such as leaving a job, leaving a marriage or relationship, or leaving one's native country to start a new life.

FIGURE 14. AMPLITUDE

Amplitude amplitude is distance from top of wave to the trough or bottom of each wave.

Here is an example that I have used in teaching stress management classes: A father whose child plays on a baseball team gets very excited when the team goes to the state championship. The father is excited, proud, and a little apprehensive. If he maintains his internal link to the life-affirming *reason* his child is playing the game, he will enjoy the experience and feel connected to the other parents and children who are part of this sporting event. As a wise elder, the father knows that the higher purpose has more to do with helping boys and girls enjoy their life and learn to relate well with each other than it does to winning a particular game. Yet a balance is needed because the striving to achieve and excel also gives valuable life lessons (and can give a child the ability to keep focus and move ahead in spite of resistance from others).

By contrast, if the father loses touch with the purpose of the game and succumbs to the spiritual entropy that is implicit in acute aggression and competitiveness, he will have a painful experience. His child will also probably have some distress and, in the extreme case, the father may suffer a heart attack on the sidelines of the game. The *amplitude* of his lifethread has gone, briefly, to a flat line. His consciousness (wavelength) has become so incoherent, and separatist from the energy of the other people involved that the fragmented wavelength has a "drag" effect on his amplitude. This example may seem quite abstract, but believe me it can be very tangible. I have counseled some fathers who had that precise experience and were entering psychological rehab (with Workers Comp total disability) after stress-related myocardial infarction (M.I.); they ranged in age from 38 to 64. As a consequence of acute emotional stresses, on top of chronic unhealthy habits, they had lost cardiac resonance, lost amplitude, and temporarily lost lifethread: the M.I. disease was an acute *occlusion of their lifethread*.

Here is where the real-world example meets the abstract model: The father who suffers a myocardial infarction while watching his child's softball game has done objective damage to his heart. We acknowledge that there have been years of contributing factors preceding the sudden onset of illness: genetics, family diet history, family and individual health history, exercise, smoking, and others. Any attribution of causality needs to acknowledge this complex of factors.

Other factors certainly combine with the current condition of one's lifethread to affect amplitude. In the example above, the lifethread of the father became "at risk" because of a gap between his purpose-in-the-moment (amplitude) and the stresses (bad diet, lack of exercise, etc.) that were leaning on the thread. The stresses, by definition, become manifest through consciousness. Sitting on a bench and watching young humans hit a small white ball with a long stick does not involve any physical threat to one's life. If it had been our cousin Neanderthal sitting on that bench, he might have been curious about the actions of the players, but he would not have felt threatened in the same way that the modern father did.

And yet, a particular combination of genetics / brain / emotions / beliefs in the *Homo sapiens* father led to a sudden onset of pain and illness. When the thread became occluded, he had a *heart attack*. The occlusion of his lifethread can be imagined as an electrical brownout of his brain-heart circuit. There was resistance, the circuit heated up, the full pulse of his purpose could no longer get through —he had a literal "disconnect"—and the electrical resistance in the system produced a sudden drop in amplitude (just like a city in the summer with too many home air-conditioners turned on at 6:00 PM).

The wisdom lesson about lifethread that can be shared with younger generations is that being *on-purpose* keeps us alive. When we drift off-purpose—however we define that term in our own lives—we risk a brownout and possible early death in the extreme and, less dramatically, we risk other chronic health problems and anxieties.

The Consciousness Thread

Now, we turn to the second template. The *consciousness thread* is a mental and emotional analog to the energy component called *wavelength*. Consciousness expresses all the thousands and millions and billions and megazillions of wave patterns that are possible in the human brain. From neurology, neurocardiology, and other interdisciplinary fields, we know that many cells in the body have *memory*, and therefore contribute to our integral sense of depth or spatial contact. That is what wavelength expresses: contact through *space*. The wave pattern goes from Here to There. The diagram below is a generic representation of wavelength.

FIGURE 15. WAVELENGTH

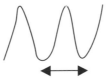

Wavelength is distance between
the troughs of each wave.

While lifethread expresses height (amplitude), which we experience as "purpose," the consciousness thread expresses depth (wavelength), which we experience as "meaning." Depth is a crucial dimension through which *Homo sapiens* touch each other and meet in relationship as self–other, and thereby make meaning in our lives. We learn who we are by touching the *other*, whether it is touching a hot stove as a child, touching a friend's arm in support or betrayal, or touching a neighborhood in generosity or isolation or rejection. Through the wavelength function of our existence, we meet in recognition of *mutual meaning*, which has as many flavors as there are thoughts and feelings. Listen to the meaning(s) imparted in the following comments:

"That sweet and sour sauce has never agreed with me."

"Whatever you do, don't laugh when he does his Elvis impersonation. It's really a core thing for him."

"Hi, I'm from Iowa too. What county are you from?"

"Yes, I do meditation, but it's none of those fancy kinds listed in books. I mostly tune into the sound of wind in the trees."

"The only time I think of it as a disability is when we go swimming at the lake, and the other women have two boobs."

"He passed over quickly, and I'm glad to know they are together again. I'm OK, but it feels strange, as if half of me is gone."

The statements above express how meaning is packed into language, and in addition the statements hint at how wavelength can vary tremendously with our affect. Imagine how one of the statements above changes if it is said aloud with *irony*—with *anger*—with *humor*—with *sadness*—with *fear*. Those are major ways of varying the patterns of wavelengths contained in the message. As we will discuss further in Part Four, one of the challenges of children who are now being born in the *Homo deva* transition is that they are extremely sentient to the wavelengths of human speech. They don't always have cues about how to filter out the many conflicting nonverbal messages when adults are "saying one thing, and meaning another." This is an area in which the *Homo deva* children may become our teachers, in order to help the adult culture express themselves with more integrity between thoughts, words, and deeds.

Let us phrase the metaphor of touch in terms of the two templates of wave patterns: The *consciousness thread* helps us touch our meaning, through contact between here and there (space). The *lifethread* helps us touch our purpose, through contact between now and longer time frames (time)... and if we extrapolate the question of purpose, the issue extends unto eternity. As you will realize when you think about it, most members of the animal kingdom are quite young or primitive in their capacity to touch meaning, to communicate in articulated consciousness.

Consciousness has been a primary medium of growth for *Homo sapiens*, particularly in the past 30,000 years with language, and then the past 400 years of cultural expansion and geographical exploration.

Plants and animals do have something that might be described as pre-consciousness (see Eldredge; Pearce; Sheldrake). However, their sentiency is of much shorter wavelength, and not nearly as complex in its interactions or its self-reflection. The more primitive animal species do not grieve for their dead relatives, as chimps and elephants and dogs have been known to do. Plants do not communicate empathy or love, although they have been shown to have complex responsiveness to individual humans. Consciousness has indeed grown over the course of the past million years, leading to modern *Homo sapiens* with our wavelengths that are literally astronomical. We are truly masters of the wavelength game, sending sophisticated greetings beyond the solar system.

We, the *sapient* "knowing" species, with our senses extended through satellites and computers, now threaten to rival the heavenly bodies with our extensive information databases. Yet, this threat is precisely the core of our problems: We are constantly threatening to "rival" someone, somewhere. It has become a habit, a habit that we need to outgrow—ASAP.

Zipping the Threads

Now, an exciting development emerges in the configuration between these two threads. *Lifethread* and *consciousness thread* are two streams of energy, and yet they are not actually separate. One is the melody, and the other is the lyrics. You would have difficulty describing a wave's height without also referring to its length or depth.

Here is a key element in our understanding of these two streams, and through them the new wisdom of *Homo deva*: The lifethread and the consciousness thread are connected at the top and bottom, somewhat like a cosmic zipper. One side of the zipper is the consciousness thread (making meaning, through the senses, in the external, three-dimensional world), and the other side of the zipper is the lifethread (our link to purpose and higher knowing beyond the sensory world). The zipper's sides begin to touch and intermesh as the zipper closes.

A central mystery in the transformation that is now occurring for our species is that, metaphorically, this zipper is coming together, or "sealing" — fusing from the top and the bottom *simultaneously*. The zipper is becoming a unified pattern from top and bottom — which we call the ascent movement and the descent movement — at the same time.

What is the nature of this "closing" of the zipper between life and consciousness? It has to do with the third parameter of a wave pattern, its *frequency*. Look back at the two small figures of wave patterns above: one shows amplitude, and the other shows wavelength. But you, the reader, have no way of inferring from those graphs how fast the waves are moving. Frequency gives us that vital part of the puzzle by describing the wave as *energy that moves through time*. And as we saw in an earlier chapter, one of the special gifts of *Homo deva* is to process and handle sensory capacities more efficiently and over much greater time frames than *Homo sapiens* can. That includes, by the way, interpreting sensory input from modalities or dimensions that we may not yet have consensual names for.

Thus, *Homo devas* will have the capacity to link life and consciousness, amplitude and wavelength, into a coherent whole by means of the greatly increased frequency of their wave patterns — as frequency accelerates without limit and approaches infinity / eternity. Yes, we need the slash in that terminology, precisely because the nature of frequency is "distance over time," e.g., 100 miles per hour. The linking of multiple amplitudes and multiple wavelengths, through frequency-without-limits, is a core gift of the *Homo deva* species. From this gift they will assist us in deriving many practical solutions to our problems. Not by being the "answer box" for us, but by pointing us in the direction we want to go.

Let us put the dimensions of the wave patterns together, and see what happens:

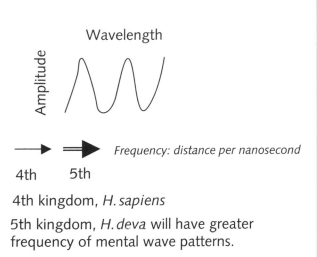

FIGURE 16.
WAVE PATTERNS THROUGH TIME: FREQUENCY

Wavelength

Amplitude

Frequency: distance per nanosecond

4th   5th

4th kingdom, *H. sapiens*
5th kingdom, *H. deva* will have greater
frequency of mental wave patterns.

In the figure above, the double-line arrow for frequency of the fifth kingdom indicates that the *Homo deva* mental functioning will be at much greater frequency (distance / time period) than is normally demonstrated by *Homo sapiens*. This will be across a range that will vary with childhood training and life experience.

In Part Four, we will examine several of the specific implications of these wave pattern relationships in terms of the characteristics of *Homo deva* children.

The Wisdom of Our Indigenous Elders

We turn now to the second concept of this chapter about wisdom that derives from the emergence of a new species. The concept relates to the great wisdom of indigenous peoples and their spiritual and healing traditions. There are native peoples on all six continents whose family and community heritage provide them with a *living thread* of reverence for and relationship with the Earth.

In many cases, sadly, a different, dominant tribe has abused this heritage over the past three centuries. The thread from the indigenous peoples to their native community and to the Earth has been, in too many cases, officially scorned, ignored, ripped in pieces, and brutalized in countless rituals of persecution. The cultural practice in 18th, 19th, and early 20th-century United States of sending the children of native families to mission schools and forbidding them to speak their own languages is a painful example of such thread-ripping. Alternately, this heritage has been pimped by the dominant culture for exploitation by the tourist industry (see LaDuke, 1999, for a discussion of some central issues in the evolving self-identity of native peoples).

The suggestion that I wish to offer is that the healing of native peoples is an important microcosm for the healing of *Homo sapiens* and, prognostically, for our collective chances of reaching the year 2050. There is wisdom in each of us and our unique cultural heritage. Yet a distinction needs to be recognized and acknowledged between those who were born in the Industrial and Information State, and those who come to that state as a foreign land after being born from the womb of an eco-village. Hear this statement clearly—such differentiation is not intended to imply that the indigenous perspective is more innocent, or holy, or that indigenous people are "noble" or somehow closer to God. In fact, given the path we are on, it might take some native groups a longer time to birth their own representatives of *Homo deva.* That remains to be seen, and it depends on a complex of factors beyond the scope of this introductory book.

Here is what I am meaning to say: A worldview that advocates taking each action "unto the seventh generation" is intrinsically intimate with longer timeframes, is deeply conversant with a knowing that includes a personal relationship with Earth. The maxim of conserving energy for future generations is but one example from the ethos of the hundreds of First Peoples. They have traditions of thinking in longer waves than we in the postmodern culture. They are our friends and co-workers in many cases, and fortunately there are increasing numbers of ecologically trained members of the younger generation who have embraced the longer timeframe as the natural way to breathe.

However they reached this historic time, indigenous peoples can help us with some of the *reorientation steps* that are crucial for all of humanity. I am not familiar with the current literature or grassroots organizations that are working on issues of native peoples. But certainly, the online resources are extensive, and the crossover fertilization for our collective healing and creativity is ready to happen.

The Wisdom of the Physical Body

We are moving now to the third major concept of this chapter, which concerns the *wisdom of the physical body*. This relates, in part, to the wisdom of healing traditions among Eastern cultures, native peoples in the West, and the centuries-old wisdom of women healers in both East and West. One such contribution is their great knowledge of herbal approaches to restoring balance and removing toxicities. Another is the wisdom of utilizing other senses in healing besides words, such as tonal sounds or the 1,000-year-old tradition of healing touch that has been recently reintroduced in the West (see Kabat-Zinn; Chopra; Murphy; and Friedman & Moon, for very exciting developments in this area).

In the epoch that is emerging, the wisdom of the body will be particularly redemptive in terms of the relationship between genders. Because we as incarnated souls love each other so much, we (men and women) have *temporally* forgotten within timespace (= temporarily asleep to the fact) that we are actually one body, so that we can undertake the task of finding each other. Here is a core truth to consider: The remembering of the spiritual fact of unity, of *being one within incarnation*, involves deep loving and joy and smiles. The daily realization, indeed making-real, of that fact is part of the gift of *Homo deva*. The daily remembering, through practice, of how we live and breathe at-one is a central aspect of being divine.

The union of the lifethread and consciousness thread serves as impetus to this at-onement from the path of ascent, as we proceed through normal growth and development. The same union is a creative result of the at-onement from the path of descent, as we as souls embody further into matter. Both aspects of our existence are coming into deeper dialogue.

Let us move from the abstract level of this "zipping of threads" back toward real life now, and talk about what this wisdom looks like, in health and illness of the human body.

The *lifethread* keeps us incarnate, keeps us alive, keeps us in touch with purpose.

- It objectively anchors in our heart.
- It is now shifting to subjectively anchor in our head—in the brain / mind interface.

The *consciousness thread* keeps us growing and self-aware, in touch with meaning.

- It objectively anchors in our physical brain.
- It subjectively anchors in the heart (possibly in the "fifth brain" that has been described in recent research; see Pearce).

In diverse spiritual traditions,

Lifethread has been called the *thread of gold.*

Consciousness thread has been called the *silver cord.*

In terms of everyday life experience, the basic impacts of lifethread and consciousness are known to most schoolchildren: If a person's *brain* were to stop working suddenly, he would "fall in a faint." He would still be alive but would be as if asleep. If he recovered, it would be as if he suddenly woke up. Children can usually grasp the concept that people's brains stop working, mostly, at night when we sleep. The seeing and thinking and talking slow down a lot when we are asleep. When our awake brain stops working, our consciousness changes and slows to almost nothing. But our heart keeps pulsing, consistently and hopefully regularly, all the time we are asleep. It is a truism of *Homo sapiens* wisdom that the heart is in charge of keeping us alive. If the brain is knocked out, we may be asleep, but the heart keeps beating.

In contrast, if a person's *heart* were to stop working suddenly, he or she usually dies. It has only been in the past 30 years or so (a mere eye-blink in species-time) that heart-lung machines and transplant operation procedures have enabled humans to postpone death for days or months, or even longer, after a heart has stopped.

The next major step in our understanding is this: Think of the head and heart as the "two foci" within the human organism. There is a laser beam that grows between head and heart during a person's entire lifetime. As we discussed earlier, the human organism in its evolutionary growth gains the capacity to govern progressively greater polarities. The head and heart are a primary polarity that humanity as a whole is learning to govern — it is a polarity of two energy streams, similar in some ways to two foci of genetic DNA strands, or two parts of a binary star, or the dyad of soul-and-personality, or even the two foci of the left and right eye.

At a later stage of development, as an individual human evolves psychologically and spiritually, *the person and the human species eventually become like tuning forks for each other.* This step of creating a larger integrated system is what is happening as the *Homo deva* children are emerging. The individual and the whole are vibrating in synchronicity with each other, deeply and continuously. The brain and heart in each individual become an exact, living microcosm for the energy circuit between *person* and the *whole species.* The brain and the heart *tune-with* each other, transmitting ever more coherent and effective internal electromagnetic patterns. This process of increasing the coherence of your brain-heart circuitry through its internal electrical patterns can enhance the whole system of your self-expression, much as an upgrade enhances the performance of your personal computer.

Imagine the increase in creativity and efficiency if your computer were to get an upgrade every week, or even every day! It would work faster and better, and it would communicate with other electronic brains in a cleaner fashion. As people are transitioning to *Homo deva,* their organic brain and heart are undergoing a similar "upgrade," becoming intimately networked with the *world brain-heart* as an integrated circuit.

That resonance in the circuit grows as we watch movies, read books, have conversations with new friends from other cities or states, visit other cities and other nations, experience diverse cultures — and even as we sit in front of our TVs or PCs and vicariously experience the triumphs and tragedies of our fellow hominids. With the resonance comes bonding, and for some people this leads to directed action to help others, to serve their community or an adopted community. Through the greater circuit and resonance of their brain-and-heart, they become *dedicated* to their local action. By serving a chosen part of the world, they serve the whole of humankind. Even further, the circuit extends outward through this kind of service to aid the healing of all beings in the intertwined, breathing ecology of life on Earth.

∾

In this new century, an *incarnation of the lifethread* of Earth is happening. The Earth's lifethread is precipitating down through specific humans, and eventually through a network of millions of humans as a core cluster. (I use the term *down* in the technical sense, referring to the transmission of electrical voltage to slower levels, and in turn, the revelation of the next kingdom, *Homo deva.*) These humans who are serving as Earth-threads number in the thousands now. By the end of this decade, there will be many more people who are disciplined in their caring and service, and passionate in their creativity. These people will build tremendous coherence in their life pulse, sufficient to help transmit the electrical voltage of the planet's throat and step it down effectively and safely to bring new energy to the rest of humanity. This species-wide team, residing in over 200 nations, will bring the *life fire* from the higher / future levels, transmitting wisdom and innovation into our diverse cultures on six continents and through hundreds of human languages.

Recall, for a moment, our earlier discussion of meaning and purpose. The appearance of a *tangible lifethread*, appearing through the new fifth kingdom, implies that the throat of the planet will be able, for the first time, to express creativity related to the purpose of the entire planet. Hear that statement lightly, as a seed for future thought. It is part of the story of why we are here, and why we have had so much difficulty accepting and have felt such ambivalence about the notion that we are meant to be a divine species. Often, the *repression of the sublime* is one of the last and toughest barriers — whether we are looking at the growth and development of a person, a family, a nation, or a species.

As the life breath of Earth's throat begins to move through these people — the core international team of pioneers — their daily lives become direct emanations of Earth's voice, as spirit incarnate. This is the arc of descent, the precipitation, the higher pulse shapechanging to fit into the slower wave patterns. You may want to consider this idea carefully: *The higher pulse shapechanges to fit within the slower wave patterns;* in other words, it conforms itself to be visible to the human eye and mind. The level of spirit sacrifices or temporally lets go of other dimensions in order to exist within fewer degrees of freedom, in order to vitalize and bring nourishment to our dense realms of the senses.

The practical effects of this higher nourishment for individuals will include a greatly enhanced immunity to disease (there would be minimal molecular *self-other* repelling) and less need for sleep. And on behavioral levels, this would nurture personalities with characteristics such as (1) natural impulses of altruism and generosity, (2) creativity in thought, arts, and gifting, (3) innovations in scientific and mechanical fields, and (4) synchronicity in their lives—their thoughts and decisions would become permeable to the larger coherence in the community and region. The result is that the "best" patterns in terms of harmony, beauty, and goodness will become self-amplifying, at first through the core group of creatives who now number in the millions. The amplification itself radiates, naturally and steadily, as the *lifeseed* process blossoms.

What will this imply about human aging? *Homo sapiens* (and all lower kingdoms) wear down, grow old, and the physical form disintegrates. But the inevitability of death will have a new meaning for *Homo deva*. Death will come as a welcome transition after a life lived with meaning and purpose. Death will be recognized as a doorway to even greater spiritual love and creativity. There will be far fewer deaths by accident or by acts of violence, because all humans will know by direct experience the reality of the soul (future Self), its limitless love for the individual person, and its power for good.

In this chapter, we have presented an introduction to three kinds of wisdom that will blossom during the era of *Homo deva*. The first is the closer integration of the consciousness thread and lifethread, as expressing the wave functions of meaning and purpose, respectively. The second kind of wisdom is the special contribution of those tribes and individuals among *Homo sapiens* who have retained a visceral connection with the Earth during the past 400 years. This subset of humanity has a specific part to play in the healing of the whole. Their role will emerge more clearly as the intuitive power of a critical mass of humanity is activated. And the third kind of wisdom is that of the body and its inherent connection to aging, healing, and creativity; such wisdom has been the particular gift of the divine feminine principle, and the cultural groups that have embraced this healing energy.

The era of *Homo deva* is, at its core, a blossoming of the *Creator-creation relationship*. The wisdom to access and develop this relationship will be a gift that we give to our children and grandchildren. The lifethread will contribute to our learning, enabling us to link more steadfastly to purpose. The indigenous bond to the planet will make a deep contribution, as we learn to welcome and cherish Earth as our friend-home. And lastly, the song of the body and the feminine link to the body (and identification with matter) will contribute deeply—as we learn to listen to the music within our very breath, the cells of our body vibrating with the touch of wholeness and the *song of return* to the world self.

～

Chapter 15

EVOLUTION AND REVELATION AS PARTNERS

For millennia, the message has been coming from our highest aspiration: "There is something more." The faith traditions of revelation, as well as the more recent scientific concepts about biological evolution, have given us hints about the larger identity toward which we are moving.

In this chapter, we will focus directly on kingdom identity levels, and some of the psychological and sociological implications of a paradigm of five kingdoms. It is generally agreed that humans who are alive today exist on all four of the primary levels of identity. In other words, our physical bodies (all 6.3 billion of us) are constituted of all the kingdoms, to date: Our cells participate in the rhythms of the atomic structure of minerals, the circulation of plant matter, the impulses and instincts of our animal nature, and the multilayered emotions, thoughts, and language of our humanity. Who are we? We are deeply constituted of the first four kingdoms of Earth. We breathe through all four, move through all four, and have our being through all four.

Now the fifth kingdom is beginning to precipitate down to the physical level . . . and to arise through maturation from the earlier four. Many of us have been sensing this approach for years. We have been vibrating at faster levels, sometimes even in unstable and incoherent wave patterns. The initial effect of the impact has been an increase in brain wavelength (wider ways of making sense of our world, making meaning through greater knowledge about other nations and peoples, cross-cultural learning, trade and commerce among ethnic groups, and "consciousness raising"); this is particularly evident during the past 400 years.

In the 20ᵗʰ century the impact shifted to an increase in brain amplitude (greater questioning of purpose, individuals asking "why?", development of existential schools of philosophy and psychology, issues of environmentalism, sexism, speciesism raising the bar on our ethical sense of responsibility for life on Earth). Now, as we move warily into the 21ˢᵗ century, we already sense that the momentum has taken another quantum leap. We are shifting from wavelength stimulation and amplitude stimulation into an era that combines much greater frequency rate, as well as acceleration of the wavelength and amplitude. It is a time of tremendous upheaval, surely! You have noticed that in world events, and probably in your local scene as well. The topics that we thought were solved last year, aren't. The areas that had seemed stable last year have become fluid.

We need to look for a moment at a little-recognized fact: The human family stretches from the top of the planetary energy field to the bottom. In other words, there are human beings at every level of identification in the planetary kingdoms.

This means that there are human beings alive today whose energy-identity is from the earlier kingdoms prior to *Homo sapiens*. This energy-identity is from our species subconscious; it is not something that these individuals are aware of at all. They are asleep to where their lifethread has its anchoring within the planetary body. That is, for each kingdom, there is a corresponding level of *mental vibration*, which gradually permeates through the personality. In my opinion, the great majority of humans now alive have the core of their *identity* at the level of either animal or human kingdom. In other words, many biological *Homo sapiens* are still at the animal level of identity in their subjective energy (locus of lifethread), even though they are objectively bipedal primates with language. Take a brief look at the daily newspaper, and you will see reports on some of them. It would not be therapeutic for anyone to suggest this concept to them, because they are not ready to use it for their own growth and development.

The majority of us have deep identity at the human kingdom level, where our primary development is *through the rational mind and heart*. By this, we mean that most people you will meet in your lifetime are working on some phase of psychospiritual development focused on the integration of mental and affective, the *mindheart*. Their emotional nature is fully individuated, but not yet fully integrated.

As *Homo deva* emerges through a hybrid process of evolution and revelation, all the people at the earlier four levels of identity (the four kingdoms) are being *systemically* stimulated to grow up fast and take their next step. For many people, taking their next step of identity will happen within this decade. It is a decade of immense psychospiritual opportunity for all peoples.

However, for some persons, it will take many years. As those of you who practice gardening know, when good quality fertilizer and sunshine are readily available, the conditions stimulate the weeds and invasive plants as well as the flowers and vegetables. An individual person might metabolize the inflow of energy in a coherent way and take the next step of more inclusive identity, or they might squander the energy on *acting out* at their primary identity level. The outcome is indeterminate, because free will exists. Each person gets to choose, and this choice clearly depends on multiple factors. That shift is more than a linear process, and a full examination of the variables influencing the identity shift is beyond the scope of this book.

Humanity as a species is being stimulated to take the step from planetary heart upward to throat, to upgrade our passions and ideological beliefs to the realm of harmonies, creative expression, and direct governance of power over matter. Earth is preparing to open her throat, steadily and gloriously, over the next 2,000 years. The throat is a living bridge between inclusiveness (the heart) and purpose (the head); *throat energy* links these two great energy centers. In this decade, that same dual pulse of *inclusive creativity* and *purposeful governing* is becoming more focused through our daily lives—you, me, and our friends and neighbors. It is no longer limited to the Michelangelos, the Leonardos, the Medici families, or to the brilliance of Shakespeare, Mozart, and Beethoven. The pulse of creativity is also the laser beam of healing—the creative restructuring of matter in direct responsiveness to spirit. The founders of the United States, including Ben Franklin, Thomas Jefferson, and George Washington, knew this. The founders whom we usually think of rarely, perhaps momentarily on the legal holidays for them, were a very special breed. They as a group were geniuses at governing and bringing spiritual energy to bear on strategic political issues. One reason that the U.S. Declaration of Independence is such a potent document and talisman for peoples yearning for freedom in many nations is that the language embodies an early direct pulse of Earth's throat—the brilliance of reason and the passion of caring brought together in a voice that rings out across the centuries in a fusion statement of high amplitude, wavelength, and frequency.

The founders consciously received that energy and grounded the pulse such that they created a nation held by the ideal of creative equality and freedom. The 21st century will see their legacy brought to full fruition (see Appendix 4 for a fuller exposition of this topic). And eventually, every person on Earth will take the step to throat identity, expressing in unique ways the beauty of their national and ethnic traditions. In the meantime, there is much resistance. The boundaries are shaking.

We have learned from psychology that when a person is preparing to take a step in personality integration, all the resistance rises to the surface to fight the next step. The resistance concentrates at the *boundary* between the current personality complex and its next level of functioning. Such moments are wonderful opportunities to do deep healing, to bring all our conscious awareness to bear on these old patterns and habits, and excise them from our lives. That is what is indeed happening, in the first decade of the new century. But the shift is occurring at a species level. *Each of the four kingdoms is a boundary in the planetary personality.*

One consequence of the planetary systemic stimulation now under way is that people who embody in concentrated form an identity of our past steps (e.g., plants, animals) are also having their personalities become more activated, along with the more highly developed members of our species. The species-wide stimulation is provoking these less developed thread layers of humanity to act up, with some dysfunctional results all around, especially for the individuals involved.

The following examples are five brief (composite) descriptions of individuals with whom I have worked between 1985 and 2001. In my experience, they exemplify energy identities at the various kingdom levels. If you know or recognize some of these patterns in yourself, then you have an opportunity to help our collective progress. By responding with encouragement and firmness about these patterns in friends, co-workers, clients, family members, or yourself, you can have a positive effect and encourage them to move onward to the next level. Giving and receiving the gift of feedback is how we all learn, at whatever step we are on. (The names below are pseudonyms.)

Figure 17. Kingdom Identity Levels

Mineral identity

Laura, the lard lady

"I eat lard to make me steady." An inpatient at Emory University Hospital, weighing over 300 pounds, Laura was having surgery for intestinal resection, so the lard that she ate daily would pass directly through her body and out. Her physician and psychologist had tried many other ways to help her stop eating lard. (Note: I fainted after meeting her, from the very deep energy sink that radiated from her. She was polite and soft-spoken, yet the experience of our ten-minute conversation felt as if my body heat were being steadily sucked away.)

Plant identity

Donna and Liz, flowers of the consumer culture

Both these young women readily agree that they were "born to shop." When the sale ads for clothes, shoes, or CDs appear in the newspaper, they are at the stores by lunchtime. They turn instinctively toward the buzz of a sale like flowers turning toward sunshine after a cloudy day; there is no weighing of options or awareness of consequences. Donna and Liz are the hothouse plants that the mass media adore, the young seedlings that are fed the fertilizer of new charge card offers each month and who automatically ingest the energy when offered. Liz says she feels more alive after a spree. Donna remarks that her favorite form of recreation is to visit two big sales on the same day. She rolls her eyes and laughs, "It just feels so good."

Animal identity

Ed, urban predator

A 17-year-old teenager with average grades, Ed resides in state youth prison on a second charge of rape. He has a young face. There is no remorse or trace of empathy. During the year he has been incarcerated, he had just two visitors, a cousin and his high school counselor. He remarks, "Once I get out, I'll find me another [female]." His affect and eye contact are that of an alpha-predator, with confident aggression toward weaker animals, especially females. His beliefs and the social environment he grew up in (urban metropolis) support the imposition of his will on others. The complex of domination is more than an affective impulse; it is the underlying motive of the culture that he has lived in and breathed through for 17 years. His criminal behaviors are a natural extension from his core of identification, of "who he is" at the biological level. He has not had any role models of another way to be; and he is quite sentient and responsive to the verbal and nonverbal messages of the social and economic environment. His language and behavior reflect the jungle because that is how the culture behaves toward him. He has no use for empty proscriptive words of how nice people "should be." Nurturing behaviors are, in his experience, a quick way not to survive.

Homo sapiens identity

Kim, master of finite resources

A 29-year-old high achiever with a cheerful smile, Kim works as an investment banker and has already received encouragement about a potential promotion to Officer. She learns new and complex customer service protocols every month as part of her work with investors. She volunteers at the local blood bank and has many friends. Her husband manages a steakhouse restaurant. She wants to retire at age 40; she and her husband already own a house in an exclusive area and drive a large SUV. They have a time-share condo at Lake Tahoe for weekends. She already worries a little about where their (future) children will go to college. She has stopped reading newspapers, because "all the news gets so discouraging," but loves to watch TV programs several nights a week.

Early Homo deva identity

Johnny, a "cultural creative" and environmental advocate

Johnny, who works as a planner for the county, is saving money to open a graphic arts consulting business. For the past two years, he has used a car-share to commute to work and for weekend trips. His best friend plays for the San Francisco Giants. They enjoy conversations about the zen of sports over seafood dinners. He reads the newspaper only occasionally but does listen regularly to the news on public radio. Johnny is a tutor for sixth graders at the local school, and he attends a nondenominational church in his neighborhood. One of his favorite weekly activities is going with friends to a nearby nursing home and giving art lessons. He describes his spirituality as "bringing beauty back into people's lives, and greening the world, one family and business at a time." His longtime girlfriend lives in Montana, so they use frequent-flyer miles a lot. When asked about any retirement plans, he laughs and says he looks forward to doing his drawing until he is 90.

∼

These five thumbnail composite sketches are meant to evoke thought about human growth within the larger context of species development. They are intended to invite further reflection about *human identity* and what makes us who we are. As you see, the question of who we are interfaces very intimately with why we are here and how we relate to each other.

The key hypothesis that I am presenting in this section is that all levels of Earth-life are represented within the family of humanity. *Hominids* stretch from the very highest to the very lowest, in terms of the planet's energy patterns. Because we are the embodiment of Earth's heart, we include connections to all the higher and lower kingdoms as well as expressing the many variations of heart energy. Somehow we have known this intuitively, and now it is time to look at it more carefully. We can look at it because we are now capable of doing so without making anyone "bad." The view of *Homo deva* is without judgment. We are talking of helping human beings to grow and develop, wherever they are on the continuum of the planetary life. Clearly, some are more ready for giant steps than others.

The future of all our children depends on our helping the *higher reaches* to be accessible to a critical mass of pioneers. Those pioneers will serve as trail guides, helping the rest of us lift upward into the fifth kingdom and, in so doing, bringing back solutions to help humanity itself survive. It is clear to me that the holographic effect is on our side, as of the year 2002. That is, we now have the coherent power to lift the whole of humanity. What we need is a critical mass of about 10,000 persons at the third phase (lifeseed), with corresponding larger groups at the innovator and creative levels, in order to fully lift the approximately 7.2 billion people, as of 2015, beyond the risk of biological overshoot (where the species extinction would accelerate). As those 10,000 lifeseeds blossom, the danger of ecologic and economic collapse will diminish significantly. It is not a sure thing, but the risk is more manageable now than it was a few short years ago.

An Overview of Approaching Divinity

Figure 18 provides a graphic view of the major kingdoms of Earth and their correspondences with the planetary energy centers. We, as the heart center, have been developing about 2 million years since we clearly differentiated from the animal kingdom (planetary solar plexus center). Then by about 150,000 years ago, we had become anatomically modern, the walking upright species with large brain. Only about 40,000 years ago, we began to use verbal speech and developed art forms.

Figure 19 presents a related view, this time with a focus on the spiritual pioneers who will lead us into the fifth kingdom: the creatives, the innovators, and the lifeseeds. The energy centers, or chakras, have been described for hundreds of years in relation to individual human development. Now we are seeing that the same energy relationships occur in the development of greater beings, such as a species or planet. What is reassuring in this view is that the uplift from *Homo sapiens* to *Homo deva* will occur—whether you and I sleep through the next decade or not (and please don't take that as a suggestion! We need the good work of every one of you).

Evolution and revelation are doing their good work, night and day. The issue is not whether this transition of Earth's life-forms will happen. The issue is how many *Homo sapiens* will be living here when the transition has run its course.

Figure 18. Earth Kingdoms as Planetary Energy Centers

View circa 2100

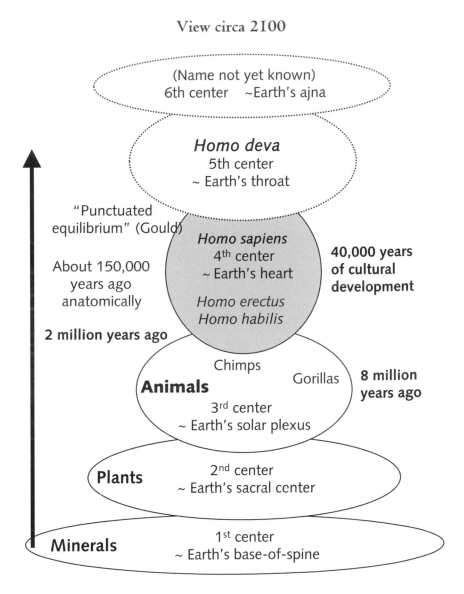

FIGURE 19. INCARNATION OF SPIRITUAL PIONEERS

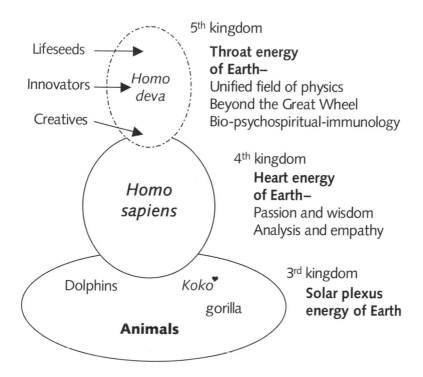

We will conclude Part Three with an exercise in identifying and mapping our pioneers: Where would you place the following organizations on the above diagram? Habitat for Humanity, Greenpeace, Jobs with Justice, Village Banking Network, Genome Project, County Search and Rescue Team, Family Hospice Care, Organic Farmers' Co-op, Committee for Responsive Philanthropy, Doctors Without Borders, Children's Theatre Workshop, Students Against Driving Drunk, Ecumenical Women's Caucus, Constitutional Issues in Technology, Youth for Environmental Sanity? Where would you put your own mentors and heroes? The projects and community efforts you are familiar with?

As the fourth kingdom opens to the wisdom, love, and guidance of the fifth kingdom, the interface species of *Homo deva* is birthed. *Revelation* and *evolution* are becoming intimate partners in the full sense of the term:

Through their interplay, the soul of our species emerges directly into physical incarnation. This will translate, in my view, as approximately 5,000 to 10,000 persons, on six continents, as the growing nucleus of Phase 3 by year 2020. (Refer to Ray and Anderson's description of *cultural creatives*, estimated at 50 million persons in United States and 300 million worldwide who are living in what we are describing as Phase 1, the creatives). Between now and 2020, we need the Phase 2 pioneers to grow in number and accelerate their contribution of social, technological, and spiritual innovations. The synergy of their emergence with the continued growth of the creatives in Phase 1 will serve as a powerful catalyst to assist the nucleus group in moving into Phase 3.

We have considered in this section some general characteristics of the biophysics of humanity's imminent divinity. What will this step look like in the lives of individual people?

We will discuss this in Part Four, as we look at *Homo deva* children.

∽

PART FOUR

OUR *Homo deva* CHILDREN

We Have a Dream

We have a dream
from the future—
no more, no less.

A dream does not
require proof.
It IS...
and in its be-ness
breathes a sigh
of hope that sings
gently over sleepers
and those who are
moving half-awake.

Homo deva,
breath of life eternal,
touches the Now
as infusion of
fire platelets for
those who are close
to death in deep
unknowing.

Birthing a language
of song to tell of
the new creation,
a quiet ecolife of I-Thou
even now replaces
aggression, execution of plan,
dominance, and
market share.

Perhaps the best way
is to use language
that comes naturally.

We have a dream about you...

Chapter 16

Each Child Is a Seed of the Future

As we witness and participate in the revelation of the Earth's throat, our first responsibility is to help the many children who are bewildered by the current chaos and violence. They need reassurance that something better is coming and that the future will be OK. The acute question is: How can we offer reassurance for the children when we adults are having difficulty reassuring ourselves? As Charlie Brown once asked, "Who comforts the comforters?"

To prepare ourselves to help the children, there are two central steps: (1) to recognize and accept the longer time-horizon and (2) to begin looking at every negative event as a knot of resistance to a more inclusive, just, and creative world that is struggling to birth. The knots of resistance are exactly like the pain and complications of a difficult delivery. We are working through them, breathing and yelling if necessary to ensure a healthy future for mother and child.

Based on 30 years of working with children, often in situations where they were suffering considerably, I have concluded that children often respond to and interact with the *Homo deva* viewpoint more easily than adults do. Perhaps this is because at their young age they are still identified with their physical bodies and the *energy* that they gather through their senses as they walk, run, skip, climb, jump, and move around. They have not yet absorbed all the beliefs about the impossible and finding someone to blame. Whatever the reason, if you give children the wider view, suggesting that this hard time is a good chance to hug their friends and learn what other people do when they are scared, they will work with the ideas quite readily. Many adults, on the other hand, are already numb from the stresses of the great transition or are *mentally calcified* in their outmoded beliefs. They need more encouragement to let their *deva child* come out and play.

Here is an example of a longer time frame concept that can be adapted for older children and adolescents as they learn about the ecosystem of which they are a part:

> **Minerals** *are Earth's base-of-spine center, about 5 billion years old*
> *as* **Plants** *are her fertile, growing center, a couple of billion years old*
> *as* **Animals** *are her solar-plexus, exploring center, which is many millions of years old*
> *as* **Homo sapiens** *or humanity are her heart center, which is only about one million years old*
> *as Homo devas will be her throat center*
> *as* ∼ *will be her ajna center (we will learn the name later)*

Making these energy levels come alive in a curriculum on ecology, or human biology, or community development is a wonderful entry for older children to get a sense of helping their world to grow and improve. Many of our children will have a deep relationship with these energy centers of Earth, all the way to their objective occupations in the 2020s. Through the occupations and life-experience of *Homo devas*, we will become creative masters in agriculture, aqua-culture, transportation, nanotechnology—precisely because devahood is, by definition, in kinship with the mineral, plant, and animal kingdoms. As *Homo sapiens* we are embedded in Nature, but we have differentiated ourselves in consciousness. Slowly, over millennia, we have recognized that we are distinct from the realms of matter. We each have an "I," which has the capacity for self-reflection. With that self-reflection, we know that we will die. We recognize that our relatives, friends, and ourselves are part of a network of mortality, of being born and of dying.

Now, in the next major step, we are transcending the separation. The "I" is an integral breathing unit of a larger breath of the world. We come into incarnation, *remembering the unity*, and will steadily learn to guide others into I-Thou relationship—including, and this is important, the I-Thou of me and the Earth itself. As *Homo devas*, we are Nature—a nature that is radiating the inner qualities, creativity, and life-juice that can be released for the benefit of all peoples. In becoming more aware of how other people experience the Earth, children can begin to articulate their own sense of life's wholeness. For example, some of the children who are described by Carroll and Tober (1999) in their marvelous volume, *The Indigo Children*, are quite clear at a young age about their life purpose. They have incarnated to help in a specific way and have a deep visceral connection to other people and parts of nature that are linked to that purpose. Their relationship with Earth's throat appears to be steadily opening in creative ways, even before they enter the school system.

Another central idea that can be adapted to give some children and youth a flavor for the long time frame is the general story of Cro-Magnons and other early *Homo sapiens.* These humans were our cousins of about 40,000 years ago, as we moved from early to physically modern *Homo sapiens.* The human kingdom was starting to live in different bioregions, and migrating across several continents. Then there was a great cultural expansion, sometimes called the *cultural big bang*, about 35,000 to 40,000 years ago. Many of our cousins developed new and more complex brain organization. From that greater brain function, they were able to do amazing things. This brain shift came in the same period when they started making paintings, carvings, jewelry, complex tools, and other signs of being modern (see Klein; Arsuaga).

We of the 21st century have a similar challenge and destiny that may bring an amazing burst of creativity. Clearly, the challenges are looking difficult. We stand at a threshold between the fourth and fifth kingdoms, as these earlier cousins bridged from third to fourth kingdoms (animal to human). The mystery and challenge ahead of us is this: Which choices bring us further across the species bridge into a more healthy life, and which choices no longer have survival value—for ourselves as a global life form, or for our friend-home, Mother Earth? As we examine our specific choices, the wisest steps for each of us will become clear.

Another connection that older children and adolescents can make involves the experiences of modern people who have been immigrants to a new country or new continent. The relatives or friends whose journey they are familiar with can be a springboard to looking at how all of us, humanity as a whole, are now making a journey to new territory. How is our journey similar in some ways to the earlier journeys of thousands of years ago? How is it different? Our predecessors, the Cro-Magnons of Europe and the other early *Homo sapiens* on the African and Asian continents, made wise choices that enabled them to survive and thrive. Their choices enabled courageous pioneers to migrate later to the other three continents—Australia about 50,000 years ago, and North and South America about 12,000 years ago. We can ask students questions about how our choices in the next few years can help make our journey a success. Their perspective is very valuable and useful, in seeing what choices the local community and neighborhood need to make. You might be surprised at how aware some of the children at junior high age are to these issues. What they need is a perspective in which to put new words about living now and being dedicated to help each other for the long future.

The choices facing our species are, of course, different in one fundamental and profound way from the choices of Cro-Magnons. It is crucial that we look at this difference, and also help our adolescents and young adults see this difference. *Homo sapiens* at the dawn of the 21st century are intelligent and awake enough to see the planetary consequences if we do not make wise choices. At the time of the transition from third to fourth kingdom, the horizon of the individual primate / human reached only as far as daily survival for himself and his immediate dozen or so clan members. At the transition from fourth to fifth kingdom, our horizon is tremendously wider and deeper. This greater vision is, in some people's opinion, both a blessing and a curse. We see the horrible possibilities of

10 or 20 years from now, as well as the beautiful and nurturing possibilities. If we make very un-wise choices this time, there could be a massive die-off for much of life on Earth. We see that scenario.

A considerable amount of emotional energy gets locked up inside children when the "possible bad future" is swept under the rug and not mentioned. It's like the old image of tiptoeing through the living-room and not mentioning the elephant in the center of the room. As we articulate the positive and negative scenarios, what happens inside us (both children and adults) can be very healing. By verbalizing and then releasing the source of our despair about the future, the positive scenarios gain psychological space to grow more. Joanna Macy and Molly Brown, in their wonderful book, *Coming Back to Life* (1998), describe a variety of exercises and approaches that can help liberate the hope energy in relation to world crises. These can be adapted for work with local community groups as well as school groups. Our choices of how to liberate the hope energy in our children is a crucial aspect of the next decade. I know directly, from having worked in juvenile justice for four years, the tremendous paralysis and waste in human spirit (as well as public funds and staffing) that occur when children fall into the well of despair. Each of them is a seed of our future, and we need to help them as a step of helping ourselves. We each have knots of resistance to facing the negative scenarios. It is clearly a difficult task to do. And yet, the knots of resistance are like blood clots that have formed in the arteries of our species, and we are working to clear them out before a severe health crisis ensues.

How are we to avoid despairing over the knots of resistance, which can seem insurmountable in these days of violence and greed? My advice is to focus on the real hope, the excitement of this period. This advice is for you as well as for your children or students or clients. The next five to ten years will demonstrate whether the *heart of Earth* is ready to lift upward and open fully to the throat center—for *Homo devas* to begin actively and tangibly energizing human culture and human institutions—for *Homo devas* to emerge as the fifth physical kingdom on the planet. You may already see this fact, but I'll state it anyway for emphasis: A realm beyond intellect, into higher intuition, does not imply nonrationality. The next level will include all the considerable intelligence, analytic capacity, empathy, and caring that *Homo sapiens* have evolved in our best moments (see Appendix 6 on *Homo sapiens* associations). The new realm that we are entering involves all the best of *Homo sapiens*, as well as the intuition of multidimensional patterns percolating downward into the more limited, four-dimensional world of human space-and-time. In a very literal sense, the next species expresses the best of both worlds.

> My choices, today and every day, affect
> how Earth's throat opens in song—
> to celebrate the one life incarnate through
> billions of voices blending in unison—
> *mineral, plant, animal, human, and deva.*

Here is a mental exercise to explore what it means for us to be pioneers—not just of a new millennium but of 10 millennia into the future. Take a slow breath, suspend critical disbelief for 60 seconds—and read the next sentence *aloud* to yourself. It is important to hear yourself say this.

> A healthy and alert caveman
> is to Shakespeare *
> As Shakespeare
> is to me.

* Note: Shakespeare's name was selected for this exercise because of his contribution to human culture through written and spoken language, a core attribute of *Homo sapiens*. If you prefer, you may substitute the name of another articulate *Homo sapiens* who lived prior to 1600. We have tagged 1600 as a general timeline marker, indicating the transition from mid-*Homo sapiens* to high *Homo sapiens*.

Let's say it again, in another font. Again, it will be helpful for you to read the statement aloud:

A healthy and alert caveman
is to Shakespeare
As Shakespeare
is to me.

Can you hold that concept for one minute without flinching? (Silent laughter is allowed.) Here is another version, more left-brain, but equally true:

A **Cro-Magnon** of 20,000 years ago
is to mid-*Homo sapiens* (400 years ago)
As mid-*Homo sapiens* is
to early *Homo deva*.

The next time you are on a plane, ready to leap into the sky, and are talking to your loved one via cell phone about being home (four time zones away) for dinner, in time for the special family celebration that evening—remember the sentence above about the caveman, Shakespeare, and you. You are a marvel of the evolutionary process. You and your family are a *seed of the future*, living and breathing today.

∾

Seeds Need Nourishment

The difficulty, of course, is that many people in this period of transition are suffering. As we saw in Part Two, many of them are children or young adults who don't have the awareness, capacity, or authority to make other choices. Their life potential is being warped and crumpled. Their lifethread is being woven in terrible ways by the local and worldwide stresses at this period of reorientation.

For example, some of the children and youth with very high amplitude and thin wavelength (see chapter 14) are manifesting illnesses. In my opinion, that includes some (not all) of the children with anorexia, and autism. This has yet to be shown clinically and therapeutically. Some of the children and youth with very wide wavelength and narrow amplitude are also manifesting illnesses; in my opinion, these include the chemical addictions, which involve a significant number of persons. This also has yet to be shown clinically and therapeutically, but I believe that future research will demonstrate this relationship.

Both these groups with skewed wave patterns are responding as best they can to the pressures within our species. The pressures are only increasing for these subsets of our children (as "outliers," in statistical jargon) across the distribution of higher mental wave patterns. A cultural term for this kind of early warning of massive pressures, or enhanced sensitivity to toxicity, is what we described in Part Two: Children are functioning as *canaries in a mine shaft*, as early warning signals that toxicities and pressures are rising to harmful levels on a global scale.

Either way, whether we use the epidemiological view of outliers or the cultural view of canaries in a mine, these thousands of children are suffering. The incidence is increasing for several major diseases or emotional dysfunctions; and in several cases these conditions are clearly related to the environmental stresses in the culture. We very much need to understand better the nature, quality, and source of the pressures, in order to design and plan therapeutic interventions. This approach can enhance the good work that is already being done in these areas.

Figure 20 is a graphic comparison across the third, fourth, and fifth kingdoms, with representative examples from each. You may wish to think of additional names that belong on the list of examples.

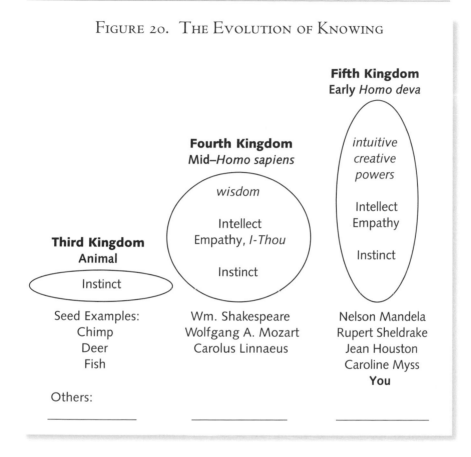

FIGURE 20. THE EVOLUTION OF KNOWING

Fifth Kingdom
Early *Homo deva*

intuitive creative powers

Intellect
Empathy

Instinct

Fourth Kingdom
Mid–*Homo sapiens*

wisdom

Intellect
Empathy, *I-Thou*

Instinct

Third Kingdom
Animal

Instinct

Seed Examples:
Chimp
Deer
Fish

Wm. Shakespeare
Wolfgang A. Mozart
Carolus Linnaeus

Nelson Mandela
Rupert Sheldrake
Jean Houston
Caroline Myss
You

Others:

_____   _____   _____

Remember that we are looking for ways in which children's energetic and psychospiritual identity can help uplift their physiological functioning. Such research is on the edge of what science has thus far demonstrated about the mind-body connection. On the edge of scientific consensual knowledge is, by definition, where we find the most potent seeds of evolution. As we learn more about the evolutionary process leading *Homo sapiens* to the next level, we will garner precious understanding that can translate directly into healing interventions for our children. Many of them are hurting, right now, as seeds of the transition phase of birth. Soon, the children will become seeds of the new species itself. At that time, the processes that are chaotic and traumatic from our *Homo sapiens* perspective will appear more comprehensible.

Figure 21 summarizes some of the main trends that we see happening in the species and kingdom transition that is occurring.

FIGURE 21. EVOLUTION OF EARTH'S UNIFIED FIELD

Top of Third Kingdom	Fourth Kingdom	Start of fifth Kingdom
Primates (chimps)	*Homo sapiens*	*Homo deva*
Early Hominids		
A.afarensis *Homo habilis* *Homo erectus*		
Sensory brain Survival heart	Analytic mind Empathic heart	Intuitive mind Healing heart
Identify with matter	Identify with consciousness	Identify with purpose/life
Know **instinctively**	Know **intelligently, compassionately,** and instinctively	Know **intuitively, etherically,** intelligently, compassionately, and instinctively
World to react to	World to dominate or incorporate	World to cherish/create and let go
Fear	Love and pride	Joy and be-ness

From this brief discussion, I hope you have a sense of the variety of opportunities that will open for our children in the next few years. Those with chronic illnesses that are exacerbated by the culture and species pressures will receive some much-welcome relief. Those who have been constricted about expressing their own special gifts or ways of being creative will have encouragement to bring out that gift. Each of them is a seed of our future, living in the present. In order for us to reinforce their hope about the future, we need to recognize and understand more about the nourishment that they need.

In the next chapter, we will look specifically at the three phases of development for people who are in transition to *Homo deva*.

Chapter 17

SPECIES DISTRIBUTION —
THREE PHASES OF _Homo deva_

Although the general approach of this book is to focus on individual children and the need to offer new approaches to helping them, in this chapter we are looking at large aggregates of people. I want to share with you the view I have of the "seeds" of _Homo deva_ in all nations. This is a composite of analytic background research and intuitive looking at longer time horizons. I make no claim of certainty on this information, but offer it as another resource for others to use in their own reflections. We need a cross-fertilization of many kinds of research during this very important decade.

Figure 22 presents a table with rough estimates of population distribution for the current phases of _Homo sapiens_ and _Homo deva_ development. The numbers are based on extensive readings and intuition, extrapolation from 2000 U.N. Population Bureau statistics, and trends described by authors listed in the Resources section. The conclusions and comments are my own.

FIGURE 22. HOMO SAPIENS AND HOMO DEVA— DISTRIBUTION AT YEAR 2000

Homo sapiens

Species phase	Generalized description	Estimated Distribution
Early *H. sapiens*	• Hunter-gatherers • Preliterate peasants • Indigenous peoples with oral tradition • High mortality rates • Communal land ownership • Ancient healing practices • Communities often lack potable water, sewage systems, and electricity • Distributed primarily in South America, Africa, Asia	50,000,000 (50 million)
Mid–*H. sapiens*	• Literate rural residents • Literate urban dwellers • Distributed across all continents, with largest frequency in China, India, and agricultural areas of Europe and North & South America • Also found in regions of ethnic / tribal warfare	2,800,000,000 (2.8 billion)
High *H. sapiens*	• Technologically literate people interested in other cultures and looking at ways to bring economic growth • Highly literate; and cultures value education / literacy of girls and women.	3,100,000,000 (3.1 billion)

Species phase	Generalized Description	Estimated Distribution
High *H. sapiens* (*continued*)	• Distributed across high-density urban areas of six continents and in rural areas connected by telecommunications • Continue to wage economic and sometimes ethnic warfare	3,100,000,000 (3.1 billion)
Homo deva		
Early *Homo deva* (Phase I)	• Individuals who contribute time & / or money to local / regional / world projects, including some leaders in environmental and "green economy" movements • Activists for worldwide causes; individuals who read and write for purposes of improving the "common good" • People who look at ways to balance sustainability with economic growth • Early *Homo devas* may be active in faith traditions as they apply to community concerns; examples include prayer groups, study groups, outreach in social service agencies. • The "cultural creatives" (Ray and Anderson) • Individuals whose positive intention is expressed in commitment and in taking specific actions to ground the unified field (e.g., using carshare or buying smaller car, decreasing caloric intake and proportion of sugars in diet, writing letters to elected officials and community groups)	300,000,000 worldwide (300 million) (~50 million in USA)

Species phase	Generalized Description	Estimated Distribution
Mid– *Homo deva* **(Phase 2)**	• Those who express their specific intuitive capacities publicly (e.g., medical intuitives, research teams on communication between species, members of nonviolent activist organizations such as Greenpeace and gardens maintained by public-private peace groups) • The "innovators" of regional and transnational organizations • Persons who are emerging slowly through the electromagnetic resistance of the four earlier phases (shown above) • People with a capacity for awake-state at high brain-amplitudes • **Hypothesis:** Phase 2 may be characterized by physiologic effects such as autism, asthma, and other neuro-expressive disorders, reflecting brain activity and stresses at the species level. • Distributed on all six continents	**3,000,000 worldwide** (3 million)
High *Homo deva* **(Phase 3)**	• Individuals with a physiological ability to "sleep" or "wake" at will and the capacity to abstract from body at moment of death fully by choice • People whose artistic and language abilities transcend the analytic mind and involve song-thought as well as words • Individuals with innovative skills who work naturally in teams to solve complex social and technological problems	

Species phase	Generalized Description	Estimated Distribution
High *Homo deva* (Phase 3) (continued)	• Individuals with intuitive knowing of social and technical events, needs, patterns, and scientific concepts & relationships • Characterized by communication skills across national / ethnic / language / occupation groups • Will reside on all six continents • Other abilities to be observed and shared as they emerge	3,000 to 10,000 worldwide To emerge more fully by year 2020

This chapter focuses on the three phases of the emerging *Homo deva*. Like wavepatterns at different depths in the ocean, the phases are, of course, occurring simultaneously. Each person will experience and demonstrate behaviors in one of the three phases as their primary identification. Yet, they may exhibit behaviors in two different phases, because these are living, breathing patterns that interpenetrate. As with the behavior of teenagers, our new species will act childlike and mature within the same day.

The phase of early *Homo deva* corresponds to the cultural creatives (Ray and Anderson, 2000), and I have adopted their terminology in calling this first phase the *creatives*. The second phase, mid *Homo deva*, is here called the *innovators*. And high *Homo deva* phase is when individual people become *lifeseeds*. Each will be described in turn.

Phase 1: The Creatives

FIGURE 23. PHASE 1: "TALK THE TALK"

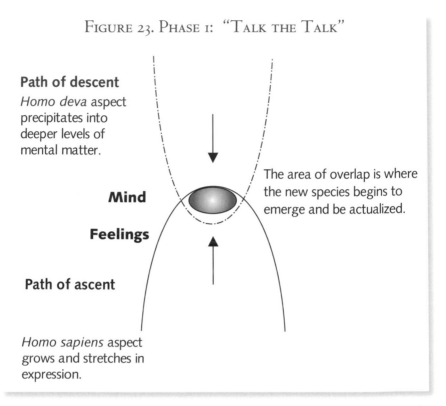

Path of descent
Homo deva aspect precipitates into deeper levels of mental matter.

Mind

The area of overlap is where the new species begins to emerge and be actualized.

Feelings

Path of ascent

Homo sapiens aspect grows and stretches in expression.

The two arrows facing each other signify the two directions of growth, one on ascent and the other on descent. Each of these two foci of this organic laser is interpenetrating the other, more and more each month and year. As the *Homo sapiens* aspect develops upward (toward the future), the *Homo deva* aspect develops downward (from the future). They blend ever deeper into each other as a unified whole. This doesn't need to be programmed. Nature / the Creator has made us this way from the beginning. We need to recognize that this is happening and welcome the process. As we open in trust, while retaining our capacity for intelligent and rational discrimination, each new step will appear.

In Phase 1, the overlap between *Homo sapiens* and *Homo deva* is through our *brain-body*, the "awake mind" that we use for everyday sensory input and physical functioning. The impact of Phase 1 blending of the etheric-brain can appear in a wide variety of activities. You may experience it as an impulse to pursue some kind of creative expression in your life. It may be the emerging sense that it's time to expand your horizons, to make some changes that express what you believe more fully. Your most deeply held values may shift to more inclusive concerns about peace and justice, community building, about more long-term planning in whatever groups you affiliate with.

A person who has fully reached Phase 1 might attend community events, read books, or participate in programs for improving parts of local community life. Or the expression of Phase 1 may appear in your seeking to learn about specific concerns in a wider region or state. These activities may be a part of the person's job or may be an avocation. In either case, the combination of mental attention and empathic caring for the *other* seeks expression through your life, and you welcome that inflow of creative energy. Your impulse to help others, however you define that term, leads you to describe yourself in deeper ways of connection to other groups, other nations. You are likely to be interested in the cluster of issues that Ray and Anderson reported on, including environmental topics, sustainability, social justice, and access to literacy. You see this happening and choose to "go with the flow."

This step can also be manifested in how we spend our money and our time. If you have ever done volunteer work, served as a local leader for children's groups or youth organizations, or have made financial contributions to a worthy cause, these impulses are likely related to your movement into Phase 1. This takes many different forms, depending on your interests, skills, capacities, and life experience.

Examples of persons whose work at Phase 1 has become visible to the public eye:

Fritjof Capra, in science

Millard Fuller, founder of Habitat for Humanity

Mel Levine, in health care for adolescents

Daniel Quinn, in nurturing cultural and interspecies perspectives

John Robbins, in the food and health revolution

Stephen Spielberg, in the visual arts

Phase 1 has been described in psychology as the integration of mind and feelings, bringing our intellect and passion into a potent synthesis that allows the light of the soul to shine forth. These pioneers are serving to guide our species across the early part of the threshold into the new epoch, and are each raising critical issues that are part of our transition to a more healthy life on Earth.

Phase I: Their brain is afire with Wisdom for the world.

∾

Phase 2: The Innovators

Persons in Phase 2 of *Homo deva* development are the regional innovators, the mid–*Homo devas*. They are participating directly in a deeper step of integration, grounding the future pulse all the way through the emotional body of our species. They are the steadfast innovators who work quietly over years and years to manifest the *one work* in many diverse ways across all fields of human endeavor. They realize and understand deeply that they are part of a long-term effort. Their dedication and perseverance are focused on birthing a healing life force larger than their individual life. They assist many other people to *walk the walk* of dedication to healing all Earth's children.

At Phase 2, the boundary between "my job" and "my life" becomes much more permeable. Dedication to serving the spirit of healing and justice in the world, in whatever field you have chosen, becomes more natural. The effort to overcome personal and local community inertia faces less resistance, although during this decade of decision it can still be difficult. In a few cases, you might face some kind of danger or confront specific forms of cultural resistance in expressing your life commitment to soul values. By linking with other persons at Phase 2, you are able to maintain your focus and radiatory power for good. Community networking becomes crucial. Innovators do not travel alone; now more than ever, we need each other's feedback and guidance. The will-to-good expresses potently and effectively through these people precisely because they realize that they are part of a larger team. The urge to make big *Homo sapiens* accomplishments is past; the remaining years of these people's lives are quietly dedicated to serving humanity as deeply as they can on a daily basis.

Figure 24. Phase 2: "Walk the Walk"

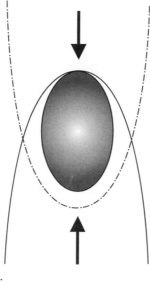

Path of Descent
Homo deva aspect leads the person to make willing sacrifices to protect the greater good.

Path of Ascent
In their *Homo sapiens* aspect, individuals become more focused in their life purpose, with outward expression of soul-commitment across months and years.

Soul
The area of overlap has grown through the person's emotional body, as a potent microcosm of humanity's compassionate and fiery heart.

Personality

The healing pulse of Phase 2 comes through your awareness of your lifework as a mission, calling, or vocation. Whenever your creative expression touches someone else's life, whether the two of you have met or not, healing occurs. The radiatory or energy impact of your work, which you may not be aware of, reaches people of many ages and stretches out at least to national levels.

Many people in our communities are quietly entering Phase 2 without public fanfare or attention. They are working at the local level to improve the quality of life for everyone. This is one of the great strengths of *Homo sapiens / Homo deva* in this transition: The willingness to "go the extra mile" in serving the good of the whole, and being unsung heroes for neighbors whom we may never meet.

Examples of persons whose work at Phase 2 has become visible to the public eye (there are many others at local levels, so this list is meant to be evocative to spark your thinking of other people whom you know about in your region):

Deepak Chopra, physician and spiritual teacher
Matthew Fox, theologian and urban mage
Jane Goodall, primatologist and ecologist
Julia Butterfly Hill, environmentalist and activist
Joanna Macy, buddhist teacher and activist
Nelson Mandela, national leader for healing race relations
Caroline Myss, psychologist and medical intuitive
Rachel Naomi Remen, physician, healer, and counselor
William Irwin Thompson, director of Lindisfarne

Phase 2 has been described in psychology as the integration of the soul and personality. This integration happens gradually and encompasses many different life paths. There are more people on Earth at this phase now than ever before. Their full pulse of *heart fire* may be expressed in a field of particular specialization or in a more general approach to one's life-purpose. Each person who reaches Phase 2 has a deep commitment to speaking heart truth, and teaching others to do so.

**Phase 2: Their life is afire with the soul's
compassion for humanity and all living beings.**

∾

Phase 3: The Lifeseeds

The third phase of *Homo deva* development is what we are calling the *lifeseeds*. In our species transition to Earth's throat, those who reach Phase 3 have evolved to high *Homo deva* functioning. They will serve as spontaneous energy nodes for millions of other persons. They will be the fusion generators of the next epoch, and by their presence in human daily life will accelerate the momentum for all the rest of us. The steady pulse from their brain, heart, and head will radiate as a unified morphological field of healing — in some spiritual traditions, this field is called the "presence of God," in other traditions it is called "the touch of grace," and in medical history there have been many reports of extraordinary healings related to such contact (e.g., see Hirshberg & Barasch, 1995). This phase will be characterized by a significant acceleration of the processes of physiological regeneration. Such acceleration will occur for individuals, groups, and larger human associations. And it will no longer appear as "ineffable," but will be rationally understood — and indeed will be taught in our universities and healing colleges.

Because we anticipate the effect of this acceleration to impact all humans (on all continents), it is truly important that all of us "do our homework" in the decade 2015–2025, so that our local projects and community affiliations are based in as clear relationships as possible. Our alignment with the nurturing and healing purposes of our community groups (and professional groups) needs to be as inclusive, trustworthy, and efficient as possible. Otherwise, the impact of the Phase 3 emergence would stimulate out-of-balance wounds; you can imagine those scenarios yourself, just extrapolating widely from the current news stories. In truth, would we wish it otherwise? The creativity that is bubbling somewhere in each child, each person, deserves to be seen and heard and celebrated. Now is our opportunity to clean house, and make space for the creative juices to come out and be shared!

As described earlier, we estimate that 3,000 to 10,000 persons will actively be entering the level of Phase 3 by about 2020. To state this clearly: 3,000 to 10,000 *lifeseeds*, with names and addresses, will be actively and consciously functioning as a divine ring of fire, gently holding human and animal and plant and mineral populations on all continents—as their presence helps all of us lift into stable identity as a five-part family: the five kingdoms of a peaceable Earth.

Phase 3: Their presence is afire with the touch of Life itself.

FIGURE 25. PHASE 3: "BREATHE THE BREATH"

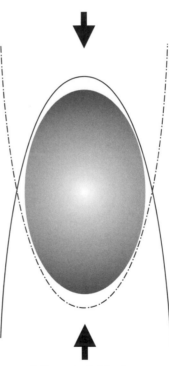

Path of Descent

Homo deva aspect is fully present in personality and now extends deeper into physiology.

Phase 3 brings the overlap fully through the analytical mind, as well as integrating the emotions and the etheric brain from the earlier phases

Path of Ascent

In their *Homo sapiens* aspect, these individuals are mentors to other people, trusted in the community, and well-respected advocates for greater wholeness. Their physical presence will be a healing force, observable and replicable. With their energy as *lifeseeds*, they will function as fusion generators and transmitters within a larger unified field. Eventually they will demonstrate the presence of light-body in human realms.

Examples of persons whose work at Phase 3 has become visible to the public eye:
None as yet.

Although the work of this phase is not yet apparent in regular human life, I believe that hundreds of people at this phase are now growing and learning to live in the present. In essence, they are learning to function as breaths of the Eternal within timespace. They will be emerging during the next 20 years. Many of them are now children or teenagers. They live in dozens of countries and will speak the native languages of their country of origin. Their gift to us is that they quite naturally see and sense and talk and walk and breathe the higher reaches, where humanity needs to grow. They are our guiding stars in the night sky, those who will help us see the way ahead.

Here is one evocative anecdote from a dedicated father, counselor, and author: Barry Kaufman, in his book *Son-Rise: The Miracle Continues* (1994), describes the deeply trusting circle of friends in which he and his wife Samahria held their autistic son, Raun. One morning when Raun was 17 months old, he was spending hours spinning round objects on the kitchen floor. He found a rectangular box, and proceeded to hold it in his hands for 25 minutes; his parent and friend observed and held him in trust, not pushing an observer's agenda or making judgments in their minds. Raun moved the focus of his gaze along the edges of the box during that 25 minutes. Then, he suddenly placed the rectangular box on the floor with the tip of one corner touching, and set it to spinning with his other hand. Without any trial and error as most children (and adults) would do, he had mentally analyzed the possibilities and then created a placement of box to floor that perfectly fit the parameters and character of the physical objects.

In my view, this story describes an early Phase 3 *Homo deva*, gently playing in silence — while in human personality he was a 17-month-old autistic toddler with no speech at all, no eye contact or social interaction. In a very real sense, I believe that Raun, and others like him, are waiting for us to grow up and find them. They will welcome our approach, and will be able to teach us a lot about our world, its potential—and the corresponding potential latent in each human being.

Phase 3 has been described in transpersonal psychology as the full integration of Spirit and Matter. We do not yet understand this phase as clearly as we understand the two earlier phases because humans are still standing on tiptoe to reach and touch this level. The third phase of *Homo deva* unfolding can also be described as opening a new chapter in physics—beyond both black holes and white holes, to full magnetic fusion. A black hole, by definition, swallows all light / energy and does not radiate anything outward. Energy that enters the region of a black hole cannot escape because of the massive implosion of gravitational collapse; because gravity is a manifestation of the curvature of space-time, an object with huge mass tends to distort the geometries of space and time. A particular result of this distortion is the "event horizon" of a black hole, the region beyond which you (or any object) cannot escape unless you were traveling faster than the speed of light. From what certain mystics and cutting-edge researchers have reported, the evolutionary stage that I am calling *Homo deva* will enable us to pass across that event horizon precisely because our identity is precipitated from a level beyond the source of "light." In other words, a being can (potentially) achieve sufficient escape velocity to move out of the black hole known to *Homo sapiens* science, by participating in unified mind of Earth and exercising what we might term the "speed of thought," or even the "speed of will." Today, these concepts may sound like a fairy tale or even elements from pandora's box. Yet within twenty years, these concepts will revolutionize our approach to astrophysics, and eventually will enhance such direct applications as educational curricula for many children who cannot speak, or who have explosions of brain activity that no medication can calm. They need help traveling across the black hole's event horizon in their own brains.

In contrast to a black hole that swallows everything, the theoretical entity of a white hole is the inverse: It spits everything out. A white hole radiates all light / energy and cannot hold anything back. It radiates (pushes away) all the energy that passes by, and does not absorb or metabolize any.

As an aside to those of you who have worked in any capacity in our current justice system, you may recognize some of our clients' behavior in these descriptions of extreme either / or relationship to external energy. I firmly believe that one reason we have such a growth industry of building prisons at this point in our history is that thousands of people with a reasonably stable "I" or ego are getting shoved around fiercely by the forces of our species' collective brain activity. They are indeed accountable, as individuals, for their actions; and at the same time they are pawns in a larger game of planetary bio-physics, as our species is making the transit from Earth's heart to throat. This is especially the case if they are quite sentient already. By exploring these issues at the human / physics interface, we will eventually be able to help many of the adults and youth who are currently living behind bars.

After that practical digression, here is a research field that appears quite fruitful: A future application of *Homo deva* science is that a black hole and a white hole are mathematical inverses of each other. And the transformation of one to the other is mathematically possible because of a basic assumption of *Homo sapiens* science: the symmetry of time. When you solve the equations to derive a black hole, and then imagine that time flows backwards instead of forwards and solve those equations, you get the (theoretical) object known as a white hole.

Now, recall for a moment our earlier discussion about *Homo devas* being masters of the long time horizon. Take a steady breath, and realize as deeply as you can a simple fact: The horizon stretches out in both directions. The past exists and the future exists. You, in the present, can look first one way and then the other; or if you wish, look both ways at once. This conceptual exercise relates directly to the spiritual traditions of several native peoples, in which young people are taught *lucid dreaming* as a form of travel — through time. What we are approaching in the 21st century is the capacity for humanity to utilize the properties of the time horizon to create new ways of being whole, of being more alive, harmonious, and healthy — in the best sense of that term.

When we say that the third phase *Homo deva* is a *lifeseed*, we are pointing to the bio-physical fact that these persons will embody a synthesis of black hole and white hole. They are the hominid version of a solar entity, a being at the planetary throat level of development. They will function as energy generators with full ability to govern the fusion reactions within their own bodies (think cellular, atomic) and within their immediate environment. Clearly, this has implications for creating solutions for some of the problems facing humanity (for pertinent discussion of issues around solar power, see Berman & O'Connor, 1996). For example, there are current developments in human science in the area of burning plasmas and other nonlinear complex systems as a major component in our plan for practical fusion. This work, both in its theoretical understanding and its development of plasma and fusion technologies, is crucial for bringing fusion power to humanity — and will simultaneously bring great synergy to the contributions of the early *lifeseeds*. Having *Homo sapiens* and *Homo deva* pioneers working as visible partners will be particularly important in these frontier projects of basic research that can provide many practical applications, as well as provide role models for other projects.

Turning for a moment to the relatively better known field of psychology, the third phase *Homo deva* will be a person who lives and breathes without the contractions of fear in any of the personality's three major levels: physical, emotional, or mental. Note that this statement says "without the *contractions of* fear," not "without the fears." A fully developed, mature *Homo deva* will experience the events that we do, but because their identity is vibrating at frequency of the planet, they will not have the "contractions" of self-preservation that a separate-individual (with ego-field) has. "Fear" comes from an intimation of annihilation, of a perceived threat to *identity*, to one's existence. By evolutionary growth, the *Homo devas* sense and know that they exist beyond the physical body, beyond the emotional body, and beyond the mental body; and in fact, beyond the consciousness body, and beyond the spiritual-will body. They are each a seed of *being*, incarnating directly from the planet's throat into human realms. For some readers, this idea of direct incarnation will sound familiar, in terms of various spiritual traditions of "heaven on earth." However, the step of *lifeseeds* is arising from a common river beyond any one particular spiritual tradition; the high *Homo devas* come as planetary pioneers, in great compassion and detachment from any religion or ethnicity or gender or nation. They are willingly entering "our" territory, and are being born into human bodies as voluntary (and joyful) pioneers from our own future.

In metaphysical terms, the lifeseed phase implies the gradual transformation of the human physical body to the mayavirupa or *body of light* referred to for many centuries in various spiritual traditions. This third phase of the transition beyond *Homo sapiens* will enable people to manifest the mayavirupa into wavelengths that are visible to the human optical range. You may find useful a metaphor that a friend provided me last year: The *Homo devas* at Phase 3 have brought the slower edge of their mental frequency down into human range, like a hummingbird that slows its wings until we can see it fly. The *Homo devas* are temporarily slowing their frequency in order to blend with us and stimulate us to increase our frequency; and the synchronizing of the mental wavepatterns between us will produce the healing results that have been described in these pages.

We will see and understand this step more clearly as people begin to describe their own approach to Phase 3 during the coming decade.

~

Chapter 18

Characteristics of *Homo deva*

In chapter 17, we looked at an abstract and sometimes theoretical overview of the three phases. In this chapter, we will describe the three phases of transition to *Homo deva* from a more practical perspective. Here are capsule descriptions of some practical issues at each phase:

Phase 1, the creatives, are moving beyond the Conquest Era: Moving from "conquest" and aggressive control of the environment to empathy and creative intuition; looking at issues of balance between altruism and self-interest, between economic growth of poor countries and sustainability; at community and regional levels, moving from territoriality and intimidation to mutual respect and creation of new solutions.

Phase 2, the innovators, are moving beyond the Information Era: Moving from linear complexity of information to chaotic innovation; this becomes possible through the integrated personality of humanity. Expressing soul values and nurturing direct knowledge at deeper levels of reality. Identification with all of humanity brings more creative problem-solving abilities, more focused empathy and use of *body language* to bring healing (I use this term to include the deeper language of the body by which intuitives can diagnose illness by "reading" the physical body). As children in the coming decades learn to read the well-being of their own bodies, their intimate bond with the natural world will be steadily rejuvenated. This will directly impact the available healing approaches for children with allergies, heavy metal imbalances, addictions, eating disorders, and other syndromes at the inside / outside boundaries. As the innovators of Phase 2 bring new understanding to these boundary issues, the nature of the whole as greater than the sum of the parts will become more widely recognized as a physical truth.

Phase 3, the lifeseeds, move beyond the Fear-of-Mortality Era: People will evolve into living and breathing a unified field of physics, a bio-psycho-immunology that transcends illness and brings us direct experience as incarnated immortals, in full communion with our friend-home, the Earth.

Some of the specific characteristics of *Homo devas*, alluded to in previous chapters, will include the following:

Homo devas recognize each other. As you and your friends perhaps have already discovered, there is an emerging transnational culture of *creatives* who bond across national and ethnic lines for interests in new projects that help the community or a larger group. They are not bound by traditional notions of "my tribe / my nation, right or wrong." They develop new ways of expressing their identification with the family of humanity and their yearning to help bring peace.

They express their life-work through creative modes and see life as an artistic expression. There is an interdependence between new media and individual self-expression. While they may have a traditional-looking occupation, they are increasingly attracted to alternative approaches to doing business, to making investments, to participating in community transportation pools, gardening co-ops, service projects that are intergenerational, and many other ways of making life more enjoyable.

Homo devas can be described as "planet children": They are committed to bifocal vision that considers the long-term as well as short-term goals. They are committed to needs of the whole of humanity and the Earth while continuing to affirm the needs and worth of the individual. They have natural affinity for animals and plants, recognize kinship with other persons of widely different backgrounds, whether or not of same class, caste, gender, or tribe. They have an articulate intelligence and empathy that will infuse tomorrow's businesspeople with a global / local mission that will move beyond "market share" to a concept I call *whole share*. The whole share is greater than the sum of the market shares. This will become widely recognized and objectively true, even in the financial services industry.

Self-healing and approaches to health are becoming more customized to the person's workstyle and life-space. The immune system is strengthened by choices for foods that have natural nutrients (e.g., see Robbins, 2001; Lappé & DuBois, 1994), and for clothing and exercise that support a regular and comfortable circadian rhythm. The need for sleep may decrease during Phase 2; physical healing and homeostatic systems will be better balanced. Other indicators will also emerge.

Lifethread and consciousness thread will become more integrated (see chapters 11 and 14). In the final period of Phase 3, the *body of light* will emerge, with concomitant effects on creativity and healing, including enhanced sensitivity to energy-exchange with others.

The individual *Homo deva* learns by intuiting and extrapolating to wider resonance with energy patterns, both those from the human kingdom and those from the other kingdoms. These people will know what is effective, or most coherent, by receiving input and feedback from diverse sources. This is an important point to emphasize: The *Homo devas* are not all-knowing. They are, rather, extremely efficient at receiving and processing feedback from other people and their environment. Where other people notice events, they notice greater patterns because their locus of identification lies within larger living groups and longer timeframes. It will be analogous to our putting a powerful laptop computer into the brain of a three-year-old child; much of their own internal hardwiring they will not understand for years. But they will be able to access coherent databases in milliseconds, even at a young age. This is important to note, because it is in great contrast to the description by Temple Grandin referenced in an early chapter. After more than four decades of careful self-study, Grandin as an autistic adult remains unable to "retrieve" facts from her brain without laborious sifting through what she calls internal videos. This process will not be needed for the fully developed *Homo deva*, because the accessing procedures will come through the common (shared) brain of humanity as an integrated system. Temple Grandin, Raun Kaufman, and many other courageous pioneers who have struggled out of autism are breaking new ground to bring coherence from a very high place in our planet's mind but without the leverage that will be possible within two decades. In effect, they are doing their thinking "offline" from the mass of humanity and each insight they gain is hard-fought by moving against the current of *Homo sapiens'* inertia. By the year 2020, such individuals will be riding *with the current* of the mass of humanity; or more accurately, the mass of humanity will be riding with us on an uplift to a greater integrated brain-system. Therefore, fewer people will be forced to function mentally offline as outliers among the rest of *Homo sapiens.* That's the plan.

Homo devas will contribute greatly to the collective wisdom of faith traditions. For over 8,000 years, humans have developed faith traditions based on revelation, the "revealed wisdom" of allegory and myth. Allegory and myth work to expand the degrees of freedom in language, to amplify meaning. We will still definitely have need for this in the *Homo deva* era. The rhythm of human language stretches upward toward higher amplitude in allegory and myth, yet sometimes it loses frequency and coherence in the process. The creativity of *Homo devas* will teach us, through our diverse and wonderful cultural traditions, to seek and recognize new ways to tell the stories of humanity. Indeed, *Homo devas* will most likely bring marvelous new perspectives to the faith traditions of earthlings. It is a time to renew our many fountains of wisdom that flow from a common source; for an inspiring early voice in this endeavor, see Matthew Fox, *One River, Many Wells* (2000).

One particular gift of *Homo devas* is that they will bring a higher knowing that has quite high amplitude (link to purpose) and yet also keeps high frequency (creativity). They will not have the "cold detachment" which has been historically associated with *Homo sapiens* who are extremely focused and purposeful. In other words, they will embody the synthesis of Love and Will. They will do this by keeping an openness to new experience, new input—a *vulnerable knowing* that is receptive to others' wisdom. By its nature, vulnerable knowing will invite cross-fertilization from peoples of many backgrounds and ages. This collective knowing will steadily expand and will be shared and accessible to others seeking their own steps.

Figure 26 illustrates several of the interfaces involved in the emergence of *Homo deva.* This diagram is a work-in-progress, because it will evolve as the dialogue grows between those who self-identify as *Homo sapiens* and those who self-identify as *Homo devas.* As the figure indicates, the characteristics described in the paragraphs above always involve two interfaces: the top growing-edge (path of *ascent* from matter), and the bottom growing-edge (path of *descent* from spirit). As you reflect on this figure, you may find more insights about the relationship between the emerging species and the earlier kingdoms.

FIGURE 26.   INTERFACE OF KINGDOMS

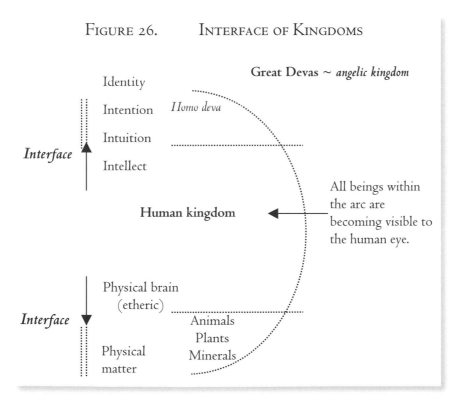

As the figure shows, in this great transition *two* interfaces or boundaries are always involved, as a dyad through which the laser of spirit and matter aligns its fusion beam. In terms of physics, these are the two reference beams through which life tunes itself.

In the evolutionary steps shown in the figure, the intellect-to-intuition interface is the upward arc, corresponding to the physical brain–to–dense matter interface on the downward arc. These two interfaces work together. For instance, both interfaces are deeply involved in the situation of adolescents who use painting and other art forms to manage pain during chronic illness. As another example, the struggle of young women to overcome anorexia and develop a wholesome relationship to food and "ingesting" external energy involves the upward arc of mind to intention, and the downward arc of feelings to physical body. Both the upward arc and the downward arc are part of the same evolutionary impulse. Thus, both are "divine" aspects of humanity's self-expression. Our understanding these relationships in more depth will help us develop more effective approaches to treatment of many health issues.

One of the important dynamics of this decade, 2015-2025, is that the boundary between human vision and the other realms is becoming more permeable, for better and worse. Those beings who exist as energy patterns that are now beyond human visual wavelengths will become more visible as our species moves higher into *Homo deva* sentiency. At each point on the arc in Figure 26, our divine nature (future) and our dense nature (past) are wrestling. As a species, our soul and shadow are wrestling, and it is a battle to the death. The result will be a unified identity. The dense part of the arc will be incorporated more fully than ever before into the divine. The arc becomes more permeable, gradually more kinetic in the present. This is another way of saying that *Homo devas* will be at home with all electromagnetic amplitudes, all heights on the diagram. They, as incarnate members of a hybrid species, will be literally *at-one* with the minerals, plants, animals, humans, and the great devas beyond. The creativity and scientific insights implicit in their relationships will be enormous because they will see patterns and implications that *Homo sapiens* simply cannot perceive.

In conclusion, our *Homo deva* children will be moving beyond what we have known as familiar territory. They will bring us with them, into a kinder place and time. They will move beyond the conquest era to embrace the values and projects of altruism, community building, sustainability, and co-creation. In the second phase, they will move beyond information gathering to direct vision and knowledge of deeper aspects of physical reality and will teach others how to access such knowing for practical applications. From this vantage point, they will be able to read their own bodies' health, the health of other persons and groups, and will provide creative insight into the treatment approaches for many syndromes of imbalance.

And in Phase 3, our *Homo deva* children will help guide us beyond the primordial human fear of mortality, into a direct realization and scientific understanding of the life-and-death cycle. Their presence at moments of birth and death will enable many people to have the visceral experience of a companion and trusted friend with them in their passage to and fro across the veil. We will no longer need to feel alone.

∼

Chapter 19

RISKS TO THE LIFETHREAD

As with all newborn beings, there is risk for the children who arrive from higher realms. Their lifethread and consciousness thread are at risk of trauma during this decade of transition. This is true for the species as a whole, just as it is true in the birth process of individual human newborns. And in particular, there is risk of misunderstanding, lack of recognition, and rejection for those children whose sensitivities and potential are totally new to their parents, teachers, peers, and other caregivers.

This chapter presents a brief discussion of some of the risks that *Homo devas* will need to face. As described by many scholars in spiritual traditions, the *lifethread* is vitalized when we come into incarnation at the beginning of our life. It is the energetic field that bounces back and forth between our heart and the heart of the world, giving us the "pulse" of life. The *consciousness thread* is what becomes more-and-less active as we go through daily sleep and waking cycles, as we grow and mature during our lifetime, as we learn and expand our matrix of meaning, and finally (within the perspective of reincarnation) as we grow and mature over lifetimes.

Let's state again the hypothesis regarding the shift in these two threads, now that you have read several chapters about the amazing developments that may occur in the wider world of science and faith traditions. There is a singular shift that is happening for each of us as individuals, because we are part of the living organism of humanity. The hypothesis: Our lifethread is in process of migrating "upward" from the human heart to the human head. As we move further into the *Homo deva* era, our lifethread will be anchored in the head-heart as an integrated system rather than primarily in the heart alone; this implies that the personality of humanity is opening to a greater identification from the soul of humanity. To use the terminology of spiritual traditions, we can say that humanity itself is going through the process of transfiguration; a critical mass of people are shifting upward to values of healing, gratitude, gentleness, and creativity within a long time horizon. All humans carry these soul values deep within their hearts, but up until now, many have not experienced life as a "safe place" to bring those values out. We are going to help each other learn when and how it is safe to do so. The bio-electromagnetic shift of the lifethread anchoring in the head-heart of a critical mass of people is an important step in this process.

Figure 27 is a simple representation of the two threads and how they interweave in a couple of different human experiences.

While asleep, a normal baby is both close to and far from death. She is close to death in that her brainwaves and metabolism functions have slowed down. Yet, her sleep state is far from death in that sleep does not cause her identity to "fall" into the mineral kingdom, the earliest step of Earth's evolution. The sleep state remains healthy throughout the human's life as long as she can revivify a regular wave pattern with the lifethread during sleep. You can think of this process as a small amplitude wave moving in-synch with a much larger wave, similar to octave overtones in music. The revivifying process provides us with that marvelous feeling of waking in the morning and feeling rested, the blessing that has been called "the sleep that doth refresh." This is a simplified explanation of the wave pattern during sleep and awakeness; its various permutations and dysfunctions during illness (e.g., heart attack, stroke) or accident (e.g., coma, toxicities) are beyond the scope of this book.

FIGURE 27. LIFETHREAD AND CONSCIOUSNESS THREAD

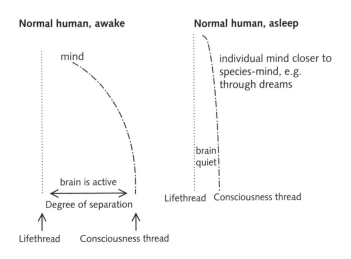

Normal human, awake

mind

brain is active

Degree of separation

Lifethread   Consciousness thread

Normal human, asleep

individual mind closer to species-mind, e.g. through dreams

brain quiet

Lifethread Consciousness thread

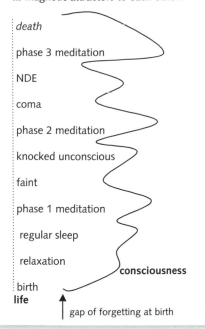

Homo sapiens
Lifethread and consciousness thread as magnetic attractors to each other.

death

phase 3 meditation

NDE

coma

phase 2 meditation

knocked unconscious

faint

phase 1 meditation

regular sleep

relaxation

consciousness

birth
life

gap of forgetting at birth

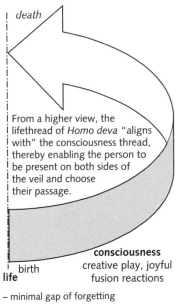

Homo deva
Lifethread and consciousness thread as binary laser in fusion reactions.

death

From a higher view, the lifethread of *Homo deva* "aligns with" the consciousness thread, thereby enabling the person to be present on both sides of the veil and choose their passage.

consciousness
creative play, joyful fusion reactions

birth
life

– minimal gap of forgetting

A person who has practiced meditation for some years and uses that state to rejuvenate the link to higher mental states is able to sustain longer periods of being "conscious," without losing brain-awareness. Such a person will require shorter periods of sleep and he will have less need for unconscious sleep. Similarly, the new emerging species will eventually, by the third phase, grow out of the diurnal awake-asleep cycles that humans have. Evolution has a new pattern in the blueprints for the fifth kingdom.

Homo devas will grow into their biological heritage over several generations of transition. The capacity for radiating energy continuously during the day, and having less need for recharging one's batteries during sleep, will be both modeled by parents and learned from peers. We anticipate that this process will be ongoing for several million young people by the middle of the 21st century.

To consider briefly a specific example, look again at Figure 27. The *lifethread* and the *consciousness thread* might make electrical "contact" at the bottom of the diagram without the person's voluntary choice. For instance, perhaps a man falls off a diving board, suffers head trauma, and goes through a NDE, *near-death experience.* The trauma can stimulate an expanded loop in his electromagnetic field. This will have both electric repelling and electric attraction properties. The specifics of how the balance of repelling and attractive mental energies will express depends, naturally, on how the person integrates the experience — physically, psychologically, and spiritually. One quite common experience is that the person can "lose his fear" of death after the NDE. His consciousness has grown to incorporate that portion of the higher loop of his lifethread, thereby bringing more energy through his entire life system.

The choice of incorporating a NDE into one's life (and learning to approach life more joyously as a result) used to be a relatively rare experience. Now, more people are reporting such a crisis and transition. During the coming decade, my hunch is that we will have several NDE's together as a human family. It makes sense, because we are approaching a fork in the road between continuing toward self-destruction or shifting into higher gear and making the transition. The possibility for massive die-off (in the magnitude of several billion people) is increasingly real. But it won't be the result of an "act of God." We have used that excuse too long. It cannot retain validity in an era when we understand quite clearly the multiple causation models that predict species extinction, resource depletion, global warming, famine, nuclear winter, and other macro-results of our choices as a human family.

There is a choice coming whether to affirm life and make the future better. The choice is real. Even within the context of all the evolutionary pressures to bring forth the new species that the preceding chapters have presented, there is a choice. We do have free will as part of the evolutionary plan. We can choose how to be a teenager, even though we can't choose to skip the teenage years entirely. Likewise, we can choose how to be a teenage species (metaphorically it has a loose fit, in terms of the vocalizing of teens and our migration to the Earth's throat), but we can't avoid the choice altogether. However, even with all the signposts and increasing number of stressors telling us that we are taking a risk, many people don't yet see the message. The addiction to consumerism and material acquisition, to use but one example, is a difficult pressure to overcome. What is needed is a clear vision, on a very macro-level, that presents humanity with the stark choice. And in that moment, humanity chooses to affirm life—the higher life of trust and joy, rather than the life of hoarding and defending. I don't see what that stark choice will be, but I can feel it coming.

The choice is going to be increasingly real in the years between now and 2025. We are dealing with a veritable risk to the lifethread of a planet, upon which we happen to reside. The lifethread of humanity and the lifethread of the planet are intimately interwoven, more so as we take the conscious step to embody as Earth's throat. The 21st-century fork in the road lies before us, and we have the opportunity to practice being our best selves. This time, we are no longer the Neanderthals who couldn't see what was coming. This time, we see the road ahead, and we know the choices that need to be made. Our eyes are open, and the responsibility to choose is ours. And we can practice with each other—having the patience and compassion that we know is the best way to awaken our best self. As Jean Bolen has reminded us in *The Millionth Circle* (1999), it does take practice to be a part and the whole. She used the metaphor of music, saying that "To pay attention in a circle as in improvising music / Is to know when to come in and solo / And when to provide backup with a listening heart / Playing together as equals takes practice and presence."

We also need to acknowledge that for most people now alive, it won't be an either / or choice of moving to Phase 2 of the transition. They won't be ready to take that step themselves. But by vigorously supporting the Phase 1 values and serving as creatives in their own community and vocalizing their support of elected officials who champion the Phase 1 values, they will help tremendously. And in so doing, *they are responsive* to the energy-field of those who are ready to be regional innovators in Phase 2. Therefore, all of us who are further along the path have a moral and sacred responsibility to plan and create civic and social structures that nurture each individual and enable each to reach as high as possible. For some, this will mean simply nurturing the goodness, truth, and beauty of their own lives as mid–*Homo sapiens*. That in itself will be a blessing for all the people whom they meet. At the end of the transition, they will be living in a much more peaceable and life-affirming world.

∾

Chapter 20

Hope for Tomorrow

A Message for Sentient Beings

This is a message to read with someone you love. The beloved friend could be a person, a cat, a tree, a waterfall—any sentient being whose presence touches your heart and who has a visceral investment in the next five to ten years. The message is intended for *sentient* beings for the simple reason that we each have many kinds of relationships, but this book has been about those relationships that are mutual. These relationships are mutual in the fullest sense, with a responsiveness back and forth, an *energy exchange*. Every sentient being, whether person, animal, plant, or mountain is a potential ally in the journey. An ally protects your energy by giving its own. Whoever you see as your ally is the one that will enjoy the journey with you.

The message to read with your loved one is this:

After 40,000 to 100,000 years of struggling as *Homo sapiens* to meet our basic survival needs, our social (and sexual) satisfactions, and our achievement goals, can you conceive of a joy large enough to *sing as a counterpoint* to that struggle? Can you, right now, conceive of a joy great enough to make it all worthwhile? Perhaps that is asking too much all at once. The message of *Homo deva* breathes a joy that transcends time, money, and mortality. The joy is breathing above your head and around your heart, ready to make the final connection, but the choice is yours. That is a key issue. If we cannot conceive of even a glimmer of such a joy, and if we aren't willing to take a risk and choose it, then it won't happen. I am suggesting that you give it a try.

We as a human family have reached the end of a long tunnel. Some initial streams of light are starting to come through. The children who are stretching upward into the realm of *Homo deva* want to bring encouraging news about that light to others. The light comes with love and creative power, and so we have talked briefly about those also. What you already know from your life experience and learning from others can be further grounded here (see Part Five, and the appendices and the Resources section for further ideas). Learn more about the children suffering and children laughing, about families struggling with chronic illness, about a teenager in juvenile prison, about mothers with young children in homeless shelters or those who have had to send their children to group homes. Learn as well about children's creativity and amazing resilience, about spontaneous healing powers through love, laughter, and prayer, about eyes that look decades and centuries into our future, and about the promise that we will never leave someone alone.

We all have stories to share about the members of our family who have fallen "off the map" of the current mainstream culture. Some of us have fallen off in the hospital with illness; some have fallen off in youth centers or prisons, or halfway houses for recovery; some have fallen off in runaway shelters, homes for battered women and children, classes for debtors and those seeking affordable housing, lines of people seeking advice on immigration or unemployment, and those who sit in silence at home. Some who have fallen off have children who are gifted and bored or bewildered and lost in schools where the mission has sunk to "maintaining order," or schools that are struggling even to pay the utility bill and keep from closing. Some of us are burned out and depressed by our jobs, and some are secretly enjoying what we do but are afraid to mention it to others because it's so rare and "weird." A few of us have forsaken civilization and gone to the mountains (or the islands) to escape the urban stresses, and many of us are numbed out by long commutes and suburban 24/7 routines that accomplish much and lead nowhere.

And yet some of us have fallen off the map of the mainstream culture onto a new and different road. In a sense, we have fallen "up" rather than "down." Some of us are actively committed to our communities and the next steps of building grassroots trust. The progress is real, but seems too little, too late when we look at the national and international scene.

These are all symptoms of our civilization's crisis, and our culture's climax. There is nothing wrong with you, or your family or friends. The message I am bringing today is — *There is something deeply right about where we are going*. Beyond the evolutionary climax for our culture is an opening that will help us breathe, and hope, and dream again.

It is extremely hard to move ahead and be born. It is damn scary! Especially when the pressures are giving us a daily message, "If you stay here in the tightness, you might die, but 'out there' is unknown and may be worse." We are all facing a historic moment that challenges us to take a leap of faith, with the combined support of our rational beliefs, emotional trust, life experience, and our circle of friends. The step of suspending disbelief and welcoming that quiet voice of intuitive, vulnerable knowing is truly a leap. And it is a critical one. Release a breath, and listen.... You may find that deep inside, you already knew the sound of that quiet inner wisdom. The spark is there for you... it just needs time to grow.

The stories of hope we have shared in these pages are about *our future-self coming down* ... and incarnating as the children of humanity's tomorrow. These children of tomorrow will grow up to be teachers, farmers, scientists, ministers and rabbis, managers in manufacturing and finance, retail store owners, authors, painters, friends, and in turn will become parents of the next generation. I am talking about the story of our future coming down to dwell among us, in the form of thousands and eventually millions of humans who are evolution's next step.

We have touched on many technical concepts in the preceding chapters. Yet, the underlying message is more than concepts for our intellect, although that is a necessary and vital contribution — and it is more than singing the tune of our feelings through novels, movies, or other art forms or in quiet talks with friends, although those are also crucial and necessary components. I am describing the *biological next step*—beyond concepts, beyond emotional / consciousness resonance—to the expression of unified field of will and identity, to the human-devas who live and move and breathe as threads of a *unified voice of Earth.* These dearly beloved children will breathe and sing in a unified voice through many harmonies because they are in their essence the hybrid between spirit and matter, joining our origins in the sky and in the planet.

~

The Next Decade is Our Species' Moment of Truth

From children in homeless shelters to flowering prose speaking of the union of sky and Earth—that is a long stretch. And that is exactly what I am talking about: a long stretch. That stretch is the topic of our current discussion, and the focus of the coming decade. The stretch is the next step. It is nothing totally "new," because some wise elders in our species have been talking about this for 2,000–4,000 years. The voices of our collective wisdom and innovation have spoken of it more actively in the 400 years since the Renaissance, and the voices for innovation and liberation have been especially active in the past 40 years.

Now it's time to do that stretch in *your lifetime*—to bring the thread of wisdom and unified will all the way from the top of your head down to your toes. A biological climax is much more than a theory. It is what you and I are living through this month, this year. Our global civilization—indeed, our global culture—has reached its climax and needs to be transformed.

There are many practical ways that we can assist the birthing of evolution's next step. In the next section, Part Five, I will suggest a number of steps that you might take to support and accelerate your part of the species transition.

PART FIVE

YOUR NEXT STEPS

THRESHOLD

To our beloved kin in all nations
Who dare to trust the human heart—
Welcome, dear wise ones,
To the climax of an incredible and
Often frightening story, the death of an age
And the birth of a new species.

Humanity has reached the crucible of *transition*.
The child's head is in the birth passage.
You and the child are emerging as bearers of
Life's flame, blossoming outward to touch
All corners of earth in gentle, cosmic fire—
Moving upward from our familiar cave in the
Heart of the planet, our chants and prayers now
Igniting creative fires of earth's throat.

Through the coherent and unified field
Of *Homo sapiens*, earth's heart—
Now emerges the next great kingdom,
Earth's throat, *Homo deva*—your divine birthright
And wondrous gift to us all. From two hundred
Nations, you will release life powers of real
Peace on earth, as Gaia's heartbeat tunes
Upward and releases joyful rhythms of atomic life.

Thank you for coming. Please let us know
How we can help. There are many resources
Available to nurture and support the fabric of our
One work. We welcome clues from you about
How to approach in mutual recognition.

We who live and move and breathe
At the threshold between kingdoms want
Very much to be of service to evolution's plan.

Remember, dear children of the dawn,
Thy choice to come to earth as precious
Messengers of the world soul, in order to
Help us all awaken to life's generous abundance.
Listen, and hear the throatsong of our mother.
It is time. We love you as our self. Breathe.

Winter Solstice, 2002

Chapter 21

THE VERY NEXT STEP:

The First Half Hour After Reading This Book

It is important that you make a choice about your first half hour after reading this book. Trust me on this one. The choice doesn't need to result in a big action. There are no heavy expectations here. I am simply talking about being awake to who you see yourself to be—and being friends with yourself.

The first half hour is a *catalyst time*, a period of re-entry into regular life. While reading this book you have been in the land of spirit, considering unusually long time frames and big concepts. Now you have the opportunity to move gently back down into the sensory world and to link in truth and beauty with dense matter. Through this linkage, you can serve as a living emissary of the future.

How do you want those two aspects of your fusion-laser, the realm of abstract energies like beauty and peace, and the realm of familiar details of sensory life, to relate to each other? *Looking at the relationship of universal and particular today is a helpful microcosm for breathing the future, of co-creating a state of grace in your life and the world.* (Grace is the future touching us through space, while glory is the future touching us in time... and both are from the source of life, however you see that.)

What you do in the first half hour will be rooted in the sensory, grounding your future in the present. For example, you may decide to make a cup of tea or coffee and sit quietly. Or you might go for a walk. You might call a friend and talk about the crazy-wonderful book you just read. You may wish to start a "To do" list of heartfelt priorities for the next week. You may feel the impulse to gather your child and go to the park for some quality time together.

Whatever you choose to do, imagine how the activity also partakes of the eternal. Watch your breathing and how it is expanding and rippling *through time as well as space*, even as you consider the choice of how to "spend" the half hour. Think of the half hour as a breathing, living entity. Indeed, from a certain perspective, the half hour is looking forward to *being with you!*

You might want to write a journal page about your three I's—intuition, intention, and identity. Or you might even turn on the TV and watch the news from "10,000 years away"—from the past in your free-wheeling identification with Cro-Magnons or other early *Homo sapiens*, and then from the future in your new identification with mid–*Homo deva*. (This exercise can be quite a trip.)

The purpose of your chosen activity is to infuse the time with as much *reality* as you have inside, from the top of your soul to the soles of your feet. Clearly, this experience will mean something light-years away from the meaning we regularly garner from "reality TV" and other activities that focus on time as something to "kill." From the view of *Homo deva*, killing time is a violent act against life itself.

Time is a sacred breath. Your next half hour is a covenant between you and what is most whole and holy to you. This moment is a sacred commitment to yourself, to a state of *being eternal here*—in a way that is meaningful to you. In the process of choosing *how* and *who you are* in this half hour, a field of concentric waves goes out from you in all directions. You have touched your *intuition* about what is meaningful to you, brought that pulse through your *intention*, and grounded the choice from your own deepest *identity*.

The energy of the choice is pulsing outward from the high place where you are the *most you* and, simultaneously, from the beautiful *ordinary you* of daily life. Here is looking at You! That synchronized pulse is emitting back and forth between the two laser foci of this moment and the eternal... between self and Self. The pulse is zipping beyond the speed of light, beyond the speed of thought, back and forth between your past and your future . . . and between the past and future of your species. All the dynamics that we have mentioned in the past two hundred pages are present in your creative act of will.

The pulse of your half hour is spreading outward, as if you have nudged a small round stone off the top of a cliff onto a sloping hillside. You watch the small stone begin to roll down the hillside, and you wish it well on its journey. You initiate the wave and then let it go. Yes, let it go. It has a life of its own to follow, just like each breath. The energy wave of your half hour is a commitment by you to *be you*, in whatever way that commitment fits. There is no way to "fail" at being you. Release another breath, and realize that you do believe that.

From another view, you can consider the half hour as a fun investiture in your role as a member of the Earth team. Whatever you choose to do is an actual commitment to a gentle transition for your species, with the result already known somewhere deep within you. You choose how you will *spend* the 30 minutes. And you *choose* how you will spend the 30 minutes. You choose *who* will spend the 30 minutes. Three aspects of your human-divine self now breathing at one, as an integrated circuit, a unified field: The nature and quality of how you "spend time" is from intuition; the purposeful "choosing" is from intention; and, naturally, "who" is spending the minutes comes from your source identity.

The more awake you are in the initial choice, the greater your return on investment will be in life energy percolating through all the levels of your daily existence. That percolating energy is working each minute and second, because the laser beam of humanity's mindheart is working within you. The dual beam of mind-and-heart is coming together and expressing through your throat, amplifying the pulse from that half hour outward through the hours . . . weeks . . . months . . . years . . . decades to come.

Whatever you do in the next half hour, above all be gentle with yourself. Mercy begins at home.

∾

Chapter 22

The First Week

The first week after reading this book is an excellent time to clean out a closet in your house, right? You have had a glimpse of the big future, with lots of abstract concepts, diagrams, and some scary scenarios of species extinction for good measure. It's time to get back to the reality of daily life, where divinity usually diffuses into mists of "good intentions," of overreaching our New Year's resolutions.

During this coming week, take all the energy that was stimulated by the earlier chapters and ground it in the *most dense matter* in your life. If closets don't do it for you, perhaps jogging, or racquetball, or clearing out the car trunk. Or gardening. Perhaps you will find that you have energy to purge last month's leftovers from the refrigerator, or even to tackle the far corner of the garage.

We are dealing with the *spirit to matter* connection here. And when spirit wants to ground fully, it needs a dense garden plot to work—preferably with lots of chaotic, messy loose ends and substantial physical details. You get the picture. I am confident that you can come up with some part of your life that fits the description.

One of the tasks that comes to my mind is to purge from the closet clothes that I haven't worn in three years and place them in a big sack to donate to the local thrift shop. Next I think of weeding out several piles of unread magazines that often seem to reproduce while I am asleep.

᪥

Celebrate our Species' Rite of Passage

My second suggestion for the next week is to covenant with yourself and your family to have some kind of quiet celebration. I don't mean *quiet* as in no noise. I mean quiet as in no fuss or hassles, no complex planning. This is a celebration of being alive! No more, no less. As a high *Homo sapiens*—to—early *Homo deva*, you have survived a lot. Now is the time to create a spontaneous ritual, a rite of passage for you and your loved ones. We are going to be part of an amazing new chapter on this planet! We are all reorienting in a very good direction. Even though most of our public leaders don't see it yet, they will eventually. You and I will be able to help them. We do this first of all by being ourselves. And that calls for a little celebration.

Here are a few celebration suggestions your family might like:

• **Storytelling**. We need to tell each other stories about what we want to have happen in the next few years. What is the ideal scenario? What is the feared scenario? Lay them out visibly in words, and look at them together. As we look fully, the fears will shrivel in the sun of our combined gaze.

• **Laugh with a Friend**. There are many ways that we can brainstorm, and even get silly, about the tribulations of being grounded visionaries. What is your worst image of what you will be like when you go through daily life with a long time horizon? "Think globally, Act locally" needs an update. How can we include the gentle laughter of delight about this incredible, bizarre challenge that Mother Earth has given us? If we are going to be a species here on Earth for thousands of years to come, we need to get a new sense of perspective. What does perspective even look like in the context of helping embody Earth's throat? We need to welcome the divine energy of joy by our choice to celebrate. Get together with your friends and brainstorm a brief list. What kind of celebration would the early *Homo devas* in your household enjoy this week?

• **Sharing dreams.** Our collective high dreams are awakening and in that process coming into incarnation. Through this awakening, the *future-dream* evokes new strengths in us. Perhaps you have heard of the ancient traditions of dreamtime among native peoples. Having a lucid dream while in brain-awakeness is another way of describing the process in which mind breathes the potential into the actual, bringing the best and highest into creative expression through the crucible of daily life. In this celebration you might each share a dream. Everyone can talk about a dream, draw it, write about it, or even act it out.

However you choose to celebrate your future self and the future of our species, think of it as a source of strength for the road ahead. The strength that comes from sharing our stories, ideas, and dreams and looking clearly at our future will also help us face a two-sided great energy in the path ahead.

One part of that great energy has the face of our divinity. In order to see the divinity clearly, we need to overcome the *repression of the sublime*—all the reasons from our personal upbringing and our culture that we haven't wanted to be too close to our divinity before. The other face of that great energy in the path ahead has the face of our collective fears, our nightmares about the identity and destiny of humanity (take a breath, and see those old dreams lift to be dissipated like smoke: "born in mortal sin," "venal evil at its core," "destined to live and die in pain," "born in poverty, die in poverty," "it will always be a dog-eat-dog world," etc.). Those are bad dreams that humans needed to invent during the past years in order to deal with the deep wounds in humanity's heart and to face the brutal competition for resources that *Homo sapiens* survival has required. We did the best that we saw in the moment.

As we see and understand more fully the evolutionary unfolding of our nature, the unknown will become more familiar and trustworthy. The bad dreams will dissolve like static fading on the radio as we tune our lives more exactly into the energy patterns of Earth's throat. The unknown will become a deeply textured field in which we can create new ways of educating, nurturing, healing, and guiding our children.

Until we are able, as a species, to stand and be accepting of both these faces (the divine and the nightmare), we will not be able to reach our next step. These faces, like all mythological beasts, are a version of our ally in disguise. Even as celebrating our expanded identities by sharing our stories, ideas, and dreams strengthens us to face the dual-headed dragon, so in turn does facing the dragon in the safe cave of family and friends give us the courage to share more fully our most imaginative stories, our most innovative ideas, and our highest dreams. Sharing our best dreams about the future is an incredibly courageous act of will. Do you have a friend with whom you can share one of your high dreams about the future? Writing in a journal can be a first step toward expressing your intention to make the dream real.

The next couple of years are an especially critical period, as we begin to discuss with friends, family, and eventually with the larger community some implications of these future stories. Take one step this next week to share one of your high dreams.

～

Open Your Throat

My third suggestion for the week after reading this book is to use your voice, your glorious power of speech, to express your reactions to the ideas. That might include talking with a friend about the book. It might mean singing in the shower about the best and worst parts of the book for you, or the issues in the world that the book stimulated for you. Using your voice could involve making a five-minute audio recording of your responses to the book and describing what the responses have evoked in you.

The *throat* is the energy center that grounds this next big step for humanity. If you and I practice using our throats in a visceral and objective way, always aware that we are grounding the *sounds of a new species*—that step alone grounds the pulse of the future even further. You are helping the course of evolution each time you sing, each time you chant, each time you lift your voice in praise and thanksgiving—each time you use verbal language that is an authentic expression of your heart. There is no requirement to have an audience, although some of you with young children may discover that this is a wonderful way to have fun together.

Regular speech with words is fine; however, singing is more effective for this exercise, because it involves both words and opening the throat-heart connection. An activity that I have found helpful in the past few months is to sing for at least one minute each day, even if what I am singing is just the grocery list on the way to the market. The act of opening the throat naturally widens the amplitude of our mental wave pattern beyond linear speech, beyond the lyrics—and involves the melody line of the mind, linked with heart. This stretches the mental categories into more intuitive octaves and helps to energize the *mindheart channel*. You might wish to reflect on this and extrapolate to other benefits that are involved in bringing your mindheart stream all the way into audible sound waves.

You will also find that it is nearly impossible to stay stuck in any of the "dark dragons" while singing! The creative act of linking head-and-heart through audible melody may start out in tiredness or frustration for a few minutes. But there is an inherent uplift that happens in the process of sharing the breath in this way. You and the world get more closely synchronized. In the process of being receptive to outside-breath, you allow yourself to be *in-spired* by the larger breath. Spending even a couple of minutes in opening the throat in this way, as a kind of singing check-in with yourself, can assist in clearing your energy for the day's projects.

Trust yourself on this. You will have many excellent ideas about ways to invite your throat to open. Your heart and head are both intimately involved when your throat is engaged. Get to know your throat. If you are comfortable with using imagery, try this delightful exercise: Imagine your throat as a person. What would your Throat Person be wearing? Where would your Throat Person go for a local outing, or on a vacation? You know best whether this kind of exercising the imagination is useful for you.

Using your voice as a sacred instrument is a powerful way of lifting ourselves from the very real traumas and pain that come our way. *Give voice* to the life that dwells within you to celebrate, to commune, to grieve, to wonder, to reflect, to protest, to gather together, to share, to express gratitude, to heal. Enjoy the exercising of your voice as part of the future speaking through your life.

Chapter 23

THE FIRST MONTH

T he suggestions in the previous chapter, for your first week after
reading this book, were deliberately on the lighter side. Now, we
are beginning to look a little deeper. During the next month, try mental stretches beyond your comfort zone. All good *Homo sapiens* have a
comfort zone. Find where the edges of yours are. The reason for this
exploration beyond the comfort zone is that a species transition will
probably be uncomfortable at times. We are heading into uncharted
waters, and the journey may be across some rough seas. It helps, in circumstances like this, to invoke a sense of adventure—to bring out the
part of you that looks forward to a new project that requires you to dig
deeply into your problem-solving skills, and patience, and brainstorming
on a moment's notice. All of that will be useful for your contribution
to your community's transition in the days ahead.

Start the Adventure with a Book

The first suggestion is to go into a bookstore (or library) and browse
for a half hour in a section where you have never in your life selected a
book. You will know which section fits in your situation: It might include the books about puzzles, mysteries, biography, romance, horror,
philosophy, languages, true crime, metaphysics, history, science fiction,

parenting, computers, cooking, crafts, psychology, or pets. The goal is not, necessarily, to buy a book but to stretch your mental muscles. If your transition from *Homo sapiens* to early *Homo deva* were to be accelerated over the next month, what kind of book might appeal to you? Why would you reach for that kind of energy? You might be curious about this different genre and how it is reflecting a part of your species' struggle through a major transition. Stretching the edges of your identity with books is a way of breathing through larger loops of your species' mind; while there is no requirement to take a book from this new genre, it is quite useful to look at why it does or doesn't appeal to you. Isn't it fascinating to see all the aspects of *Homo sapiens*?

∼

An Imaginary Lunch Meeting

The second suggestion for this month is to plan an imaginary lunch meeting for three persons, yourself and two others. This particular gathering brings together people who might not ordinarily meet. Think of two people, two public figures, whom you would enjoy meeting and who might enjoy learning from you and from each other, even though normally you and they might not cross paths in a hundred years. Imagine hosting the luncheon at one of your favorite restaurants with these two people as your guests. By having the three of you connect and interact mentally, through the medium of your brain and imagination, you are helping to accelerate the evolutionary process. The meeting is, in effect, occurring on the amplitude level of *healing our culture.*

Recall the discussion in earlier chapters about the amplitude wave pattern relating to purpose. What is your sense of the purpose of this meeting, and what would you like to share with the two public figures? What threads of common wisdom, of compassion (or even of mutual respect) could you help nurture during the hour meeting? On the direct rational level, what do you think the three of you would talk about?

Your imaginary guests can be local figures in your community, or more widely known public figures. That distinction doesn't matter. The following list of names may be useful in stimulating your imagination about such a luncheon meeting (each pair of names is shown in alphabetical order).

A lunch meeting with you and . . .

Dick Cheney and Julia Butterfly Hill
Cher and Alan Greenspan
Stephen Hawking and Stephen Spielberg
Barry Bonds and Ralph Nader
Julia Child and Lawrence Ferlinghetti
Colin Powell and Barbra Streisand
Andrew Cohen and Richard Leakey
Jimmy Carter and James Redfield
Bruce Springsteen and Desmond Tutu
Deepak Chopra and Archbishop William Levada
William F. Buckley and Rachel Naomi Remen
Madonna and Serena Williams
Paul Ehrlich and H.H. the Dalai Lama
Ursula LeGuin and Bill Moyers
Ram Dass and Daniel Quinn

Be aware of your own assumptions in looking at these pairs. Each dyad is an example of a fusion-point, whether that is mind-feelings, rational-mystic, analytical mind—intuitive mind, mind-body, etheric physical—dense physical body, will-consciousness, or another interface. Of course, each individual has energy from both ends of these lasers in our species' development. Through the process of becoming a "public figure," each of these individuals is embodying directly a layer of the culture; their energy is a lens for many. The issue is, which part of the cultural polarity is a particular person expressing more (visibly) in their life, and how can the interaction between these persons energize a larger balance?

To imagine the interaction between you and the two guests over lunch is a creative act of will, a way of deepening your approach to life as an adventure. Each person has skills and gifts to bring to the luncheon dialogue and interaction. You are serving as a synthesis point to help the other two people as "opposites" come together in a greater whole. Have fun (and compassion) participating in your imaginary conversations! The purpose, again, is to stretch the beam of your mind to include larger strands of our cultural genetics — to open the throat and get our marvelously differentiated interests and life passions flowing in reciprocal ways. By energizing such dialogues and relationships across the arcs of your mind laser, you are truly helping connect all of us across the horizon toward a better future.

Ask yourself the following questions: Which of these pairs would I be most interested in talking with during the next month? Given the quality of energy that these dedicated persons are bringing to their lifework, what could I learn from them? In addition, given the energy that I bring to my lifework, what could they learn from me? In what way could our three-way conversation produce a pulse that brings all of us one small step forward in moving humanity across the threshold?

As a postscript to this exercise, you might invite two of your real-life friends to dinner. Tell them that they are stand-ins for Colin Powell and Barbra Streisand, or some other public pair of your choosing. See where the conversation goes! Bringing the *public* level (our local version of the *universal*) into your private life is one way of activating your high dreams. It helps us all to breathe the deeper air of possibilities, the air that comes with choosing to *enliven* (bring to life) a positive future. The art of precipitating dreams and goals is a wonderful skill that several excellent writers have focused on in the past decade. You can find many books on this topic in your local library or bookstore. A couple of the ones that I have found especially helpful are Adrienne (1998), Cameron (1992), Goldberg (1993), and Luhrs (1997).

∿

All the News That's Fit to Read

The third suggestion for this next month is to read the newspaper. I realize that you may already do this regularly or, conversely, that you may avoid this activity like the plague. And indeed, the news is in a way a plague. In several respects, the mental field of the mass media is "stuck" in early *Homo sapiens* mode. There are some exceptions that touch higher vision, but the solar plexus vibration level (and lower) is definitely what sells newspapers and TV commercials.

As you may recall from an earlier chapter, the solar plexus energies are what stir our gut, the desire nature that has its roots in our animal nature—the sensationalism, the hype that implies something dreadful will happen if we miss an installment, if we don't read or tune in every day...the innuendoes and focus on lower feelings such as fear, guilt, shame, greed, acquisitiveness, jealousy, and aggression. The subtle (and often not so subtle) messages assault us with the thought that we will die—or become lonely or unattractive, whichever is worse—if we don't hurry to the nearest store or phone and buy XX. In daily mass media, our collective mind is saturated with a plague of dark dragons. Need I mention telemarketers?

How can we take a step together to shift the media upward, from solar plexus to heart? You may have had the experience of glancing through a few days' newspapers after returning home from vacation. The ads are bad enough; in addition, the stories about human suffering, new indictments, and budget cuts are enough to give a person fever, chills, and prostration. But we can work to stop this plague from spreading. Our job—your job, because you did volunteer for this—is to help identify the transmitters of this plague ... and to look behind them to the *positive* hosts that they are feeding on. We need to energize the wisdom, compassion, and insights about the future that will help that host to thrive, and thereby assist humanity to uplift. Sounds possible, right? It is possible, especially since the half-forgotten purpose of the print and audio media is truly positive—to share the information that is useful and sought by a free citizenry in a democracy.

Now we get to the practical part. Here is a first step: Take a half-dozen index cards (scrap paper will do, if index cards are not close at hand). Write on each of the six cards, one of the following: early *Homo sapiens*, mid-*Homo sapiens*, high *Homo sapiens*, then (you guessed it) early *Homo deva*, mid-*Homo deva*, and high *Homo deva*.

Start reading any section of the newspaper that draws your attention. Then go to another section. Continue reading for a half hour. Read as if you are an *interplanetary anthropologist* on assignment. Your mission is to list on the cards some of the issues that Earth-people from each evolutionary phase are talking about. What are the mid-level *Homo sapiens* talking about, and what are they selling in the Classifieds? What are the modern, late-phase *Homo sapiens* discussing, and whom are they blasting in the Op-Ed columns? How about the early *Homo deva?* Where do you find clues to their presence? On the relevant index cards, jot down phrases about the issues you notice. Be aware that in many cases you are intuitively recognizing the differences among the six phases.

As a detached but compassionate anthropologist, also note any issues (or writers) that tend to sound like the "fleas" that carry pestilent news. Another variation on this theme is to note those problems or issues that are being handled at a particular level (e.g., mid–*Homo sapiens* strife and warfare, ethnic conflicts), and consider whether these issues could be better addressed from a more long-range perspective. You can expand this theme in several different directions, as it appeals to you. Even "Letters to the Editor" can take on a new sense of efficacy when you are able to approach them from a longer time frame and a more inclusive view. The grounding step is important: With whom in your local community could you share your note cards about some steps we need to take?

≈

Action Steps This Month

A fourth suggestion for this next month is to write down a couple of action steps that you have already taken that, in your view, qualify as Phase 1 of *Homo deva*. Here are a few examples to start your creative juices flowing:

- Volunteer at a nonprofit agency or school
- Quit smoking
- Use carshare or downgrade a vehicle for better gas usage
- Write a letter of concern to an elected official; and send copy to your newspaper editor
- Contribute funds to a charitable organization; call and thank a charitable group for their work
- Participate in a prayer-circle of friends
- Attend a meeting of your local school board, and learn about current issues

There are literally thousands of such steps, many of which you already know would be "good" for you. There are also many books in the library describing such steps. The hard part, friends, is the *persistent focus*. It is no longer a matter of "taking one good step" or "doing one good deed" once annually as a follow-up to a New Year's resolution. I recommend that *each year, for the next* 10 *years,* each of us add *two* new steps such as those above.

Lifting a species by its bootstraps is a sport for trained athletes, not weekend warriors.

I hope that one or more of the suggestions in this chapter appeals to you. My goal is to communicate the great variety of ways in which we can and will help *Homo sapiens* to make the transition upward, in as healthy a manner as possible — and that it can be fun along the way. The steps are not "magical" or other-worldly. They make common sense and, at the same time, they expand our senses into the farther reaches. That is where we are going to live in the new epoch that is dawning — in the ordinariness of *daily life* and the *farther reaches* of a divine species.

Chapter 24

The First Year

During the first year after reading this book, you may want to do a conscientious life review. You might reflect on what you've been attempting to do or reach since the decade started, and how has that been going for you? We are already approaching the mid-point of the decade in another year. A lot has happened, for your family and for the world. It's time to look around, and possibly bring some of the insights you've gained into a renewal of life direction. This chapter considers briefly a couple of areas that you may find pertinent in charting your own course through the next twelve months.

Religions in the Time of Homo deva

I suggest that in your reflections during the next year, you devote some time to considering how our religious institutions can nurture the spiritual pulse that is increasingly reaching humanity. There is much opportunity here for institutional renewal and refocusing of the mission of these human-divine organizations. As *Homo sapiens* transitions to *Homo deva* over the next years, what is the ideal use of local spiritual communities, and the best way to incorporate traditional religious institutions into such a future? Where do you see the greatest pockets of resistance to such a transformation? You might wish to discuss this with a friend who grew up in the same faith tradition as you. Then, on a different day, discuss this with a friend who grew up in a different faith tradition.

As a starting point, consider the thoughts of Matthew Fox, an Episcopal priest and founder of the University of Creation Spirituality in Oakland, California. One idea that I found particularly useful in his recent text, *One River, Many Wells*, is this: The practice of wisdom traditions needs a bias in favor of what we have in common. As simple as that. A bias to look at our commonalities, and to let each voice speak for themselves. That seems like a very good beginning.

A very long list of human experiences first elicited the religious impulses in our species over 30,000 years ago. Now we are crossing a major threshold, and it is time to revivify our link to the source. That is what the *fusion* of human lifethread and consciousness thread is all about. We are fusing the meanings that we create for our lives, and the purpose we ascribe to daily existence. That fusion brings our wavelength and our amplitude all the way into alignment, as *space approaches infinity*; and it expands our mindheart frequency all the way, as *time approaches eternity*. The mathematical solution of such a transformation includes all things, life itself made manifest. We will all be able to see more implications of this within the next couple of years.

My own view is that humanity is on the brink of truly understanding, as a species, that our link to the Creator is as close as our next breath. That is the gift that *Homo deva*—through you, me, and in all of us—will bring to Earth's children. How could you contribute to this understanding in the next year?

A New Mythology for a New Species

As we begin traversing the territory between today and that larger transformation, we need new myths. The new myths will, by their nature, be birthed within a deep ecumenism. The favorite myths of all cultures are those that heal and save the wounded people, that offer hope and solace to the frightened and hungry children, the lonely heroes, and the forgotten little ones. We need new myths—in song and dance as well as verbal and written language. Myths, like religion, challenge us to lift out of the unexamined life and make new goals for ourselves—sometimes irrational goals, like loving our enemies, or liberating all sentient beings. Although religions as we know them at the dawn of the 21st century are often practiced at low amplitudes, I maintain that religions and myths are crucial for the transition we are now facing. They help keep us awake at many moments when we would otherwise tend to fall asleep. With 7.2 billion human beings, as of 2015, struggling to see what this threshold is about, we need many new stories in order to help people see the transition in language and colors and voice and movement that make sense for them. Does any of this strike a creative spark in you for the coming year?

～

Exploring New Wisdom Sources

A third area that I suggest you ponder during the coming year is where you look for wisdom. Most of us, even with much training and practice, tend to get into a rut and go to the same sources. I would recommend that you start with the Resources list at the back of this volume, and select two authors whose work you have never read. Perhaps one of their titles attracts you, or perhaps you have heard their name mentioned by a friend or teacher. It is a good opportunity, as you begin to ground some of these insights about a new species into your life, to broaden your receptive lens—to open the aperture of your mind as wide as possible, and welcome the input from your species' collective wisdom. It is out there, waiting for you to approach. Select two books from authors that are new to you, and read them.

For instance, if you are familiar with meditation but have never owned a business, check out Roach, *The Diamond Cutter*. If your background is in liberal arts and you've never studied anthropology, I imagine you would enjoy Arsuaga's *The Neanderthal's Necklace*. If your mind tends toward the logical and technological, perhaps Burke and Ornstein's *The Axemaker's Gift* will be an eye-opener for you. And if your cultural niche has been relatively fixed by your family upbringing and mainstream schools, now is a good time to get acquainted with LaDuke, *All Our Relations*.

By widening the lens of where we look for wisdom, of whom we identify with, of whom we include in our caring and organizing for the future, we contribute directly to the successful transition of many peoples.

If This were Your Last Year ...

Start with the scenario: Your physician has gently informed you that you have only a couple of years to live. Your general health is okay for moving around. Perhaps, with all the macro changes going on, it's a good opportunity to look at your own plans. What would you like to do next? Are there areas that you would like to explore as you practice life at the edge? For instance, might this new perspective give you ideas about people you would like to visit, or family outings you would like to plan? Consider the priority concerns in your community in the fields of social justice, literacy, the arts. Would you like to get involved in local projects or join an ecumenical faith group? Whom would you like to visit in these critical next couple of years, before embarking on the physical version of our *great transition*? Would you choose to travel and see more of the world? Or perhaps your priority is to have time with close friends.

Please note that when I refer to a great transition for our species, I do not at all mean a transition where groups of people suddenly disappear, as in the scenarios predicted by certain fundamentalist groups and authors. I respect those individuals' right to their view; after all, we live in the greatest democracy on Earth, and we defend each other's right to our own opinions. And I trust that those authors are honest and sincere in their beliefs; in fact, I believe that we are all sensing the same major transition approaching. However, what I hope has been clear from the preceding chapters is that I am describing an evolutionary, bio-psycho-spiritual transition that will occur for thousands and eventually millions of people, right here on *terra firma*. There will still be schools and the mail will be delivered after *Homo devas* have emerged by 2020. This will not mean a complete restructuring of society. *Homo devas* will have Social

Security numbers (or their equivalent in other nations); they will need to learn to read and write and will buy groceries, just like you and me. But if you look forward a couple of decades, you will see that our current identity will have passed over, moved on, evolved into something new.

Journal Writing for Our Future Self

Here is a corollary idea about the new identity that is sometimes difficult to touch: Are there positive parts of you that you haven't ever let your friends see? A fondness for poetry, perhaps, or a gift for woodwork, an inner concern or longing that you have carried alone and not shared. We all have threads of deep creativity that are part of our inheritance. Each of those threads needs to be celebrated and made visible as part of who we are, as part of our own high dreams. You might consider in the next year doing some journaling about the shift to *Homo deva*, perhaps dialoguing with the future self that wants to embody aspects of the new species through you and your family.

~

Local and Regional Groups

My next suggestion for the coming year is that you attend a meeting of a local or regional group with the specific purpose of meeting more early *Homo devas!* You might be surprised to find one of your neighbors at the meeting. If you aren't sure where to start, look over the list of *Homo sapiens* Associations in Appendix 6. The list includes national and international groups, but many of them will have local affiliates that can be located in your phone directory or online. Your local library also has a wonderful reference called the *Encyclopedia of Associations: National Organizations* (published by the Gale Research Company), which you might wish to peruse for inspiration.

Once you have selected a group that fits your interests and gifts, take the next step and attend a meeting. The goal here, again, is to stretch your identity and express the passion for bonding and networking that humans have in such abundance. Whether the association is based on a common interest, a mission of bringing a specific change, or expressing caring for a particular community group or family, the act of will to join one of these groups is a wonderful step. I believe that you will enjoy such linking together in our larger family.

~

You and I and all of our extended network need a willingness to face the *greater unknown* in these next few years. No one knows for sure what shape we will be in by the year 2030. We truly don't know what the future will be like in its specifics.

What we do know, with full certainty, is that evolution is a win-win for those who care for each other and who look ahead. Make creative caring and planning twin themes for this next year. Look for ways that you can expand your ability to create your life, to express your creativity—even as you do what is needed to support yourself and your family. In this chapter I have suggested a wide array of activities, each of which can be a doorway to greater hope and wholeness. Reflecting on the role of religions in an era of *Homo deva*, looking at how you can co-create some new myths for the human journey, exploring diverse wisdom sources, pondering on what would be meaningful to you if this year were to be your last in this life, journal writing with your future self, and visiting a meeting of a local or regional group whose mission blends with yours—all these are seeds. Some of the texts in the Resources list may offer other useful ideas. I recommend that you choose the ones that evoke a welcoming sigh around your heart or a sparkle in your eye. Then water those particular seeds, and enjoy watching them grow.

~

Chapter 25

THE NEXT DECADE: 2015–2025

Throughout the next decade, cherish your friends. We are moving through this giant transition together. No human being walks alone across the threshold to a new species or into the next kingdom! We are a core team of thousands, rapidly becoming millions. No one is walking alone, although that unfortunately is the visceral experience for many people at this time. By affirming our ties of love, friendship, trust, and guidance, we help each other and help the larger whole of Earth's throat to incarnate through our lives.

I believe that there will be a psychological event horizon that we must cross together—namely, the fear of death at the species level. Facing the (potential) end of existence and defusing its terror, once and for all, is a task of the next decade. It won't necessarily come in the form of physical warfare, although that tragedy will continue for a while. Here is one issue that I see as important and, in several ways, critical in the next decade:

Spirit and Matter in Nutritional Health

We in the United States must sooner or later face a glaring health and developmental issue: our national habit of overeating. We have the greatest proportion of chronic overeating and intake-obesity (in contrast to obesity caused by genetic or metabolic disorders) in the world. During the next decade, we need to look diligently at ways to help our families, friends, and ourselves to replace the habit of overeating in terms of both quantity and content.

As we discussed in our examination of the four terrible A's (see chapter 7), obesity and overeating are partly a function of our outmoded physiology, and partly a function of our emotional desire nature becoming addicted (with massive reinforcement from cultural advertising and role modeling). We eat whenever food is available because our brains are hard-wired from 100,000 years ago to prevent starvation, and because the TV messages of the past 50 years have been saying we should. But in the United States at least, food is plentiful, the risk of outright starvation is slight, and our hard-wired impulse to eat actually works against us. On the frontier of emotional-to-physical interface, hundreds of thousands of young people, mostly women, are suffering. For young women in the United States at the beginning of the 21st century, the epidemic increase in anorexia and bulimia is a critical issue—both in terms of health and of their relationship to themselves. A reorientation is clearly needed.

But to welcome that reorientation, we need to look beyond our physiology to the cultural messages that we give teenagers and young people—and that connects directly to our species identity. In my view as a health educator and psychologist, many people's craving for the physical intake of food, and especially for sweets, is being intensified by the craving for *life-juice*, the electromagnetic voltage that is accessed precisely at the level of identity. When people are starving for a sense of "self," they stuff themselves with metabolic sugars as a surrogate for an open link along the lifethread to the level of identity. As long as the lifethread (with very high frequency wave patterns) is blocked, these people have to seek vitality through such lower versions as sugars, alcohol, or other substances (which substitute a temporary "high" of wavelength wave pattern rather than frequency).

Perhaps you have noticed in preceding chapters that I did not discuss directly some of the gender issues that have been paramount in our cultural passage of the past two decades. Here, I want to emphasize that a prime reason that young women are having difficulty with overeating and eating disorders is because of the outmoded image of the "feminine" that many of them still hear from family or local role models. There is a wealth of research and popular literature about the divine feminine aspect. Exploring that topic would take us too far afield from the core concept of the new species. However, in regard to the viability of all of us, getting a better grip on how to nurture our teenagers is near the top of the priority list.

I would highly recommend that some of the feminist-oriented organizations take on the issue of eating disorders as a project, to sponsor research and provide one-on-one support to girls and young women who are caught in this culturally driven addiction. That would be a tremendous investment in our future and in the collective healing of our culture's split about health, the feminine, and beauty.

Let me state this in other words to help clarify why I believe the illnesses related to food are a microcosm of many issues we have to face before we can reach the other side of the transition. As the species transition "heats up," the mental fuel we are using has to come from somewhere. The combined mental field of 7.2 billion people, as of 2015, is steadily lifting in vibration; our physical bodies have to receive a raised vibration also, or there is a wrenching in the system. If our energy link to the planetary level (either through nature or self-image as part of the divine) is 99.99 percent blocked (see chapters 7 and 8), then our physical personalities must look elsewhere to get that same "octane" of fuel in order to keep moving at an accelerating pace. Otherwise, there is a real experience, on mental levels, of imploding and starving to death.

You might reflect for a moment about the teenagers who are ingesting lunches of junk food from the vending machines that have replaced cafeterias at many high schools. Not just at lunch, but starting at 7:00 in the morning. Their bodies are highly dependent on the low-octane sugars to get a boost of energy to get through the day. Part of it is physiological dependency; part is emotional addiction; part is mental implosion of their focal length to focus on what is expected of them, because many of them are early *Homo deva* and are receiving greater mental (amplitude) stimulation than they are consciously aware of! Some of them may appear sullen and geared toward "getting through the day," but from a higher perspective these same kids are battling at the forefront of our species' mental growth and development—often without support or tools to handle the massive inflow of energy. They are the true warriors in the trenches, ingesting all the toxicities that our culture's shadow can throw at them, and still persisting in moving forward, often with youthful enthusiasm.

The magnetic attraction of our bodies is getting pulled *down* to the sugars, when we really need to be moving *upward* to access the same atomic velocity. As a very practical and controversial example, the current debate about removing soft drink vending machines from junior high schools relates directly to this issue. Remember our discussion in an earlier chapter about the escape velocity that is needed to get out of the energy-sink of a black hole? That applies to our teenagers' obesity problem and their physiological addictions to junk foods. The electromagnetic reorientation to a positive addiction is a difficult step, but it is absolutely crucial in order for our physical bodies to "travel with us" into the next kingdom. Ponder that last sentence from a scientific angle, then from a mystical / religious angle. Homework: Think about it for 60 seconds the next time you stare at a soft drink can at the local deli during your lunch break.

In the model I am presenting, the *Homo devas* bring greatly enhanced frequency, or "speed," to the mental functioning of our species. The most effective way to achieve that frequency is from the *top down*; that way, it precipitates as an expression of who we are (identity), doesn't have rapid fluctuations because we are mentally choosing it (intention), and can be generously shared with other people. On the days when we rely significantly on energy from fast food to get through the day, we are achieving a short-term mental acceleration from the *bottom up*. It is not intrinsically "bad," it is just terribly inefficient as a fuel, made glamorous and seductive through marketing, is quite addictive, and entropic. Ultimately, leads to early death.

The topic of spiritual dimensions underlying physical health will be one of considerable research during the next decade. The 180-degree reorientation from materialistic culture to spirit-identified culture will happen, and it will include a shift in our perspective toward food. That much is certain. The excellent work by John Robbins (2001) and others is facilitating this educational shift. Our bodies will learn to open to nourishment that comes from planetary wholeness, as the full inflow from Earth's throat streams into humanity's mental field by 2020. The question is, Do we enter into this reorientation as a voluntary choice, with graduated changes in improved health habits, or will we be yanked into it by sudden, physical crises on a huge scale? How many of our citizens will reorient before the heart attacks, the onset of diabetes, and other health crises? How many will wait until after they have been struck?

All diseases related to nutrition have increased sharply in the past decade, especially in the United States but worldwide as well. To adapt a phrase from our religious-oriented friends, it is true to say that at this moment in history, "the devil is in the sugars." I recommend that you raise the priority-rank of your own family's food habits by a big notch, and look at what you may want to change. Then, look further at what you *choose* to change. Finally, look at what you *are* changing. If you're not sure where to start, look at some of the many excellent books about the more wholesome approaches to food and general health. You may want to browse in that section of the bookstore or library sometime soon.

Another way to view this general idea is to state that the physical-identity of our culture needs to go through the same 180-degree shift. It is a reorientation to the *life fire* rather than the dense, physical *fire of matter*. And through the unfolding coherence of that higher fire and its radiating outward through our lives, more healthy food and exercise choices will be a natural consequence. Once you make one positive choice in this area, the next one, and then the next and the next come more easily. This is a vibrant example of building positive addiction, shifting those arrows in the "terrible A's" diagram to point upward instead of downward.

Health education in the new epoch will involve a widespread recognition of spirituality as a health practice. From a lived experience of unity, people will be able to work more closely *with* their health care practitioners, providing important clues and information about their own bodies, and giving their own insights about disease prevention and treatment. In the very hopeful scenarios, a majority of our fellow humans will be able to develop an experiential link to their own intuitive body wisdom. This kind of link utilizes traditional faith and goes beyond it — to provide direct knowledge of the energy patterns underlying reality (e.g., see Borysenko, 1999; Myss, 1996). Such *vulnerable knowing* will not strip the higher realms of mystery. It will bring the mystery closer as a source of healing and health.

~

Patience for the Long Term

In the next decade, we will take some steps forward and a few steps back. All the steps will eventually lead us upward to the full incarnation of the next species. Evolution is too large a wave to be stopped or even appreciably delayed. Yet we will need patience in this decade, as well as focused determination. As the third phase of *Homo deva* , the lifeseeds, begin to be visibly recognized and accepted (probably by 2020), the transition will enter a steady-state of growth and creativity. The mental acceptance by a critical mass of people will come even sooner. That is when the deeper healing can occur.

The following list includes some rough notes on both the worst and best scenarios for the next decade. These are preliminary. Such notes are a way of making our dreams visible, both the nightmares and the *high dreams.* You can add elements from your own experience and study.

2015 – 2025: Worst Scenarios
- Population pressures bring water wars.
- Biodiversity plummets, with resulting climate effects.
- Biological and cyber-terrorism occurs on several fronts.
- Regional human conflicts escalate.
- Rogue government(s) test and utilize nuclear weapons.

• Sub-Saharan Africa, Russia, and other regions slide into financial and social chaos with over 25 percent of their populations symptomatic with AIDS.

• "Random" domestic violence escalates, especially against women and children.

• Others (you fill in the blank): _____

Spend a little time reflecting on specific changes that would come in the world culture and in your community if even some of these scenarios came to pass. We need to get very specific here, in order to recognize what we have been avoiding, denying, or just plain missing.

What would happen to the global economy if AIDS brought regional economies to a standstill? How would this affect your work? Your community? How would your region respond to severe, ongoing water shortages? To a sizeable increase in global temperature? What if all of these things happened within a few years?

Stating Our Path Clearly

It would help if we could, over the next decade, clarify our intention or vision of where we are going. *Our intention, as a whole species,* is chaotic right now. We don't really know what we want. Do we want, above all, for everyone to have [at least] a middle-class "quality of life"? Do we truly wish for every one of the 200 million adult persons in the United States to own a cell phone? Do we truly wish for every family in China (all 1.2 billion people) to have a refrigerator? For every person among the 7.2 billion, as of 2015, now on Earth to live to 80 or 90 years? The social and psychological implications are staggering, let alone the financial and ecological.

Until we look at questions like these rationally and compassionately (with reason and passion together), we won't solve the issues. And if we continue to stay in fuzzy-land about our intentions, the dark dragons of fear, greed, hate, envy, doubt, and fission-paralysis will have a field day.

To help clarify our intentions, it helps to think about the best possible outcomes. Here are a few notes on possible "best scenarios," for your consideration:

2015 – 2025: Best Scenarios

- At the city council and county supervisor levels, local leaders emerge with "seventh-generation" wisdom and a willingness to sacrifice personal ambition to clear the path.
- Teachers regain a sense of mission: to help young people at all levels to maintain focus and sense of direction.
- Students at the high school level energize their school's sense of mission and purpose, with new forms of social media.
- Medical and chemical advances accelerate, as the seeding of innovation through greater coherence of mind catalyzes significant changes in these fields.
- Businesses wake up and embrace green economy policies as an efficient return on investment and to make crucial contribution as corporate citizens.
- Thousands of those persons identified in Ray and Anderson's (2000) survey data decide to take leadership roles in their local communities and to network with others for a better future.
- Others (you fill in the blank): _____

Which of the steps outlined above would you like to participate in? There is a sign-up sheet by your kitchen table.

The next decade will bring some unexpected challenges for all of us. One way to manage the unknown is to become familiar with the potential extremes, the high-risk and low-risk scenarios, and who will be the decision makers in the various scenarios. Here is an exercise in stretching the mental horizon:

Which of the following groups, in your view, might be first to adopt a task force to examine how the emergence of *Homo deva* will affect their mission and their profession? In your opinion, which group needs the concept the most, and why?

American Psychiatric Association
National Academy of Sciences
Association of Hospital Administrators

Congress of U.S. Catholic Bishops
Mortgage Bankers Association
National Football League
Juvenile Court Judges
League of Large-City Mayors

- Today, the day you are reading this book, over 50,000 children under age five died of malnutrition on this planet. Tomorrow, the same number will die. And the same the day after.... That is just one disease. We have plenty of work to do in order to bring Epoch III (Keck) or a sustainable planetary lifestyle (Quinn) to our governments, corporate leaders, and communities.

- Take as a strong hunch that most people reading this book are an early-phase *Homo deva*. There is already a cohort of 50 million in the U.S. and 300 million worldwide who subscribe to the creative phase values of *Homo deva*; soon there will be an even more vigorous group of at least 10 million innovators who can serve as teachers, mentors, and colleagues for you. The species transformation is radiating out, disseminating and cross-fertilizing new ideas, new levels of dedication, new innovations, and new energy. There is no force organized enough or of sufficient scope to stop this tide. The good guys are getting organized and learning that they can trust each other.

- The evolutionary wave of Earth's throat is greater and more powerful than any 10, or any 1,000, or 1 million, or 1 billion people. We are each part of a blossoming that is happening—whether we feel ready or not, whether we see the horizon clearly or not. It is happening in spite of our own limitations. It is unfolding in spite of our own fear of the divine, our repression of the sublime, and our habit of hiding our light under a bushel-basket! Therefore, feel free to ask for help—from friends and colleagues and from the future / above. And feel free to practice voicing your own light and love and power with friends. Look for opportunities to co-create a positive tomorrow with your friends, neighbors, and new colleagues you will meet in the days and months ahead. Keep your bifocal vision open, for the daily path and the long-term future—and see what happens. We have nothing to lose but our self-doubt.

• In order to share some compassion with a group that doesn't often receive any, here is a gentle note about the "public eye." Be aware in the next decade that the species transition will bring unexpected pressures on those people who live and move in the public eye. The most rigid and nonresponsive members of *Homo sapiens* are often those in the public eye—people like celebrities and politicians, famous athletes, and corporate honchos who must face the camera, the microphone, the crowd on a regular basis. Please notice that this statement is one of compassionate observation, not judgment. Persons in the public eye didn't start out that way. Individuals who enter the maelstrom's eye are forced to use *equal and sufficient force* on both the emotional and mental levels (and sometimes on physical levels, with bodyguards) to push back the tremendous waves coming toward them, and to avoid being crushed and ripped apart. Their personal lives are invaded and savaged. They push back to survive, in order to avoid being shattered / swallowed by the fear, hate and envy, doubt and greed of the mass. In other words, they are pushing against the dark dragons of the rest of us. They are serving as local avatars, to help in a small way to dissipate and defuse the dragons from our collective psyche that attempt to swallow humanity.

Those of us beyond the glare of the public eye, out here in anonymous-land, are pushing against those in the public eye because we sense that they stand between us and . . . and what? Between us and the fruit of our desire? Between us and the *source of energy*? Between us and the immortality-flavor-of-the-week? Between us and the "five minutes of fame" that promises to release us from a baleful life and to restore the beauty that some ogre stole from us at birth?

Think again about the myths we live by. Review some of the diagrams in this book, and think carefully about any resentment or envy you might bear toward someone in the public domain; we have all had those moments. Do you still think that those in the public eye are closer to the source of energy than you are? Where is the divinity, the *life-juice*, that millions of people search for so desperately? Is it really on MTV? Take a slow breath, and remember that the membrane between us-and-them is dissolving. The dark membrane of our fears was only a barrier to our birth, a barrier that blocked the birth canal until the time was right. Humanity is waking up. Life is here, and we are it. It is time for the throat of our planet to sing. People's hearts will recognize the voice of the future, and will know the lifethread is opening.

Right now, at this moment, what would you recommend to young teenagers who are exploring their creativity, many of whom probably have *Homo deva* sensitivities and who express a wish to go into politics? Or into public service as a local schoolteacher, county employee, police officer? Ponder the meaning of "public service" in the era of divine-humans. During the transition into an era of human-spirit hybrids, there is a great need for continuity and stability, a place to find reassurance in the midst of tremendous change. We need the steady creation of continuity along with the speedy changes. You, and your children and friends, will be part of holding the field steady, as well as bringing your own seeds of transformation.

What would you recommend to teenagers who express a wish to become an artist in the next decade? To those who express a wish to get an MBA degree and start their own business? It is helpful to clarify your own assumptions about the nature of "creativity" and "divinity" and what they look like, and don't look like. There will be many types of creative acts through the birthing of *Homo deva*. There will be many personal and unique paths along the journey to a unified humanity.

∾

Decade of Destiny

It is time to say farewell for now. We have covered a lot. Remember that evolution grows one day at a time, just like you. Know that 50 million people (at least) are working with you and walking with you on the next step—this week, this month, this year, during this decade of destiny.

I hope that the concept of *Homo deva* opens some inner doorways for you. If you are feeling the inner nudge to "move on" to the next big step, know that the message of this book was written with you in mind, whatever your background, age, ethnicity, gender, nationality, occupation, or favorite foods. The work of healing our Earth family needs you. Humanity now needs to grow up fast, and growth spurts are often painful. What we are going to need in the coming decade goes far beyond political persuasion. We need widespread, grassroots courage to talk the talk, walk the walk, and make many small and some big changes with the breath of our daily lives.

Here is one of the central truths that will liberate new energy for our unique and diverse purposes in more than 200 nations during the next decade:

Hundreds and thousands and millions of voices are being raised about a more hopeful Future. Together, we are the unified voice of that Future. We are each an integral part of the throat of Earth, our voices rising to make our message heard. We will no longer be silent and passive about what we see and who we are. The song of Earth rising is being sung in our house, our family, our community, this day, now and forevermore.

There will inevitably be moments when you waver, when you want to go hide in your neighborhood fast-food restaurant until the decade is over. Please don't succumb to that impulse. And when you do fall in a ditch, so to speak, don't waste time kicking yourself. Breathe each day in kindness.

Take a little time now to browse through the appendices, and then start the future with your covenant for the sacred half hour.

Let the Earth breathe through you, let the sky kiss the top of your head, reminding you *how much help we have*. Take a steady breath, and know that you are a beloved part of the best family that has ever been.

∽

APPENDICES

To me, freedom of speech
Represents the very dignity of
What a human being is.
That's what marks us off from
The stones and the stars . . . as
Just below the angels.

Berkeley, 1964
Mario Savio (1943–1996)

Engraved on wall of the Free Speech Café,
University of California, Berkeley

OUR FAMILY: DEFINITION OF HOMINIDS

Family
Genus (pl: *genera*)
Species

[Family] HOMINID
Any of the modern or extinct bipedal primates of the family Hominidae, including all species of the genera *Homo* and *Australopithecus*. (*Random House Dictionary*)

[Genus] *Australopithecus*
Multiple (four to seven) early hominid species; all of them were in Africa. These species had a primate-size brain, smaller than the later genus *Homo*, and a leg size intermediate between chimp and human. Height ranged from 3 feet to 5 feet. Examples of species in this genus: *A. afarensis* (the famous "Lucy"), *A. africanus*, *A. robustus*, *A. boisei*.

[Genus] *Homo* "Large brain and uses tools"
Genus of bipedal primates that includes modern humans and several extinct forms, with large brain and use of tools.
  a) member of the genus *Homo*.
  b) the species *Homo sapiens* or one of its members (Latin *humanus*).

[Species]
Homo habilis ("habilis" from Latin: "adaptable"), 2 million years ago
First appeared in eastern Africa.

Homo erectus (e.g., "Java Man"), 1.6 million years ago
First species to use fire; distributed in Africa, Asia, Europe.

Homo neanderthalensis.
Species that reached Europe from Africa and the Near East about
400,000 years ago. [Following Klein (2002), I consider it a distinct
species from *H. sapiens.*]
By 30,000 years ago, they were extinct.

Homo sapiens ("sapiens" from Latin: "rational")
1. Species of bipedal primates to which modern humans belong, with
brain capacity averaging 1400 cc (85 cu. inches), dependence upon
language, and creation and utilization of complex tools, including permanent shelters.
2. Humankind.

Homo sapiens sapiens.
Subspecies of the genus Homo in which modern humans are classi-
fied. One branch of the subspecies was the anatomically modern people
who are popularly known as Cro-Magnon. The Cro-Magnons were early
Homo sapiens who migrated from Africa to the Near East and then to
Europe. They replaced the less adaptable species *Homo neanderthalensis*
over a relatively short time (before the last ice age in Europe of 20,000
years ago). All this was prior to the first humans arriving in the Americas
about 12,000 years ago.

For thoughtful discussion of the transition to our modern species, I
particularly recommend Richard Klein, *The Dawn of Human Culture*
(2002), Leakey and Lewin, *The Sixth Extinction* (1995), and Arsuaga,
The Neanderthal's Necklace (2002).

Berkeley City Council: Two *What-if* Scenarios

Scene One: The Past

Berkeley City Council
Year: 3 million years ago
Meeting Notes (inscribed on ostrich eggshell) *

you and you and you and you and you ... Each you has to gather more berries. And hunt more run-and-squawk. After you eat, the extra goes to Lucy and her cubs. She can't run as fast. Her legs are thicker. She can't skin the meat as close. Her fingers are slow. No one will run ahead until all you's are running together. No one will eat if some you's are being hungry. This is the great thunder plan.

"Lucy" is the name given by researchers to the ancient hominid whose skeleton was found in Ethiopia in 1974 and dated at 3.5 million years ago. Lucy and her kin have the scientific name *Australopithecus afarensis.* This means that they were on the big branch (genus) of the hominid tree right before the genus *homo,* the branch that we are on. The species to which Lucy belonged was extinct by about 2 million years ago. They could not run or hunt as efficiently as the newcomers, *Homo habilis.*

Lucy's species is an important intermediate step of development between prechimps and prehumans. Tim White, an anthropologist from U.C. Berkeley and one of the scientists who found Lucy's skeleton, once remarked on the unusual hybrid nature of the skeletons of Lucy's tribe: "From the neck up they are extraordinarily primitive, and from the neck down they are just as extraordinarily modern" (Lewin, 1988, p. 59).

Lucy was 3'8" tall, with a small early primate brain and large canine teeth. She had long legs for bipedal walking and a wide pelvic bone structure to distribute the weight of the upper body in upright posture. It is clear from the fossils of several dozen individuals found at the same archaeological site that walking upright came first, and the bigger brain of prehumans evolved later, beginning about 2 million years ago. Lucy and her peers of 3 million years ago walked like us but could not think as we do.

As a very early hominid (standing upright species), Lucy and the other members of *A. afarensis* were predecessors to *Homo habilis* and *Homo erectus. Homo habilis* were the first anatomically modern humans, appearing about 2 million years ago. They had evolved smaller canine teeth, a flattened face, and a larger brain. They were the first species in the human genus, our earliest human cousins.

Members of *Homo erectus* followed, about 1.6 million years ago. They were the first to migrate out of Africa and the first to use fire. Their brains were significantly larger than their *Homo habilis* kin. The gradual and steady migration led this first wave of hominid long-distance travelers to spread out across the continents of Africa and the Middle East, then to Asia, and eventually Europe.

This brief recap of our ancestors' journey was compiled from work by several researchers, including Arsuaga, 2002; Diamond, 1992; Klein, 2002; Lewin, 1988; and Tattersall, 1998. For a delightful young people's introduction to the story of "Lucy," I highly recommend Pieg, 1996.

---

* There is clearly some narrative license in this account of Council Meeting notes, in two respects: Written language did not appear for several million years after Lucy's era and, secondly, hominids did not reach North America until about 12,000 years ago. We imagine, of course, that if language had in fact appeared by then, Berkeley would have been an active site of hominid speech and other activity.

Scene Two: The Future

Berkeley City Council
Year: 2024
Meeting Notes (inscribed on laser dot)

All Citizens, whether domiciled in or conducting business licensed by the City, shall contribute three percent (3%) of annual gross income or revenue, whichever is greater, for the operating budget of BAMHS (Benevolent Association for Maintenance of *Homo sapiens*).

This financial obligation is neither a tax nor a tithe. It is a duly designated Local Action that expresses the will of the Noble Global Whole, inasmuch as the pure strain of *H. sapiens* is in grave peril of dying out. BAMHS is the truly humanitarian way to help this difficult transition.

As a self-governing and self-emergent body, this Council cannot countenance the ineptitude and ingratitude of federal or international bodies to permit the lineage of our collective great-grandparents to go the way of the dodo or the renowned Lucy.

This Local Action shall continue in effect until the year 2100 or until there is no one left to administer it, whichever comes first.

Whether organizations such as BAMHS will, in actual fact, be needed depends on the individual choices of thousands and thousands of persons in the next decade. Notice that I did say thousands of persons, not millions. The future of the human race depends on a relatively small number of people because of the quantum-energy effects of a critical mass of change agents. As people continue to gravitate upward to an *identification with humanity as a whole*, the cultural resistance to Earth / humanity concerns will dissolve quite naturally and steadily. The resistance is now concentrated in the *Homo sapiens* preconsciousness, in a chronic level of fear about the unknown and about loss of control. Most of our fellow humans don't see the abundance of energy that will become readily available as people shift from "scarcity thinking" to the "abundance thinking" of unified field (e.g., see Badiner, 2002; Keck, 1992; Quinn, 1999; Satori, 1999). Once this primordial fear is faced directly on a species level, much greater life energy will flow, and often in surprisingly synchronous ways.

Whether *Homo sapiens* can "run or hunt as efficiently" is no longer the criterion of survival, as it was with Lucy 3 million years ago, and later with the Neanderthals 40,000 years ago. A major criterion of survival in the 21st century will be full physical *trust*, sufficient basic identification or empathy with other humans (*other-as-self*), and with the planet (*self-as-all*) such that people will not lash out at newcomers whom they perceive in some ways as more powerful. The newcomer species is highly permeable and sentient to our emotions and beliefs—both positive and negative - and in their "vulnerable knowing" they fully sense our fears. Right now, most of the young newcomers emerging among us are absorbing those fears as their own (and, as we discussed in earlier chapters, many of them are becoming ill as a result). They don't yet realize who they are and how to differentiate individual fears from the collective. They are intimately "hard-wired" to the vibrations at the species and planet levels. *Homo sapiens'* macro level is *Homo devas'* micro level. This is the gift and the challenge of our welcoming the growth of the future within our own households, local schools, and communities.

What are the best steps to help *Homo sapiens* en masse and as families to recognize, accept, and welcome the presence of a new species—a species that has more coherent brain, great wisdom and compassion, unprecedented creativity, and literally inconceivable resources of energy? That is the core question.

You are part of the solution.

The *Homo sapiens* Hall of Fame

Nominations Wanted!

If there were to be a Hall of Fame for our species, as a celebration of *Homo sapiens* skills and achievements, who would be among the nominees? This is an excellent exercise for stretching the synapses in asking *Who are we?* and, even more interesting, *What makes us who we are?*

Two criteria were followed in generating the brief list shown below:

1. Persons on the list were nominated by several of my friends and co-workers when asked, "Name a couple of persons from any time in history whom you would choose to represent *Homo sapiens* at a hypothetical interplanetary conference." These are a few respected examples of our species over the past 3,000 years. I acknowledge that the list reflects the life perspective of the respondents' European roots in this nonrandom survey.

2. No one currently living was considered for the list.

Nominations for *Homo sapiens* Hall of Fame
(in chronological order)

Lao Tzu	William Shakespeare
Plato	Ben Franklin
Alexander the Great	Charles Darwin
Kublai Khan	Abe Lincoln
Ferdinand Magellan	Carl Jung
Leonardo da Vinci	Albert Schweitzer
Martin Luther	Carl Sagan

Now it is your turn. Whom would you nominate? Use this exercise as a chance to think *outside the box*.

Note: The absence of women from the above list is striking. This in itself can provoke some good and lively discussion! Try this question at your next party: Is a female *Homo sapiens* Hall-of-Famer an oxymoron?

Prime Pioneers: Gautama Buddha and Jesus of Nazareth

There is a reason that these two individuals were not added to the *Homo sapiens* Hall of Fame. We consider them on a different pathway, an *emerging wave*. (You may have noticed that evolutionary waves tend to overlap.) As the *Homo sapiens* wave entered its cultural expansion several thousand years ago, the lives and words of these two humans brought divine pulses of early *Homo deva*.

In other words, while living fully within the fourth kingdom, these two individuals grounded pulses of high-voltage brain organization from the fifth kingdom. And naturally, their advanced neurological organization (brain-heart-mind) produced potent messages that disseminated widely through human consciousness. They were early transmitters of the next major quantum step of bio-psycho-immunology. Or, to express the same thought in physics terms, they embodied a much greater coherence of laser-energy than the humans of their time. These two served to link Light and Love (analogous to amplitude and wavelength, respectively) from the *Homo deva* level down to the *Homo sapiens* level, so that their students of over two millennia ago could understand a little of what they were thinking and saying.

Very Early *Homo deva* Trailblazers

Gautama Buddha Prime pioneer of Phase 1 'brain fire' LIGHT
Jesus of Nazareth Prime pioneer of Phase 2 'heart fire' LOVE

More than 2,500 and 2,000 years ago, respectively, these two persons served as Teachers for us. They incarnated near the end of the larger period of approximately 40,000 years of growth and development for modern *Homo sapiens*. The beginning of that 40,000-year period has been called our cultural big bang, resulting in spoken language, sophisticated tools, and creative and healing arts. Several major waves of spiritual evolution can co-exist at the same time in history, and even during your own lifetime. As one wave starts to ebb, the next wave has already begun to flow in and disseminate. The *Homo deva* wave began over two millennia ago, and is now rapidly accelerating upward. Those who are stuck in the old habits of early *Homo sapiens* will experience increasing churning in their lives during this decade.

Both Buddha and Jesus said that humans will be able to see a much greater reality when we learn to look beyond the surface of things, and to link with all living beings *as self*. These two great teachers spoke directly about the scientific and metaphysical capacities that will blossom through humanity during the next era, the era of "peace on earth." Each of these teachers, from different perspectives, described the major threshold of the fifth kingdom that humanity is now in the final phase of approaching.

Recent trailblazers within our lifetime include people of science as well as those from faith traditions. You may have noticed that many astronauts from several nations, who have circumnavigated the world, have spoken eloquently upon their return about the beauty and fragility of the "home planet," and the importance of protecting and preserving our habitat for all of Earth's peoples. The expansion in their focus from primarily national priorities to embracing humanity and world identification is striking. Their work is helping us prepare for the great step of becoming a new biological species, a species that will introduce new ways of exploring the "neighborhood."

FIGURE 28. THREE PHASES OF FUSION REACTION

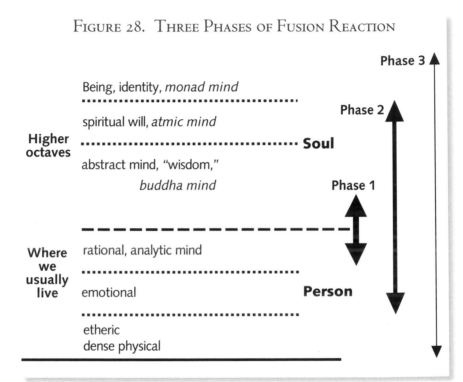

Figure 28 shows the relationship between the three phases of *Homo deva* emergence, and the corresponding fusion reactions at levels of mind / brain, spiritual will / personality, and spirit / matter.   For those readers with some background in the wisdom traditions, you may wish to study the chart with regard to the prime pioneers mentioned in this appendix, Buddha and Jesus. Here are two hypotheses that I offer as evocative seeds, and invite your discussion and reflection: 1) Abe Lincoln was a prime pioneer of the Phase 2 for *Homo deva*, with his leadership of the U.S. during a major spiritual crisis of the nation (see Appendix 4 for elaboration on this event). 2) Because each succeeding wave of prime pioneers takes the pulse of divine energy deeper into the body of humanity, the pioneers now alive are wielding mental / emotional / spiritual lasers of tremendous voltage. What needs to happen is a clear network of support by those thousands at Phase 2, in order to provide a "launching pad" for the Phase 3 individuals to emerge and become publicly effective rather than having the energy scattered inefficiently.

Our Nation, Our Self:
Spiritual Growth of the USA

Birth of USA

Considering the growth and development of the United States as a spiritual being could take us into an entire other volume of work. For now, I will sketch some themes that you may find make sense in your own experience. Notice in Figure 29 that the crisis of the 1770s was clearly the birth of our nation. The leaders of the thirteen colonies energized the focused emotional commitment and physical endurance of sufficient peoples, such that the physical integrity of a collective body was born: The colonists won a prolonged war that was driven by ideals of participatory democracy, individual freedom, and equality of opportunity. The battle to govern the physical territory was the crisis of Birth.

Baptism of USA

Ninety years later, in the 1860s, the Civil War period was the second major step in our nation's spiritual growth. At this second step, the populace faced its greatest split in the emotional life of the nation, through years of debate about self-determination and slavery, and then the crucible of four years of brother fighting brother. The nation's collective struggle entailed its people going through the agony of deepest wounds in the emotional body, which many of us still resonate with today. The battle to integrate the emotional life and govern it "as a union" is the spiritual crisis of Baptism. We as a nation went through that crisis, and emerged with re-dedication to the ideal that "government of the people, by the people, and for the people, shall not perish from the earth" (Abe Lincoln, Gettysburg Address).

Transfiguration of USA

In the 1960s, approximately ninety years after the dust settled from the Civil War, the third major step occurred, that of Transfiguration, involving much suffering and a burning through many of our nation's limitations and blindspots. During the 1960s decade and into the 1970s, the USA was forced to face the deepest splits in our mental body, the areas of mental pride—about race, gender, national origin, religious allegiance, economic station—that kept us fragmented and separate. Through the agony and ecstasy of that decade, we as a national whole took the third major step in spiritual growth. By diverse efforts in grassroots protests, civil disobedience, civil obedience to those leaders who shared our voice of conscience, anguished family conversations around dinner tables, and new identifications with our brothers and sisters in many states, we learned to utilize higher positive energy from the superconscious to integrate and then govern the analytic mind. We thereby moderated the core of mental pride and arrogance in our national character that had kept us caught in political rigidity, racism, sexism, and other isms. The soul values of inclusion, compassion, respect, and nurturance were steadily incorporated into millions of individual lives and into some of our institutions.

It is important to acknowledge, loud and clear, that our daily behaviors as a nation do not always match our high ideals. But through the burning ground of the 1960s, those ideals *precipitated deeper* than they had ever been before—into legal (and in some situations, social) expectations that guide our conduct and national self-image. What the fires of transfiguration have brought forth, through pain and sacrifice unto death in some cases, will not be undone. Evolution does not turn back. The subsequent three decades have seen steady growth of that inner fire in the core of our spine as a nation.

With great compassion and gratitude to my cohort who came of age in the 1960s, it is important to realize that we were not wrong or naïve to believe that we could change things for the better—that we could make a difference. The issue then was uplifting our nation from solar plexus to heart commitment. Fifty years later (a mere instant in planetary time), we are embroiled in the next major psychospiritual step. This is a sign of great progress, not of wasteland.

FIGURE 29. SPIRITUAL GROWTH OF THE USA

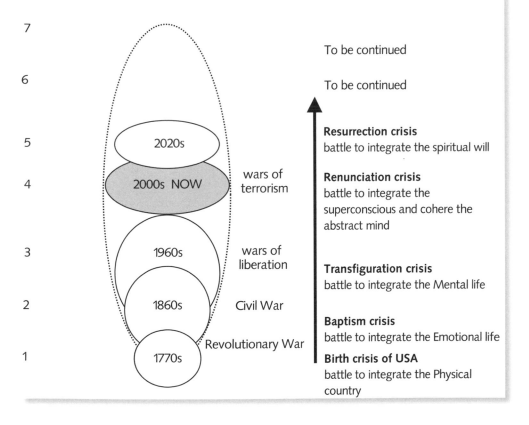

Dear brothers and sisters, exhausted ancient warriors all, we have been semi-convincing ourselves that we're trying to forget while actually trying to remember. Here is part of what we need to remember and remind each other: The flame of the 1960s was of transfiguration, and we did the job very, very well. The national leaders who embodied the knots of our collective solar plexus were sent packing. And we learned a lot about trusting our heart values; that's where the 44 million people that Ray and Anderson talked with in their survey have come from. The heart commitment is rising from a deep and grounded place in our beliefs and our daily lives.

Now, the flame is of renunciation, and we need to roll up our shirtsleeves and get dirty—whether that means participating in an organic gardening co-op, or mentoring young people who began life with a language other than English, or volunteering for committees of the local school board, or organizing a phone call-in (or e-mail campaign) to Congress about a controversial bill that is pending, or playing music for those people in your community who are in hospital or receiving hospice care.

To put it simply, the 1960s was a time to *talk the talk*. The huge pulse of Planetary Heart came through like a comet and our brains were on fire. It was the Phase 1 of *Homo deva* touching our individual and collective lives. The 1990s and into the 2000s is a time to *walk the walk*. That means doing more than zipping off a check to your favorite environmental or human rights organization. You know the difference. Let's do it. We are in Phase 2: The fire in our hearts wants to connect with the larger reason that our nation was born, and why we are here now when humanity needs us desperately.

For the record, the voices that say our efforts are hopeless, nihilistic, selfish, disorganized, retrograde, or sentimental reconstructionism have not met us in the full flower of 21st-century maturity and creative power. In addition, we are now joined by many new partners on the path, the young people who grew up in the 1970s and 1980s and who bring their incredible and unique innovative spirit to our mutual work (e.g., see O. Robbins & S. Solomon, 1994; Cohen, 2002).

Renunciation of USA

In the decade of the 2000s, we have entered the next major crisis, the next higher fire of USA's psychospiritual growth. The fourth great crisis is called Renunciation because there is a need to renounce what we know from the consensual reality, to let go of the *Homo sapiens* stance of "being in control." In response to growing pressures, we turn toward new sources of knowing; in a word, we ask for help. We choose as individuals and affiliated groups to be receptive at the superconscious level, and become an awake and intimate part of a greater spiritual force. We blend our daily lifework into a healing purpose such that our service or product or presence is governed by the direction of the greater whole. By becoming receptive to this governance by the higher level, we immediately gain velocity and momentum, because we are joining a larger stream of life energy; we have placed our boat in a fast-moving river. In religious terms, this has been described by different faith traditions as "surrender to divine will." In biological terms, the same crisis in environmental science now involves our letting go of human hubris and surrendering to the carrying capacity of the planet, which will indeed govern our future, literally, whether we like it or not.

The critical learning step in Renunciation is to traverse this crisis with the wisdom of head and heart both fully engaged. We don't relinquish our analytic mind or compassionate heart at the doorway! Both of them must come with us as integral parts of ourselves, our nation. If either head or heart is suppressed significantly, we risk falling into fanaticism or willingness to commit (or sanction or condone or legislate or even fund) violent acts. This occurs precisely because the velocity of the higher Will tends to spin any part that is not held in stable alignment into centrifugal motion. We currently bear witness, by the newspaper accounts of suicide bombers in several countries, to the tragic effects of the momentum of greater Will spinning small individual identities into violent action. These tragic effects are being produced by dedicated but warped versions of "obedience to divine will." The force of Renunciation is impacting all personalities, and they are reacting sometimes in extreme ways. Each of us, in our affiliated community groups, can learn to maintain the stability and integrity of our work, to balance the centrifugal effects of this tremendous force coming into our world culture, by linking head-and-heart upward to the source of our lives—however we each conceive of Creator, the life force, the force of evolution. The unified will of life itself comes through in the fourth great crisis, as the part dies to itself. Renunciation is about the "part" dying as a separate entity, and becoming at-one with the next greater "whole"; that is why this growth step has sometimes been called the crisis of crucifixion.

The USA as a psychospiritual being is learning (with visible resistance, on some issues) to lift upward and meld with the will of humanity, while retaining our national viewpoint and not sacrificing our distinct purpose and direction. This massive approach of unified will at the level of nation-and-species is causing deep waves of ambivalence, fear, turbulence, and retrenching of resistance points (e.g., think of the 90,000 lobbyists and 60,000 attorneys in Washington, DC alone; but only think of them in a calm, dispassionate, and forgiving way!). Every other nation that has relationships with the USA, and that includes most of the 200 countries, is resonating with this crisis. The full integration of mind-and-heart emerges through the *unified will of grace*, and that is the goal of Renunciation. *Thy Will be done*, on earth as heaven.

At this writing, the will of humanity as a whole is being expressed in quite varying degrees through 7.2 billion members, as of 2015, residing in over 200 political units called nations. How the USA relates to the greater whole of humanity by the year 2020 is the crux of this decade of destiny—in terms of social programs, humanitarian relief for refugees and oppressed groups, trade relations, healthcare policies toward other nations as well as our own children and elders, technological innovation and responses to piracy, immigration quotas, environmental priorities and conservancy projects, nuclear arms development and testing (or not), genetically engineered foods and import / export policies, the benefits and risks of nanotechnology. The list is extensive, and we clearly can't do it all in one decade. Remind yourself, when the path gets thick at times, that evolution / Creator knows what it's doing and has been moving one-day-at-a-time for billions of years. Yes, I agree that it would be fantastic to have a crystal ball, but we don't. Sigh. Renunciation is never easy.

The unified heart of humanity is alive and well; the unified mind of humanity is steadily emerging, in accelerated form since 1990 with the advent of the Web and Internet. The natural next step is to welcome the "unified will of the people," and nurture the integration of the USA as an integral part (and at times, as a natural pacemaker) of the world family. Being an integral part means serving neither as "policeman" nor as an automatic "universal donor" for any group or tribe or political party's agenda. As events in the past decade have shown, there are concerted forces that wish to block and / or derail the unified will of the people. We together—a critical mass of thousands, becoming a tsunami of millions—are going to move upward in our *daily dedication* to the children of Earth. We are going to hold steadily the circle of light, love, and creative power of Life birthing life. And by our steadfast focus we will dissolve those forces of separation, fear, and greed, and create a new chapter for the USA and our friends of many nations. Rather than a pyramid of power, we are going to energize a spiral of life-givers (see Appendix 6 and Resource list for names of some of the many groups already participating in this work).

In the next appendix, I consider in more depth the nature of the relationship between the USA and the whole of humanity.

THE UNITED STATES AND HUMANITY: 2000–2024
(written in 2002)

The United States is now entering an intense phase of its growth and development. The *unified field* of spiritual will is incarnating through the energy-field of the nation, and will eventually coalesce through scientific innovations such as practical fusion power. Each individual person, family, agency, organization, business, city, county, and state within the whole is reverberating to this great process of incarnation. The fourth major psychospiritual crisis, called *renunciation,* is both an exciting and distressing event on many levels. One result of this crisis is that stresses are exacerbated within the political decision-making bodies in many nations, because political bodies are the "willful" entities that carry out human choices for large-scale changes in daily life (i.e., everything from raising the postage rate for a letter, to licensing new foods, to waging war). What this means at the highest political level is that the relationship between the United States and the rest of humanity is entering its most severe test to date. As the USA traverses the crisis of renunciation, the whole of humanity, of which we are a part, is also reverberating (and reacting) to the higher energy.

Several writers in the popular press have made very thoughtful statements in the past year about these pressures that the USA is facing.

Some journalists are helping us look at the temptation our leaders face to use this willful energy for domination, to "get our way" on certain issues. What is required of us as the greatest democracy on earth at this moment? Anna Quindlen of *Newsweek* wrote in a recent column that we are the "petri dish of individual freedom," and that we must live up to our principles, not down to our enemies. That is the challenge in our learning to express tremendous power in life-affirming and long-term nurturing ways.

Particularly over the next decade, the will of the United States and of humanity will be tested. The relationship between the United States and the U.N. is critical at this time. The USA / humanity interface is intimately related to the humanity / planet interface. The dynamics between these interfaces will be explored in future research.

The United States will have its own growth stresses, with energy moving further up into its throat center. Figure 30 is a schematic view of the throat of the United States, as a potent microcosm of humanity during the next two decades. This diagram shows how the area of coherence grows and overall energy moves into an open-system, as the alignment of heart and head emerges fully. Clearly, there are many details to fill in on this picture. The details are where we and our families live, and move, and breathe on a daily basis! But the general direction of reducing resistance to unified field is clear.

Think of the period 2000–2024 as a quarter-century of birthing the USA's throat center. In a certain view, there will be seven mini-chapters in testing the nation's will during this period. Each of the seven chapters will be, in effect, birthing a "subchakra" of the throat. Each step is a microcosm crisis within the larger creative energy emerging. Because there are seven subchakras, with the same names as the major chakras, you will recognize them from our earlier discussion: Base-of-spine, sacral, solar plexus, heart, throat, ajna, and crown. The seven subchakras of the Throat are what we are now looking at in Figure 30.

The first such mini-chapter was in autumn of 2000, when the *will of the people* was totally in doubt for more than two months following the USA presidential election. This was a classic crisis of the base-of-spine

FIGURE 30. *Unified Will* OF THE UNITED STATES

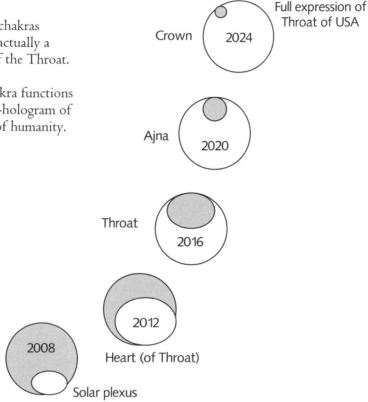

Each of the chakras indicated is actually a subchakra of the Throat.

Each subchakra functions as an energy-hologram of the Throat of humanity.

Crown 2024 — Full expression of Throat of USA

Ajna 2020

Throat 2016

2012 — Heart (of Throat)

2008 — Solar plexus

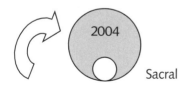

2004 — Sacral

Base of spine

2000

"Hanging chads," Nov. 2000, the millennial U.S. elections

Note: The white space at each step reflects the coherent momentum energy that is steadily growing. As mind and heart become more aligned with each other, the will emerges as their synthesis, or "baby," a unified field.

The shaded areas indicate the resistance to the unified field or, in biological metaphor, the albumin that is feeding the growing embryo.

(in this case, the base-of-spine serving holographically as first subchakra of the nation's throat). During this crisis between November 2000 and January 2001, the actual choice of direction by our citizens (i.e., identity of president as a microcosm of that choice) was swallowed by *doubt energy*. Who was the chosen president? Our choice itself was in severe doubt and swung back and forth. The base-of-spine subchakra of the nation's throat was struggling to emerge and be expressed.

The U.S. Supreme Court eventually acted as a choice-maker, to cut through the doubt, but in so doing it violated the *will of the people* as expressed in the popular vote. Longer-term consequences of this judicial preemption will become more evident as the decade progresses. The next such subchakra mini-chapter will be in 2004, when the second subchakra (sacral center) of the throat of the United States is due to emerge. The second subcrisis will involve some level of our nation's emotional well-being and how we choose to express our true feelings rather than suppressing or denying them. The crisis will express as a specific difference of direction between *spiritual* and *material* agendas, and how we collectively feel about that choice. Our citizens will need to look closely at the choice, in order to distinguish which is which, which is "spiritual" and which "material." The discernment of which choice is more aligned with the *nation's purpose* is a vital responsibility of its citizens and, in this case, will be an especially important one.

With each step and its associated crisis, the coherence of the unified field grows. That is, the expression of the nation's will (through the throat) becomes more focused, responsive, and sensitive to all the component parts of the organism. The coherence of light-and-love is being directly expressed through the will of the whole. As the will of humanity itself manifests more and more coherently, the resistance in the global political community crumbles before it. This was vividly demonstrated in 1989, when the dictatorships in Eastern Europe disintegrated and then the Berlin Wall came tumbling down before the gloriously potent and coherent will of the peoples of Europe. We are now moving rapidly forward from the political coherence of the world body (early 1990s), to the next major resistance, the economic level. As the integration of head-heart grows, the *coherent will* emerges—in concrete terms through such struggles as economic globalization and the associated WTO protests. Again, the United States is a pivotal grounding point in this struggle, for both inspiration and resistance. During this decade of decision, we will learn to "let go" even of the urge to control the world's economies. Renunciation is coming all the way through the decision-making process of our nation and our states, counties, cities, and towns.

There is one last concept that I wish to remind you about, in the context of the current spiritual crisis of the USA. In scientific terms used by physicists, "coherent" implies harmonious wave patterns, very focused emission that has minimal loss of information (by refraction, diffusion, etc.). If the emission of energy is in the range that is visible to human eyes we call it "light"; if it is in other parts of the spectrum, we call it "sound," "X-rays," "gamma rays," "nuclear radioactivity." Here is the dictionary definition of coherent light, which you might find a useful seed for reflection:

Coherent light. Light in which the electromagnetic waves maintain a fixed-phase relationship over a period of time and in which the phase relationship remains constant for various points that are perpendicular to the direction of propagation. (*Random House Dictionary*, unabridged)

We are learning to keep our "phase relationships" constant, by holding the link between now and seven generations in the future. We are learning to have "fixed-phase relationships" by building reputations among our colleagues and friends (and eventually other nations) of being dependable, that we can be relied on to guide and support and help those in need. We can solve problems and bring succor.

With physical coherence comes a focus toward maximum integrity. *Integrity* in terms of physics means something lasts a long time. Integrity in physical matter then translates to *morality* in social terms, *ethical action* in political / philosophic terms, and *joy* in spiritual terms. Here is the new concept: The power of spiritual integrity is ready to emerge, whether the global corporations and resistant political leaders are ready or not. And spiritual integrity emerges on Earth through joy.

In other words, coherent will emerges as the full synthesis of head and heart alignment, and it is expressed through the human throat as *joyful will*. Roberto Assagioli first introduced the term "joyful will" in his teachings in the 1960s and then in his volume, *The Act of Will* (1973). The emergence of joyful will through humanity is inevitable, because the cohering of human will is a creative force of evolution itself. The act of releasing joy, which by its nature is inclusive, integral, and radiatory, comes from the soul level. In our current historical era, the term "soul level" implies the throat level of the planet. *Joy* as a spiritual power originates from a realm above the destructive forces that we have witnessed, to our collective agony and despair, during the 20th century. The full joy of *being* comes from the identity level, whereas the friction of willfulness that breeds destruction comes from wounds in the level below identity.

To translate this into an oversimplification, we can say that we have the "bad guys" surrounded. The resistance points within all of us are held in a steady embrace from both above and below. This will become clearer as we move toward 2020. With the steady growth of coherent brain, gentle heart, and joyful will for humanity as a whole, there will be a concomitant reduction in friction / violence. This is a biological fact: We are learning to starve the blood supply of the cancers in our culture, and they will therefore starve to death. As humanity's head and heart are aligning with each other in this new decade, the *joyful will* that is potential in all human beings will emerge more tangibly—as a planetary energy that is available for healing, redeeming, nurturing, guiding, replenishing, and incarnating healthy children of Earth.

SAMPLE OF *Homo Sapiens* ASSOCIATIONS

Excerpted from *Encyclopedia of Associations: Regional, State, and Local Organizations,* Vol. 5 (Western States), 2001. Published by Gale Research Company

The excerpted list on the following pages is from volume 5 of *The Encyclopedia of Associations,* which has 1,235 pages of listings for the 14 Western states alone! I recommend using this list as a meditation resource or a networking tool, or both. Be receptive to the focused caring, deep compassion, passionate interests, and dedication that energize these volitional gatherings of human beings.

The list includes examples of three kinds of associations. Some of the associations are interest-based (e.g., Bicycle Coalition). Others are mission-based (e.g., Adopt-a-Creek). And then others are compassion-based (e.g., Friends of Foster Kids). The specific county and city names in some titles have been deleted because many of these associations appear in multiple cities and counties.

This brief excerpt does not include any of the thousands of professional societies and associations specific to our many human occupations, nor the associations with explicit religious or ethnic affiliations. These latter types can be found in the multiple-volume *Encyclopedia* for you to explore on your own and to enjoy the rich cultural and spiritual heritages that infuse human life. In addition, your local library and Internet search engines will have listings of many community and regional groups that are specific to your location.

Our species is truly diverse and wonderful. We obviously like to interact with others of similar interests, and to reach out to offer a helping hand. Through such voluntary organizations of people focused around a common interest or goal, we are steadily learning to focus our *caring for each other as self*. The next step is to widen our overall identification with *other* to humanity as a whole, and to find ways to express that identity coherently (which by its nature implies sustainably). The following list is offered as one resource within that process. Several of the books in the Resources section also have excellent listings of organizations and networking groups.

Adopt-a-Creek
Adults Literacy and Resources Center
Alliance Against Graffiti
Alliance for a Drug Free County
Alternative Energy Resources
Alternatives in Dispute Resolution
Association Against Domestic Violence
Association for Persons with Severe Handicaps
Association of Home-Based Businesses
Autism Coalition for Creative Educational & Social Services
Aviation Historical Society
Bicycle Coalition
Blind Babies Foundation
Business Volunteers for the Arts
Center for Ethical Leadership
Center for Independent Living
Children's Repertory Theater
Chronic Pain Outreach Support Group
Citizens Against Lawsuit Abuse

Citizens for Natural Habitat
Classroom Law Project
Coalition for Fair Liability Laws
Coalition for Habitat Conservation
Coalition on Homelessness
Committee for Clean Air and Balanced Transportation
Communities by Design
Community Arts Center
Community Citizens on Patrol
Community Concerts Association
Community Office for Resource Efficiency
Community Pantry
Community Partners
Compassion Center
Consortium on Renewing Education
Constitutional Issues in Technology
Consumer Credit Counseling Service
Corporate Council for the Arts
Council for Community Empowerment & Leadership
Council of Mediators
Council of Parent Participation Nursery Schools
County Association of Governments
County Literacy Volunteers
County Search and Rescue Team
Early Childhood Music Association
Earth Action Forum
Ecumenical Women's Caucus
Emergency Housing Consortium
Family Caregiver Alliance
Family Hospice Care
Fellowship of Reconciliation
Folk Music and Dance Society
Forest Guardians
Friends and Family of the Mentally Ill

Friends of Foster Kids
Friends of the Birds
Friends of the Lake
Friends of the Public Library
Friends of the River
Friends of the Youth Symphony Orchestra
Friends Outside
Friendship Council
Grandparents Raising Grandchildren
Gray Panthers
Greyhound Rescue Education
Grief Support Group
Habitat for Humanity
Heritage Shared
High Country Trekkers
Immigrant and Refugee Community Center
Indigenous Communications Association
Innovation Center
Jobs and Clean Air
Jobs with Justice
Joyful Births
Kids Day on the Big Hole
League of Women Voters
Lighter than Air Association
Local Earth Action Forum
Mainstream Housing
Make-a-Wish Foundation
Music Booster Club
My Home Away from Home
National Academy of Law, Ethics, and Management
National Committee for Responsive Philanthropy
Neighborhood Leadership Initiative
Nonprofit Community Network
Organ Transplant Headquarters

Organic Growers and Associates
Outdoor Science Exploration
Parents Helping Parents
Parents of Multiples
Partners in Housing
Peace and Justice Network
Physicians for Social Responsibility
Pioneer Historical Society
Poetry Society
PostPolio Network
Public Interest Law Center
Quilts from the Heart
Read-Aloud Volunteer Program
Recovery Centers
Research and Genealogy Association
Rural Cancer Care Association
Society of Association Executives
Solar Energy Society
Special Horses for Special People
Special Libraries Association
Special Olympics
Spiritual and Medical Healing Arts
Storytelling Guild
Students Against Driving Drunk
Students Taking a New Direction
Survivors of Suicide
Transplant Support Group
Tribal Law and Policy Institute
Turtle and Tortoise Club
Visions for Prisons
Volunteer Ambulance Corps
War Resisters League
Water Education Foundation
Women's International League for Peace and Freedom

Women's Multi-Cultural Resource Network
Ye Olde Walking Club
Youth Ecology Corps
Youth for Environmental Sanity
Youth Mediation and Conflict Resolution Program

H.D. Newsletter, 1988 – 1998

A Brief History

During the mid-1980s, I shared the seed thought about species-beyond —*Homo sapiens* with various friends and colleagues. Their reactions and suggestions were very helpful. Several of them encouraged me to compile my notes and ideas for a wider distribution. In early 1988 I initiated a subscription newsletter that was originally published seven times a year for a Special Interest Group (SIG) of American Mensa. The publication had a small circulation of about 75 persons. Some subscribers were fellow Mensa members, and others had heard of the newsletter from friends.

The masthead of that initial offering in 1988 began as "*Homo deus —A newsletter to help birth the 21ˢᵗ Century.*" After 11 years of publication, the newsletter was retired in 1998. The following message appeared on every issue during its publication:

> The purpose of *Homo deus Newsletter* is to review recent literature and share original articles addressing trends for the next 25 years of human life. The newsletter is based on the premise that we as a species are traversing a major quantum step in human development. The birth of this new branch of our family tree will be the emergence from *H. sapiens*

to *H. deus.* This step will be a gradual, objective physical process here on earth, brought into existence by the efforts of all 5.6 billion of us.

There is a dual-event happening. An upward movement or force, called by science the course of *evolution,* is meeting a downward movement or force, called by mystics of every culture the path of *revelation.* What we and other writers in this century are proposing is that these two paths, which have been described for several millennia, are now in the final phase of blending. Their tangible fusion will emerge within the next 20–25 years. Homo deus will celebrate the unity of life on earth, while enhancing the uniqueness of each individual person.

We each function, at times, as pioneers who blaze new trails for those around us. One of the needs of pioneers is for maps — ways to describe obstacles and paths to overcome them, to share stories with kindred souls, and to guide others forward in their own journey through territory that we may have already traversed. One goal of this newsletter is to serve as a resource of long-range maps.

A note is pertinent here about the evolution of the name of our emerging new species: The newsletter began in 1988 with the name *Homo deus.* The intent was to recognize the uplift beyond human logic to a synthesis of intellect and intuition, human and divine. After receiving useful input from several readers, we changed the name to *Homo deva* in order to (1) move beyond the historical / patriarchal connotations of the Latin *deus,* and (2) evoke explicitly the biological fusion of nature-and-humanity that is a core aspect of this evolutionary step. The biopsychospiritual dynamics that produce *Homo devas* move "upward" from humans into divinity / future, and also "downward" from us to nature as the earlier / past kingdoms. *Homo devas* are the breath of Earth's voice, the living bridge through and across time.

Implicit in every chapter of this book is a special thank-you and hug to all the subscribers and friends of the *H.D. Newsletter* of the 1990s. You are certainly early pioneers, and your feedback has been most welcome. Best wishes for your next steps in this exciting threshold decade.

FIGURE 31.

A LAYER OF THE THROAT CHAKRA OF EARTH, CIRCA 2003

With particular gratitude to 16 pioneers and authors—16 petals of a throat chakra layer giving voice to the song of our future. Their collective work creates a potent and radioactive flower of hope, wisdom, and stamina for all of Earth's children. May their creativity harmonize with the pulse, rhythms, and overtones of your life.

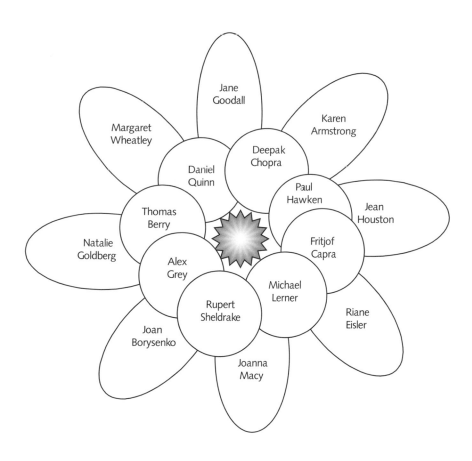

A Note About Resources

On the following pages are selected resources that are offered as door-ways to your future. These resources can serve as starting points for those of you new to the field of future-thinking. And for those of you with years of study, there are perhaps a couple of new gems to savor and enjoy. It is relevant to note that, even though the resources are written or produced from quite varied disciplines, each one is a breath of fresh air. Each author or artist listed here has gifted the human community and enriched our shared life.

We describe the unity of life on Earth through different breaths. Each breath has pulsing vitality, velocity, and a unique configuration of wave patterns; indeed, even unique colors. Each breath brings hope, as a sign that life on Earth will continue. *Breaths do not compete.* Breaths do not attempt "hostile takeovers." Breaths are the wave fronts of life itself, unfolding steadily and blending intimately within timespace.

Whether we are referring to resources as part of the *ascent wave* or the *descent wave* in the emergence of *Homo deva* depends on which end of the map we are holding. Both waves interpenetrate quite deeply and integrally in the one work we are all doing. For example, the works of Bishop Desmond Tutu in South Africa and of philosopher Ken Wilber in the United States are both helping to embody the message, "We are one." Bishop Tutu's primary work has been in the area of ethnic and racial tolerance, and in evoking redemption through spiritual witness, compassion, and forgiveness. He has guided his nation, and by at-one-ment has guided all of us, through deep trenches of human suffering, offering wisdom and hands-on solace to those who have been brutalized and those who did the brutalizing.

Wilber works in the area of philosophy and psychology, guiding us and pointing out to us the relationships between concepts at the far reaches of the human mind. In so doing, he provides useful and ele-gant models of human development, maps to guide the diverse work of fellow pioneers. Both these men are, in my view, singular pioneers and examples of early *Homo deva*.

We need guides and warriors at all depths in our earthlings' ocean of mind—visionary novelists like Daniel Quinn and James Redfield, social scientists like Paul Ray and David Loye, theologians like Robert Keck and Michael Lerner, activists like John Robbins, Julia Butterfly Hill, and Joanna Macy, artists like Alex Grey and Stephen Spielberg, healers like Deepak Chopra and Rachel Naomi Remen, biologists like Rupert Sheldrake and Fritjof Capra, futurists like Jean Houston and Barbara Marx Hubbard, therapists like Barry Kaufman and John Firman, geologians like Thomas Berry, and historians like Karen Armstrong. The power of their individual beams interacts and produces fusion reactions—within their readers, viewers, and fellow explorers. We are revitalized by the steadfast radiance of their wisdom and passion. Their contributions remind us to breathe deeply of life. And thus, we together—you and I—have a responsibility now to share that same breath and send it on to others.

A specific note regarding Figure 1, "Our Family: Hominids—Past, Present, and Future," in the front of this book: The factual dates and information about past migrations and names of species are from general historical consensus reality and can be found in the following sources: Arsuaga (2002), Diamond (1992), Klein (2002), and Leakey & Lewin (1995). The visual representation in Figure 1 of the various species and the extrapolation to the future species are original with this book. All other Figures are from work by the author.

BIBLIOGRAPHY

*Note: The resources marked with an asterisk have greatly helped my perspective recently.

For *inspiration,* **thank you . . .**

Abram, David. *The Spell of the Sensuous: Perception and Language in a More-Than-Human World.* New York: Pantheon / Random Books, 1996.

Adrienne, Carol. *The Purpose of Your Life.* New York: William Morrow & Co., 1998.

Armstrong, Karen. *A History of God: The 4,000-Year Quest for Judaism, Christianity and Islam.* New York: HarperSanFrancisco, 1994.

———. *The Battle for God: A History of Fundamentalism.* New York: Ballantine Publishing / Random House, 2000.

Arrien, Angeles. *The Four-Fold Way: Walking the Paths of the Warrior, Teacher, Healer and Visionary.* New York: HarperSanFrancisco, 1993. [Excellent Action Steps and study questions]

Arsuaga, Juan Luis. *The Neanderthal's Necklace: In Search of the First Thinkers.* New York: Four Walls Eight Windows, 2002.

Assagioli, Roberto. *The Act of Will.* New York: Viking Press, 1973.

Ayres, Ed. *God's Last Offer: Negotiating for a Sustainable Future.* New York: Four Walls Eight Windows, 1999.

Badiner, Allan Hunt (Ed.). *Dharma Gaia: A Harvest of Essays in Buddhism and Ecology.* Berkeley, CA: Parallax Press, 1990.

——— (Ed.). *Mindfulness in the Marketplace: Compassionate Responses to Consumerism.* Berkeley, CA: Parallax Press, 2002.

Barnhill, David Landis (Ed.). *At Home on the Earth: A Multicultural Anthology.* Berkeley, CA: University of California Press, 1999.

Berman, Daniel, and John T. O'Connor. *Who Owns the Sun?* White River Junction, VT: Chelsea Green Publishing, 1996.

Berry, Thomas. *The Great Work: Our Way into the Future.* New York: Bell

Tower / Random House, 1999.

Berry, Wendell. *In the Presence of Fear: Three Essays for a Changed World.* Great Barrington, MA: The Orion Society, 2001.

Bolen, Jean Shinoda. *The Millionth Circle: How to Change Ourselves and the World.* Berkeley, CA: Conari Press, 1999.

Borg, Marcus (Ed.). *Jesus at 2000.* Boulder, CO: Westview Press, 1998.

Borysenko, Joan. *A Woman's Journey to God: Finding the Feminine Path.* New York: Riverhead / Penguin Putnam, 1999.

Brand, Stewart. *The Clock of the Long Now: Time and Responsibility.* New York: Basic Books, 1999.

Brin, David. *Earth.* New York: Bantam Books, 1990.

Bruteau, Beatrice. *Radical Optimism.* Boulder, CO: Sentient Publications, 1993.

Buckley Jr., William F. *Gratitude: Reflections on What We Owe to Our Country.* New York: Random House, 1990.

———— . *Nearer, My God: An Autobiography of Faith.* New York: Harvest / Harcourt Brace, 1997.

Buhner, Stephen. *One Spirit, Many Peoples: A Manifesto for Earth Spirituality.* Niwot, CO: Roberts Rinehart, 1997.

Burke, James, and Robert Ornstein. *The Axemaker's Gift: Technology's Capture and Control of Our Minds and Culture.* New York: J.P. Tarcher / Putnam, 1997.

Cameron, Julia. *The Artist's Way: A Spiritual Path to Higher Creativity.* New York: J.P. Tarcher / Putnam, 1992.

Capra, Fritjof. *The Hidden Connections: Integrating the Biological, Cognitive, and Social Dimensions of Life into a Science of Sustainability.* New York: Doubleday, 2002.

———— . *The Web of Life: A New Scientific Understanding of Living Systems.* New York: Anchor / Doubleday, 1996.

Capra, Fritjof, and David Steindl-Rast. *Belonging to the Universe: Explorations on the Frontiers of Science and Spirituality.* New York: HarperSanFrancisco, 1991.

Carroll, Lee, and Jan Tober. *The Indigo Children.* Carlsbad, CA: Hay House, 1999.

Carter, Jimmy. *Living Faith*. New York: Times Books / Random House, 1996.

Chodron, Pema. *When Things Fall Apart*. Boston: Shambhala Publications, 1997.

Chopra, Deepak. *Ageless Body, Timeless Mind*. New York: Harmony Books / Random House, 1993.

———. *How to Know God*. New York: Harmony Books / Random House, 2000.

Christ, Carol P. *Rebirth of the Goddess*. New York: Routledge, 1997.

Cohen, Andrew. *Living Enlightenment: A Call for Evolution beyond Ego*. Lenox, MA: Moksha Press, 2002.

Combs, Allan. *The Radiance of Being*. St. Paul, MN: Paragon House, 2002 (2nd ed.).

Diamond, Jared. *The Third Chimpanzee: The Evolution and Future of the Human Animal*. New York: HarperCollins, 1992.

Ehrlich, Paul R. *Human Natures: Genes, Cultures, and the Human Prospect*. New York: Penguin Books / Island Press, 2000.

Eisler, Riane. *Tomorrow's Children*. Boulder, CO: Westview Press, 2000.

———. *The Power of Partnership*. Novato, CA: New World Library, 2002.

Eldredge, Niles. *Life in the Balance: Humanity and the Biodiversity Crisis*. Princeton, NJ: Princeton University Press, 1998.

Elgin, Duane. *Promise Ahead: A Vision of Hope and Action for Humanity's Future*. New York: William Morrow / HarperCollins, 2000.

Ellis, Joseph J. *Founding Brothers: The Revolutionary Generation*. New York: Vintage Books / Random House, 2000.

Firman, John, and Ann Gila. *Primal Wound: A Transpersonal View of Trauma, Addiction, and Growth*. Albany, NY: State University New York Press, 1997.

———. *Psychosynthesis: A Psychology of the Spirit*. Albany, NY: State University New York Press, 2002.

Foster, Richard J. *Celebration of Discipline*. San Francisco: Harper & Row, 1988.

Fox, Matthew. *The Reinvention of Work: A New Vision of Livelihood for Our Time*. New York: HarperSanFrancisco, 1995.

————. *Creativity*. New York: J.P. Tarcher / Putnam, 2002.

————. *One River, Many Wells: Wisdom Springing from Global Faiths*. New York: Putnam Publishing, 2000.

Frank, Thomas. *One Market under God*. New York: Anchor Books / Random House, 2000.

Friedman, Lenore, and Susan Moon (Eds.). *Being Bodies: Buddhist Women on the Paradox of Embodiment*. Boston: Shambhala Publications, 1997.

Gatto, John Taylor. *Dumbing Us Down*. Gabriola Isl., BC: New Society Publishers, 2002 (2nd ed.).

Gawain, Shakti. *Living in the Light*. Novato, CA: New World Library, 1998 (rev. ed.).

Gelb, Michael. *How to Think like Leonardo da Vinci*. New York: Dell Publishing / Random House, 1998.

Goldberg, Natalie. *Long Quiet Highway: Waking Up in America*. New York: Bantam Books, 1993.

————. *Thunder and Lightning*. New York: Bantam Books, 2000.

Goldsworthy, Andy. *A Collaboration with Nature*. New York: Harry N. Adams, 1990.

Goodall, Jane. *Reason for Hope: A Spiritual Journey*. New York: Warner Books, 1999.

Gore, Al. *Earth in the Balance: Ecology and the Human Spirit*. Boston: Houghton Mifflin Co., 1992.

Gorski, Terence. *Passages through Recovery*. Center City, MN: Hazelden, 1989.

Gould, Stephen Jay. *Rocks of Ages: Science and Religion in the Fullness of Life*. New York: Ballantine Books, 1999.

Grandin, Temple. *Thinking in Pictures: And Other Reports from My Life with Autism*. New York: Vintage Books / Random House, 1995.

Greene, Brian. *The Elegant Universe*. London: Random House, 1999.

Grey, Alex. *The Mission of Art*. Boston: Shambhala Publications, 1998.

Halberstam, David. *The Next Century*. New York: William Morrow & Co., 1991.

Hanh, Thich Nhat. *Living Buddha, Living Christ*. New York: Berkley Publishing, 1997.

Harman, Willis. *Global Mind Change.* Indianapolis, IN: Knowledge Systems, 1988.

———(Ed.), with Maya Porter. *The New Business of Business: Sharing Responsibility for a Positive Global Future.* San Francisco: Berrett-Koehler, 1997.

Harman, Willis, and Elisabet Sahtouris. *Biology Revisioned.* Berkeley, CA: The Institute for Noetic Sciences, 1998.

Hartmann, Thom. *Attention Deficit Disorder: A Different Perception.* Grass Valley, CA: Underwood Books, 1997.

Harvey, Andrew. *The Direct Path: Creating a Personal Journey to the Divine Using the World's Spiritual Traditions.* New York: Broadway / Doubleday, 2001.

Hawken, Paul. *The Ecology of Commerce: A Declaration of Sustainability.* New York: HarperCollins, 1993.

Heart, Bear, with Molly Larkin. *The Wind is My Mother: The Life and Teachings of a Native American Shaman.* New York: Berkley Publishing, 1996.

H.H. the Dalai Lama XIV. *An Open Heart: Practicing Compassion in Everyday Life.* Boston: Little, Brown & Co., 2001.

Hill, Julia Butterfly. *The Legacy of Luna.* New York: HarperCollins, 2000.

Hirshberg, Caryle, and Marc Ian Barasch. *Remarkable Recovery: What Extraordinary Healings Tell Us about Getting Well and Staying Well.* New York: Berkley Publishing, 1995.

Hogan, Linda. *Dwellings: A Spiritual History of the Living World.* New York: Touchstone / Simon & Schuster, 1996.

Houston, Jean. *Jump Time: Shaping Your Future in a World of Radical Change.* New York: J.P. Tarcher / Putnam, 2000.

Hubbard, Barbara Marx. *Conscious Evolution: Awakening the Power of Our Social Potential.* Novato, CA: New World Library, 1998.

———. *Emergence: The Shift from Ego to Essence.* Charlottesville, VA: Hampton Roads Publishing, 2001. [Excellent resources and calls to action.]

Hughes, K. Wind, and Linda Wolf. *Daughters of the Moon, Sisters of the Sun.* Gabriola Isl., BC: New Society Publishers, 1997.

Jones, Laurie Beth. *Jesus, CEO: Using Ancient Wisdom for Visionary Leadership.* New York: Hyperion, 1995.

Kabat-Zinn, Jon. *Full Catastrophe Living: Using the Wisdom of Your Body and Mind to Face Stress, Pain, and Illness.* New York: Delta / Bantam, 1990.

Kaufman, Barry N. *Son-Rise: The Miracle Continues.* Tiburon, CA: H.J. Kramer, 1994.

* Keck, L. Robert. *Sacred Eyes.* Boulder, CO: Synergy Associates, 1992.

Kelley, Colleen, and Anna Eblen (Eds.). *Women Who Speak for Peace.* Lanham, MA: Rowman & Littlefield, 2002.

Kelly, Petra. *Thinking Green!* Berkeley, CA: Parallax Press, 1994.

Kidd, Sue Monk. *The Dance of the Dissident Daughter: A Woman's Journey from Christian Tradition to the Sacred Feminine.* New York: HarperSanFrancisco, 1996.

* Klein, Richard, with Blake Edgar. *The Dawn of Human Culture.* New York: John Wiley & Sons, 2002.

Korten, David. *When Corporations Rule the World.* San Francisco: Berrett-Koehler, 2000 (2nd ed.).

Kozol, Jonathan. *Ordinary Resurrections: Children in the Years of Hope.* New York: Crown Publishers, 2000.

Kung, Hans, and Karl-Josef Kuschel (Eds.). *A Global Ethic: Declaration of the Parliament of the World's Religions.* New York: Continuum Publishing, 1993.

LaDuke, Winona. *All Our Relations: Native Struggles for Land and Life.* Cambridge, MA: South End Press, 1999.

Lappé, Frances Moore, and Paul Martin DuBois. *The Quickening of America: Rebuilding Our Nation, Remaking Our Lives.* San Francisco: Jossey-Bass, 1994.

Leakey, Richard, and Roger Lewin. *Origins Reconsidered: In Search of What Makes Us Human.* New York: Doubleday, 1992.

Leakey, Richard, and Roger Lewin. *The Sixth Extinction: Patterns of Life and the Future of Humankind.* New York: Anchor Books / Random House, 1995.

LeGuin, Ursula K. *Tales from Earthsea.* New York: Harcourt, 2001.

Leonard, George, and Michael Murphy. *The Life We Are Given: A Longterm Program for Realizing the Potential of Body, Mind, Heart, and Soul.* New York: G.P. Putnam's Sons, 1995.

Lerner, Michael. *Spirit Matters.* Charlottesville, VA: Hampton Roads Publishing, 2000.

Leslie, Mitchell. "Suddenly Smarter..." (examining the work of archaeologist Richard Klein), in *Stanford Magazine*, July / August 2002, pp. 57–61.

Levine, Mel. *A Mind at a Time*. New York: Simon & Schuster, 2002.

Levine, Robert. *A Geography of Time*. New York: Basic Books, 1997.

Levine, Stephen. *Turning Toward the Mystery*. New York: HarperCollins, 2002.

Lewin, Roger. *In the Age of Mankind*. Washington, DC: Smithsonian Books, 1988.

Loye, David (Ed.). *The Evolutionary Outrider: Impact of the Human Agent on Evolution*. Westport, CT: Praeger Publishers, 1998.

Luhrs, Janet. *The Simple Living Guide*. New York: Broadway Books / Bantam, 1997.

Macy, Joanna. *World as Lover, World as Self*. Berkeley, CA: Parallax Press, 1991.

Macy, Joanna, and Molly Young Brown. *Coming Back to Life: Practices to Reconnect Our Lives, Our World*. Gabriola Isl., BC: New Society Publishers, 1998.

Margulis, Lynn, and Karlene Schwartz. *Five Kingdoms*. New York: W.H. Freeman & Co., 1998.

* Marohn, Stephanie. *The Natural Medicine Guide to Autism*. Charlottesville, VA: Hampton Roads Publishing, 2002.

McLaughlin, Corinne, and Gordon Davidson. *Spiritual Politics*. New York: Ballantine / Random House, 1994.

McNiff, Shaun. *Trust the Process: An Artist's Guide to Letting Go*. Boston: Shambhala Publications, 1998.

Medicine Eagle, Brooke. *The Last Ghost Dance*. New York: Ballantine Wellspring, 2000.

Meindl, James D. (Ed.) *Brief Lessons in High Technology*. Stanford, CA: Portable Stanford Book Series, 1991.

Metzner, Ralph. *Green Psychology: Transforming Our Relationship to the Earth*. Rochester, VT: Park Street Press / Inner Traditions, 1999.

Milam, James, and Katherine Ketcham. *Under the Influence: A Guide to the Myths and Realities of Alcoholism*. New York: Bantam Books, 1983.

Moffett, James. *The Universal Schoolhouse: Spiritual Awakening through Ed-*

ucation. San Francisco: Jossey-Bass Publishers, 1994.

Morrison, Philip, and Phyllis Morrison. *Powers of Ten: About the Relative Size of Things in the Universe.* New York: Scientific American Library, 1994.

Moyers, Bill; with Joann McAllister, Mary Lou Finley, and Steven Soifer. *Doing Democracy.* Gabriola Isl., BC: New Society Publishers, 2001.

Murphy, Michael. *The Future of the Body: Explorations into the Future Evolution of Human Nature.* Los Angeles, CA: J.P. Tarcher, 1992.

Myss, Caroline. *Anatomy of the Spirit.* New York: Three Rivers Press / Random House, 1996.

Nader, Ralph. *Cutting Corporate Welfare.* New York: Seven Stories, 2000.

Naranjo, Claudio. *The End of Patriarchy.* Oakland, CA: Amber Lotus, 1994.

Neusner, Jacob, and Bruce Chilton. *Jewish-Christian Debates: God, Kingdom, Messiah.* Minneapolis, MN: Augsburg Fortress, 1998.

Nisker, Wes. *Buddha's Nature: A Practical Guide to Discovering Your Place in the Cosmos.* New York: Bantam Books, 1998.

Norris, Kathleen. *The Cloister Walk.* New York: Riverhead / G.P. Putnam's Sons, 1996.

Ornstein, Robert. *The Evolution of Consciousness: Origins of the Way We Think.* New York: Simon & Schuster, 1991.

Ornstein, Robert, and Paul Ehrlich. *New World, New Mind.* Cambridge, MA: ISHK, 2000 (orig. ed. 1989).

Packard, Edward. *Imagining the Universe.* New York: Perigee Books / Berkley Publishing, 1994.

Patten, Christopher. *East and West: China, Power, and the Future of Asia.* New York: Times Books / Random House, 1998.

Pearce, Joseph Chilton. *The Biology of Transcendence.* Rochester, VT: Park Street Press, 2002.

Peck, M. Scott. *People of the Lie.* New York: Touchstone / Simon & Schuster, 1983.

——— . *Denial of the Soul: Spiritual and Medical Perspectives on Euthanasia and Mortality.* New York: Harmony Books / Crown Publishers, 1997.

Phillips, Kevin. *Arrogant Capital: Washington, Wall Street, and the Frustration of American Politics.* Boston: Little, Brown & Co., 1995.

Pieg, Pascal, and Nicole Verrechia. *Lucy and Her Times*. New York: Henry Holt & Co., 1996.

Pipher, Mary. *The Middle of Everywhere: The World's Refugees Come to Our Town*. Orlando, FL: Harcourt, 2002.

——— . *Hunger Pains: The Modern Woman's Tragic Quest for Thinness*. New York: Ballantine Books, 1995.

Quinn, Daniel. *My Ishmael: A Sequel*. New York: Bantam Books, 1997.

——— . *Beyond Civilization: Humanity's Next Great Adventure*. New York: Harmony Books, 1999.

Ram Dass. *Still Here: Embracing Aging, Changing, and Dying*. New York: Riverhead / Penguin Putnam, 2000.

Ram Dass, and Mirabai Bush. *Compassion in Action: Setting Out on the Path of Service*. New York: Bell Tower / Harmony Books, 1992. [Excellent section on Resources and Calls to Action]

* Ray, Paul, and Sherry Ruth Anderson. *The Cultural Creatives: How 50 Million People are Changing the World*. New York: Three Rivers Press, 2000.

Redfield, James. *The Celestine Vision: Living the New Spiritual Awareness*. New York: Warner Books, 1997.

Redfield, James, and Carol Adrienne. *The Celestine Prophecy: An Experiential Guide*. New York: Warner Books, 1995.

Remen, Rachel Naomi. *My Grandfather's Blessings*. New York: Riverhead Books / Penguin Putnam, 2000.

Riedelsheimer, Thomas. *Rivers and Tides* (film), examining the work of land artist Andy Goldsworthy; winner of Grand Prize for Documentary at 2002 San Francisco International Film Festival.

Rifkin, Ira (Ed.). *Spiritual Innovators: Seventy-Five Extraordinary People Who Changed the World in the Past Century*. Woodstock, VT: SkyLight Paths Publishing, 2002.

* Roach, Geshe Michael. *The Diamond Cutter: The Buddha on Strategies for Managing Your Business and Your Life*. New York: Doubleday, 2000.

Robbins, John. *The Food Revolution: How Your Diet can Help Save Your Life and Our World*. Berkeley, CA: Conari Press, 2001.

Robbins, Ocean, and Sol Solomon. *Choices for Our Future: A Generation Rising for Life on Earth*. Summertown, TN: Book Publishing Co., 1994. [Very good section on Resources.]

Roberts, Elizabeth, and Elias Amidon. *Life Prayers*. New York: Harper-Collins, 1996.

Rocha, Adriana, and Kristi Jorde. *A Child of Eternity*. New York: Ballantine Books, 1995.

Roszak, Theodore. *Longevity Revolution: As Boomers become Elders*. Berkeley, CA: Berkeley Hills Books, 2001.

Ruether, Rosemary R. *Gaia and God*. New York: HarperCollins, 1992.

Ryan, M.J. (Ed.) *The Fabric of the Future: Women Visionaries Illuminate the Path to Tomorrow*. Berkeley, CA: Conari Press, 1998.

Salzberg, Sharon. *Lovingkindness: The Revolutionary Art of Happiness*. Boston: Shambhala, 1995.

Satori, Jessika. *Synchronicity: The Entrepreneur's Edge*. Boston: Butterworth-Heinemann, 1999.

Schachter-Shalomi, Zalman, and Ronald Miller. *From Age-ing to Sage-ing: A Profound New Vision of Growing Older*. New York: Warner Books, 1995.

Shabecoff, Philip. *Earth Rising: American Environmentalism in the 21st Century*. Washington, DC: Island Press, 2000.

Sheldrake, Rupert. *The Rebirth of Nature: The Greening of Science and God*. Rochester, VT: Park Street Press, 1991.

* Sheldrake, Rupert, Terence McKenna, and Ralph Abraham. *Chaos, Creativity, and Cosmic Consciousness*. Rochester, VT: Park Street Press / Inner Traditions, 2001.

Sinetar, Marsha. *Spiritual Intelligence: What We Can Learn from the Early Awakening Child*. Maryknoll, NY: Orbis Books, 2000.

——— . *Developing a 21st-Century Mind*. New York: Villard / Random House, 1991.

Smith, Huston. *Why Religion Matters: The Fate of the Human Spirit in an Age of Disbelief*. New York: HarperCollins, 2001.

Somé, Malidoma Patrice. *Healing Wisdom of Africa: Finding Life Purpose through Nature, Ritual, and Community*. New York: J.P. Tarcher / Putnam, 1999.

Spangler, David. *Blessing: The Art and the Practice*. New York: Riverhead Books, 2001.

Spangler, David, and William Irwin Thompson. *Reimagination of the World.* Sante Fe, NM: Bear & Co., 1991.

Spielberg, Stephen. *Minority Report* (film), 2001.

Spignesi, Angelyn. *Starving Women: A Psychology of Anorexia Nervosa.* Dallas, TX: Spring Publications, 1985.

Spong, Bishop John Shelby. *Why Christianity Must Change or Die.* New York: HarperSanFrancisco, 1999.

Stiglitz, Joseph E. *Globalization and Its Discontents.* New York: W.W. Norton & Co., 2002.

Suu Kyi, Aung San. *The Voice of Hope.* New York: Seven Stories, 1997.

Swimme, Brian. *The Universe Is a Green Dragon.* Santa Fe, NM: Bear & Co., 1984.

Swimme, Brian, and Thomas Berry. *The Universe Story.* New York: HarperSanFrancisco, 1992.

Tattersall, Ian. *Becoming Human: Evolution and Human Uniqueness.* New York: Harvest Book / Harcourt Brace & Co., 1998.

Terkel, Studs. *Will the Circle Be Unbroken? Reflections on Death, Rebirth, and Hunger for a Faith.* New York: Ballantine / Random House, 2001.

Thomas, Lewis. *The Fragile Species.* New York: Collier / Macmillan, 1992.

Thurman, Robert. *Inner Revolution: Life, Liberty, and the Pursuit of Real Happiness.* New York: Riverhead Books, 1998.

Toms, Michael. *A Time for Choices: Deep Dialogues for Deep Democracy.* Gabriola Isl., BC: New Society Publishers, 2002.

Tutu, Desmond. *No Future without Forgiveness.* New York: Doubleday, 1999.

Vargiu, James G. (Editor). *Synthesis Journal,* vol. 4. San Francisco: Psychosynthesis Institute, 1978.

Vaughan, Frances. *Shadows of the Sacred.* Wheaton, IL: Quest Books, 1995.

Wallach, Lori, and Michelle Sforza. *The WTO: Five Years of Reasons to Resist Corporate Globalization.* New York: Seven Stories (Open Media Pamphlet Series), 1999.

Walsch, Neale Donald. *ReCreating Your Self.* Ashland, OR: Millennium Legacies, 1995.

Walsh, Roger. *Essential Spirituality.* New York: John Wiley & Sons, 1999.

Wauters, Ambika. *Life Changes: With the Energy of the Chakras.* Freedom, CA: Crossing Press, 1999.

* Wheatley, Margaret. *Leadership and the New Science: Learning about Organization from an Orderly Universe.* San Francisco: Berrett-Koehler, 1994.

Wilber, Ken. *The Marriage of Sense and Soul: Integrating Science and Religion.* New York: Random House, 1998.

Wills, Garry. *A Necessary Evil: A History of American Distrust of Government.* New York: Simon & Schuster, 1999.

Wilson, Jon, publisher. *HOPE: Inspiring People, Encouraging Change* (magazine).

Wolf, Fred Alan. *The Spiritual Universe: One Physicist's Vision of Spirit, Soul, Matter, and Self.* Portsmouth, NH: Moment Point Press, 1999.

Zukav, Gary. *The Seat of the Soul.* New York: Fireside / Simon & Schuster, 1990.

NAME INDEX

APPRECIATION

The many children I have met and worked with over the years have been a continuous source of inspiration for me. To each of them and their families, my heartfelt thanks. You have given the gift of trust, and demonstrated the many faces of grace under great stress. You are each my teacher.

My kin family stretches from here in the Bay Area northward to our adopted state of Washington. My parents, Jack and Martha Morgan, and three siblings have been a wonderful home-team through the years. Thank you all for being an integral part of my journey. Our early years in Iowa taught me the healing nature of rural rhythms and introduced me to several young cows who were my first playmates. I was blessed to begin life within the embrace of the big trees, creeks, and cornfields that provided a deeply textural sense of place.

My maternal grandmother, Gail Jackson, a Quaker lady and farmer's wife, was a central early influence for me. She would say with a gentle smile to a very inquisitive three-year-old, "Mary Gail, thee has the answer to that one in thy noggin." I am grateful for my extended family and the community of activist Methodists that encouraged me to think and reflect within on questions of belief, faith, and service.

For excellent early schooling and training in music performance in Long Beach, thank you to the wonderful teachers and the taxpayers of California. Some of my fondest memories of high school are of participating as a member in symphony orchestras, creating glorious sounds as a unified voice of many people. Especially, I thank the caring educators who opened doorways and in a hundred ways told me it was OK to have ideas that stretched and even pushed the envelope. I also appreciate the many wonderful opportunities to travel with my family. Those trips helped me get acquainted with our country's national parks, wilderness areas, beautiful cities, and the incredible diversity of our people's voices and stories. I am very grateful for my years of college and grad school that helped me discover the many sides of wisdom and human love. Growing up in the 1960s came fast, with friends leaving for war in Vietnam, or not leaving, and both groups holding pieces of my heart.

A warm greeting goes to my companions from the 1970s in health education and psychology, and to my colleagues at Three Mountains Foundation. To those who journeyed east in the fall of 1980 to join the dragon wars, and also to those who stayed in California to hold the beacon steady and clear, I send gratitude. I love each of you, and wish you well.

During a sojourn of 10 years in the state of Georgia, I met many wonderful friends and colleagues. That chapter also brought opportunities / challenges in applying the ideas about *Homo deva* in public institutions of education, juvenile justice, social welfare, and rehabilitation. Appreciation for steady dedication under siege conditions goes to my colleagues of the 1980s at Emory University Hospital, Georgia Youth Services, and Fulton County Superior Court.

Into the 1990s, I appreciate the lessons learned with the City of Anaheim Community Development, Redevelopment Agency and Housing Agency. A special hug to the dedicated program directors and other staff members, past and present, at the San Francisco / Marin / San Mateo County agencies of Catholic Charities. You all are awesome! With help from above, we performed a deep act of healing. You have my respect for practicing integrity and daily caring for your clients in the midst of what was, at that time, institutional bedlam.

And to my recent colleagues in the financial services industry, the story is still unfolding. Excellent seeds are appearing, such as the training programs for entrepreneurship both from bottom-up and top-down, and the beginning of self-questioning and—dare we say—soul searching in the accounting industry. With thousands of people focusing on this arena, we can bring the top-line and bottom-line together in more integral ways. One possibility concerns creative approaches to investment in an era of unified field (perhaps the *market-share of a white hole?* Just kidding). It is going to get better, as we work together to redefine "better."

Each of the authors and artists listed in the Resources section has provided valuable guidance through their works. Several of them have offered specific advice that has been quite useful. I consider you all my intellectual and spiritual mentors.

During the past decade, I have been blessed with a trio of friends and counselors who helped me keep my balance during the re-entry to mass culture after years of solitary contemplation: Lew Southern, educational film expert, Mensa best-bud, and raconteur extraordinaire; Marty Fiebert, international peace-sower and southern California yoda; and John Firman, teacher and psychologist, who walked with me along the path when the way was fierce with dragons. You each are cherished in my heart.

The grace and wisdom of Julie Rebecca Belknap has blessed my life. Julie is an anthropologist and alternate-energy activist. I am grateful that she chose to enter this cycle as my daughter, to share the joys of times together and the traumas of times apart. We have done much healing, and the two of us will continue sharing the trust and redemption we have earned with those whose lives we touch in the years ahead.

For technical guidance in the adventure of book publishing, thanks to Dan Poynter of *The Self-Publishing Manual,* and Deborah Herman and Cynthia Black, authors of *Spiritual Writing.* Your books appeared on my horizon at exactly the right time. Each of you has gifted the authors' community with beautiful links between the visioning stage and the practical steps of bookcrafting and production. Carol Adrienne, special thanks for helping focus my momentum in the final months. The dharma path of turtle-island is steady and true. Patricia Heinicke Jr., you are a gem of an editor, and I look forward to co-creating more of the future with you. Thank you to Irene Elmer for the index.

To Cypress House, literary consultants, kudos for introducing me to the complex business of books in a manner that also celebrates the humanity of business. I salute your beacons of light.

And to you, the readers, thanks for being part of the journey. See you on the trail.

The mission of Lifethread Institute: *Breath for the 21ˢᵗ Century.*

ABOUT THE AUTHOR

Mary Belknap trained as an educational psychologist and attorney. Over the past four decades, she has worked as a teacher, researcher, and administrator in juvenile justice and in social service agencies including homeless shelters, healthcare facilities, and private foundations.

After undergraduate studies at Stanford, Mary completed graduate programs at U.C. Berkeley (MPH, health education; Ph.D. with honors in educational psychology), and later received a J.D. from Georgia State University. She is a member of the California Bar (inactive), and is a longtime member of Mensa. In 1999 – 2000, Mary served as operations director for Family and Children's Services of Catholic Charities for San Francisco, Marin, and San Mateo Counties. During the eight years leading up to Autumn 2008, she worked as a catalyst in the financial services industry. In the past five years, 2010- 2014, Mary has focused on projects in her local community in areas of sustainability, healthcare for elders, and nurturing a better relationship of religion and spirituality.

Mary began studying human potential in 1973 as a member of a project on alternative approaches to medical education. For over 11 years, she published the *H. D. Newsletter,* which explored the emergence of a new humanity. Her writings and observation are based on 40 years of exploration at the frontiers of human development and cultural climax. She is founder and director of Lifethread Institute. Mary has five special links to the future of humanity—her daughter, granddaughter, and three nephews—plus many wonderful friends who all make this lifetime a journey of joy. *Homo deva* is her first book.

Book Orders

Send postal orders to: Lifethread Institute
Mary Belknap, Director
PO Box 2285
Vashon, WA 98070

Please send the following books:

Homo deva _____ @ $16.00 USD = $_____

8.6% Washington state sales tax $1.38 ea _____

Shipping: Within the U.S., for first copy $4.00 _____
$1.00 for each additional copy _____

Total: $ _____
Check (or money order) in U.S. dollars payable to *Lifethread Institute*

Please allow 2–4 weeks for delivery.
Send book(s) to:
Your Name _____

Address _____

City _____ State _____ Zip _____

E-mail (optional) _____

Online orders for *Homo deva* are available from:

www.Indiebound.org
www.Amazon.com
www.bn.com
www.vashonbookshop.com
www.cypresshouse.com

For more information contact:
Lifethreadinstitute@gmail.com
Thank you for your order!